DIGGERS
IN FRANCE

DIGGERS IN FRANCE

AUSTRALIAN SOLDIERS ON THE WESTERN FRONT

RICHARD TRAVERS

ABC
Books

Published by ABC Books for the
AUSTRALIAN BROADCASTING CORPORATION
GPO Box 9994 Sydney NSW 2001

ISBN 978 0 7333 2342 3

Cover design by Josh Durham, Design by Committee
Typeset in 11/16 pt Bembo by Kirby Jones
Printed in Hong Kong, China, by Quality Printing
Cover photograph: Diggers of the 5th Division take a smoko in December 1916
during the coldest and wettest winter of the war. AWM E00019

5 4 3 2 1

For John William Holmes Travers

CONTENTS

INTRODUCTION

In its first serious engagement in France, at Fromelles in July 1916, the Australian 5th Division suffered 5533 casualties in one night. In their first seven weeks' fighting on the western front, culminating in the Battle of Pozières, the Australians suffered 28 000 casualties. This compared with the 26 000 casualties suffered in eight months at Gallipoli.

After the diggers had suffered heavily at Pozières, the British Commander-in-Chief, General Haig, did not hesitate to lecture Generals Birdwood and White, the commanders of the Anzac Corps, that 'You're not fighting the Bashi-Bazouks now.' White was offended, but there was no denying the stakes were higher on the western front than they had been at Gallipoli. As Haig said, 'This is serious, scientific war, and you are up against the most scientific and most military nation in Europe.'

Eventually, through bitter experience, the Australians learned to fight a 'serious, scientific war'. The Australian volunteers who tasted defeat at Gallipoli came to the western front early in 1916. Over the next two years, they learned on the job — fighting under British commanders in the Battle of the Somme, at Bullecourt, at Messines and at Passchendaele.

Initially, the diggers suffered terribly under the impetuosity of Generals Haig, Haking and Gough. At Messines and in the later stages of the Passchendaele battle, they came under the command of two British generals of quite a different stripe: the avuncular General Plumer, and his chief of staff, General Harington.

From these two generals, the Australians (from the generals down) learned the elements of the bite-and-hold tactic. They learned the importance of thorough planning. They learned how to use all the elements of their force — tanks, machine guns, artillery, aircraft, forward observers, and underground mines — to facilitate attacks across open ground. Above all, they learned from Plumer and Harington the inclusive style of 'leadership by trust' which Plumer and Harington regarded as the foundation of their success. It later became the foundation of the diggers' success.

In 1918, the diggers finally came together under an Australian commander, General Monash, and under Australian officers, to form a single Australian (not Anzac) Army Corps. By this time, they — the Australian generals and soldiers — had honed their fighting skills and methods. They were in the peak of fitness, training and morale. Monash adopted the leadership style of Plumer and Harington. He believed that

the true role of the infantry was not to expend itself upon heroic physical effort, nor to whither away under merciless machine gun fire, nor to impale itself on hostile bayonets, nor to tear itself to pieces in hostile entanglements ... but, on the contrary, to advance under the maximum possible array of mechanical resources, in the form of guns, machine guns, tanks, mortars and aeroplanes; to advance with as little impediment as possible; to be relieved as far as possible of the obligation to *fight* their way forward; to march resolutely ... to the appointed goal; and there to hold and defend the territory gained; and to gather in the form of prisoners, guns and stores the fruits of victory.

These were winning tactics.

Fighting together in 1918, the diggers played a vital part in defeating the 'most scientific and most military nation in Europe'. On Anzac Day 1918, the diggers used rifles, bayonets and tough hand-to-hand fighting to drive the Germans out of Villers-Bretonneux. This was the battle that finally halted the German advance that had begun on 21 March 1918.

With the Canadians, the diggers led the offensive on 8 August 1918. This was the offensive that eventually drove the Germans back out of the Somme valley. General Ludendorff called 8 August 1918 'the black day of the German army in the war'. Alone, without the support of tanks or artillery, the diggers took the imposing landmark of Mont St Quentin. This was the victory which opened the way to the Hindenburg line.

The battles that the diggers fought in the second half of 1918 were as sustained and relentless as any battles fought in the twentieth century. The battles themselves are not, however, the only focus of *Diggers in France.*

For three years between 1916 and 1918, Australia maintained a standing army of up to 150 000 fit young men in northern France, England and Belgium. A single battle might last three days — indeed, the Hamel battle lasted only 93 minutes. If the average digger fought in ten battles (few did), he would have been engaged in battles for only one month of the 36 months of his service.

This left the diggers with large amounts of spare time. Most spare time was devoted to training, but there was also ample time to mingle with the French and the Belgians, whose lives continued, almost normally, quite close to the front. There was time for leave, which might be taken in England or in France. Many of the diggers were wounded. They received treatment in hospitals in France and England. Many others were taken prisoner of war. Accommodating, feeding, clothing and equipping the force on the front line was a task that demanded great ingenuity and organisational skills, which may be compared to the ingenuity and skills that the diggers devoted to the courtship of the women of France and England.

By using the letters, diaries, autobiographies and biographies of the diggers themselves, *Diggers in France* describes the experience of the diggers in the authentic voice of the young soldiers who offered their lives in service of their country.

CHAPTER ONE

THE LEGACY OF GALLIPOLI

When war broke out on 4 August 1914, Australia immediately offered to send a force of 20 000 men to Britain. The British government asked that the men be sent as soon as possible.[1] Recruiting began on 10 August 1914.

The convoy carrying the first contingent of Australians left Albany, Western Australia, on 1 November 1914 and arrived in Egypt on 3 December 1914.[2] Aboard was the 1st Australian Division under the command of General Bridges. Colonel Brudenell White was his chief of staff. The division consisted of 12 000 infantrymen. One brigade came from New South Wales; one from Victoria; and one from the other states. There was also a regiment of Light Horse from Victoria, three brigades of artillery, each of twelve field guns drawn by six-horse teams, a horse-drawn ammunition column, three field companies of engineers, three field ambulances and a divisional train supplying horse transport. In all, the 1st Division numbered 18 000 men.

Also aboard was the 1st Light Horse. It comprised 2226 men divided into three brigades.[3] The convoy included ten ships transporting the

New Zealand contingent. A second Australian contingent arrived in Egypt in February 1915.

In Egypt, these troops were formed into an Anzac Corps under the overall command of General Birdwood.[4] The Anzac Corps headquarters was staffed by British officers, hand-picked in India by General Birdwood. The corps had two divisions, the 1st Australian Division, commanded by General Bridges, and a New Zealand and Australian Division, commanded by General Godley. For three months, the men trained in Egypt, believing their destination was the western front. It was not until April 1915 that they learned that their destination would be the Dardanelles, not France.

On 25 April 1915, in the legendary attack at Gallipoli, the Anzacs forged their reputation. In Charles Bean's assessment, 'Anzac stood, and still stands, for reckless valour in a good cause, for enterprise, resourcefulness, fidelity, comradeship, and endurance that will never own defeat.'[5] All of these are individual qualities — strengths that make an individual a great soldier. The Anzacs proved themselves to be great individual soldiers. Their initiative and guts became the stuff of legend. The Australians were rightly proud of the qualities they had shown at Gallipoli.

Yet Gallipoli was a highly unusual campaign. It was a seaborne invasion in which the invading force never moved far from the sea. Most of the fighting took place at close quarters, in steep seaside gullies. Unlike conditions on the western front, conditions were so cramped that the Anzacs had no chance of respite from the shellfire; no chance of rest in peaceful conditions.[6] The base at Anzac Beach was crowded and busy — it was only half a mile from the centre of the front line.

The terrain of the battlefield made it difficult, if not impossible, for the invading force to use artillery to any serious effect. The only howitzers at Gallipoli were those of the New Zealand battery of (which was equipped with 4½ inch guns), until a Scottish division brought a battery of 5-inch howitzers in June 1915. According to Birdwood, these 'made a lovely noise, but they were, I fear, far from accurate weapons'.[7]

By the time of the evacuation, there were 100 guns in total at Anzac.[8] The Anzacs also improvised bombs and catapults.[9] Given the close quarters of the battlefield, naval artillery could only be used in limited circumstances, for fear of hitting the Anzacs instead of the Turks.

Everything the Anzacs needed had to be brought by sea. Equally, the Anzac wounded had to be evacuated, first to hospital ships, then to hospitals on Lemnos or in Egypt. On Anzac itself, disease flourished — dysentery and typhoid in summer, and colds and influenza in winter. Water was scarce.[10] The troops received no regular canteen or Red Cross stores until late in the campaign.[11] By contrast, the Turks were supplied by land, in the conventional way. It was only a matter of time before the Turks would receive German ammunition and equipment in sufficient quantities to tip the scales of the battle in their favour.[12]

At Gallipoli, the Anzacs were invaders, not liberators. In France and Belgium, they were welcomed as heroes. In Gallipoli, their only contact with the Turkish people was in the bizarre, yet sometimes sympathetic, communications with 'Johnny Turk' which occasionally occurred, so close were the opposing trenches.[13]

In these adverse circumstances, the individual qualities of the Anzacs came to the fore. After the invasion stalled, there was no way to restore momentum by a sweeping attack on a broad front, as might have been possible on the western front. There was no room for mass attacks from the cramped Anzac trenches, nor could artillery be used to support an attack in the same way it might be used in Belgium or France.

So the diggers — for that was what other nationalities called them, and they, in turn, came to call one another[14] — learned to trust their resolve and courage. They learned to hold their own in the toughest of scrapes. They realised they were equal to any challenge that war might set them.

Having started as a volunteer force in August 1914, they had made brilliant progress by the time they left Gallipoli in December 1915, only eighteen months later. As Bean said, 'They were now a military force with strongly established, definite traditions.'[15] They had not, however, learned many of the skills they would need to fight on the flat and open plains of Belgium and northern France. Gallipoli had not taught them much about artillery, and less still about the challenges of the massed battles they could expect on the western front, such as the battles that had taken place at Ypres and Loos in 1915. Although they fought in trenches at Gallipoli, and often at close quarters, trench warfare on the western front was quite a different proposition. The Australian force had little experience of the logistic and administrative support it would need to sustain itself in France and Belgium.

The invasion of Gallipoli dragged on for three or four more months after the 2nd Division arrived in August 1915. The last of the troops from Anzac, now hardened veterans, were evacuated on 19 and 20 December 1915. They returned to their training camps in Egypt to rest, refit and reorganise.

Rest meant leave which, for the diggers, meant release from military discipline. For Lieutenant Maxwell, who later won the Victoria Cross, leave was spent experiencing the 'fleshpots and pintpots of Alexandria':

> What memories flood back! Memories of 'Sister Street', Alexandria, where the sensuous odalisques from a dozen nations hawked their charms. Hard bitten and raucous, silky voiced and seductive, languorous as a purring cat, deceptive, powdered, dissipated, decked out in blazonries like some lithe tiger moving in the gloom. Not a single English or American girl gave you that knowing glance of the lady who seems to have known you for an age. Filled with the chivalry of eighteen years I felt proud of the fact that girls of our race were not as the mystery women of Sister Street who flaunted Sex before the weary warrior. I was young. I was destined to live and learn and see much.[16]

Lieutenant-Colonel MacNaghten, CMG, was an Englishman. He had fought with great personal bravery on Gallipoli. Educated at Eton and Cambridge, and a solicitor by profession, he was popular with his men, not only for his courage, but also for his unorthodoxy.[17] The men in his company were drawn from some of the roughest areas of Woolloomooloo and King's Cross. When it had rained whilst MacNaghten's men were training on Randwick racecourse, he had commandeered a supply of rum from the local pub: 'a matter which caused slight unpleasantness (not altogether unusual) with the army financial authorities'.[18]

MacNaghten knew exactly what the men would get up to in Cairo. He thought it was natural that 'these heroes should play up a bit after the great heat and then great cold, flies, shells, ghastly wounds, and maggots from the dead … they can suddenly have alcohol (mostly filthy, drugged and brain-maddening), and females of sorts — just what do you expect of them?'[19]

MacNaghten claimed that he would discipline men who 'cut loose', but the claim does not ring entirely true — MacNaghten was one of that breed of Englishmen who understands Australians, and the distinction Australians draw between doing their duty, and letting their hair down afterwards.★ Sadly, in September 1916, MacNaghten was invalided back to Australia, suffering from 'shell-shock' as a result of his experiences of Gallipoli.[20]

In Cairo, Lieutenant Rule experienced the 'delights of the Wozzer':

The famous Wozzer was the most notorious [attraction in Cairo] and generally came first. Turning off the main street, we had gone a very short way when two military policemen darted out of one house and into another. Screams of, 'Abdul! Abdul! Mahomet!' echoed in the building, as the police chased the male lovers upstairs and down, knocking the furniture all ways.[21]

Private Bishop found his way to the same place. He saw 'a perfectly nude brownish-black woman' who 'smiled at us, turned herself slowly

---

★ 'Home is beautiful, orgies are vile, but you need an orgy once in a while': Ogden Nash.

around as if to show off her attractiveness from all angles'.[22] He had never seen a naked woman before. He paid two piastres to see a show:

> The room was crowded, an empty space in the middle. Two girls and two donkey-boys, all nude, took up station in the open space, and the show commenced. The show, of course, did not lend itself to respectable reporting. It had just about reached its climax when someone in the rear threw a crunched-up Egyptian Times, well alight, into the centre of the performance.
>
> The girls shrieked, the donkey-boys yelled, and a wild melée took over. Nude girls and women were running up and down the corridors, men were scrambling to get out of the room, the doorway was jammed. Our foursome, heads down and pushing hard, got through the doorway, found a down staircase and we really travelled. We took wrong turnings here and there, nude girls were everywhere, screaming their heads off as they ran.[23]

The diggers were getting an education in more things than soldiering.

The Wozzer was actually a street of brothels. Its name was 'Haret el Wasser', and it was near the famous Shepheard's Hotel. Bean describes two 'not very creditable riots' which took place in the Wozzer.[24] The first involved Australians of the 1st Division and some of the New Zealand Maori. The second involved Australians of the 2nd Division. The diggers gave these incidents names: first battle of the Wozzer; and second battle of the Wozzer.

At first Wozzer, 'bad drink sold in the neighbourhood led this demonstration to greater lengths than were intended — beds, mattresses and clothing from several houses were thrown out of the windows and piled in a bonfire in the street'.[25] British military police were called — 'always a red rag to the Australian soldier' — and the MPs used their revolvers in an attempt to disperse the crowd. In fact, the shooting had the opposite effect, attracting a bigger and rowdier crowd to come and watch the party.[26]

Second Wozzer was similar to first Wozzer in scale and nature. Bean was happy to write both 'battles' off to high spirits: 'These two affairs made a good deal of noise at the time. They were not heroic, but they also differed very little from what at Oxford and Cambridge and in Australian universities is known as a "rag".'[27]

Sister Donnell saw a quieter side of Egypt:

Yesterday a party of fifty of us [nursing sisters] went for a ride on camels and donkeys to the Sakkara Pyramids, and then to see some old Tombs that date back to 3,500 years before Christ … Seeing Cairo and the Eastern life is interesting. The natives make excellent servants; you can't help admiring their keen perception. By a look they know what you want, but what I think is so appalling about the place is its filth, and the influence it has on some of our boys. They say if you live in Egypt long you are sure to grow into Egyptian ways. I don't feel afraid, though I can watch and see things now that first used to make me shrink.[28]

Things that might have made Sister Donnell shrink from the streets of Cairo were 'the poor, the blind, the maimed, the horrible deformed creatures of humanity, freaks of nature, the starving, all crying for: "Bakshish! Bakshish!"'[29]

Leave was short-lived. Soon it was back to the business of war.

In Australia and New Zealand, news of Gallipoli had boosted recruitment. Between 35 000 and 40 000 Australian and New Zealand reinforcements had arrived in Egypt ready to join the veterans. More troops were expected at the rate of 12 000 per month.[30] These new recruits were not attached to any existing formation. A plan would need to be devised to absorb and assimilate them into the fighting force.

There were also issues of command. General Bridges had died of wounds at Gallipoli. A Turkish sniper shot him, severing his femoral artery. Knowing he had only a short time to live Bridges told a friend, 'Anyhow, I have commanded an Australian Division.'[31] There was just time for Birdwood to cable the King, asking him to confer an immediate knighthood on the general. Bridges was informed of the honour shortly before he died.[32]

At Gallipoli, General Birdwood was given responsibility to command the evacuation of the Dardanelles Army. With that task successfully accomplished, he was free to resume command of the Anzac Corps.[33]

After Gallipoli, the Australians had to apply themselves to the task of preparing for a different form of warfare. In January 1916, it was still not clear whether their next role would be in repelling the attack the Turks and Germans threatened to make on the Suez Canal, or whether they would be sent as reinforcements to the western front.

In either case, it would be necessary to form the Anzacs into divisions which conformed to the model of the British Army, and to complete the training which, in some cases (notably among the 2nd Division), had been cut short by urgent calls to reinforce the troops at Gallipoli.[34]

CHAPTER TWO

SPLITTING THE DIVISIONS

General Birdwood, with General White as chief of staff, took charge of the reorganisation. They adopted a three-point plan. First, the recruits still in Australia would form a new 3rd Australian Division. Second, the Australian divisions in Egypt would be divided to form two new Australian divisions: the 4th and 5th. This would be achieved by splitting the existing 1st and 2nd Divisions and using the reserves arriving from Australia to bring all four divisions up to full strength. Third, the New Zealanders would form a single New Zealand Division.[1]

All five Australian divisions would adopt the organisational structure of a division of the British Army.[2] The division was the basic strategic unit of the army. The structure and strength of a British division in 1914 are shown (approximately) in the following chart.[3]

Unit	Officers and men	Horses
Headquarters	82	54
Infantry		
3 x Infantry Brigades each with four Battalions	12 165	741

Unit	Officers and men	Horses
Artillery		
Artillery Headquarters	22	20
3 x Field Artillery Brigades	2385	2244
1 x Field Artillery (howitzer) Brigade	755	697
1 x Heavy Battery and Ammunition Column	198	144
1 x Divisional Ammunition Column	568	709
Engineers		
Divisional Engineers Headquarters	13	8
2 x Field Companies, Royal Engineers	434	152
1 x Signal Company	162	80
Other Supporting Units		
1 x Cavalry Squadron	159	167
1 x Divisional Train	428	378
3 x Field Ambulances	702	198
Total strength	18 073	5592

An infantry division, therefore, consisted of three brigades of infantry, each with a nominal strength of about 4000. A brigade consisted, in turn, of four battalions, each with a nominal strength of 35 officers and 970 other ranks. A battalion was organised as four companies, each of four platoons, each of four sections.

Each battalion had a transport establishment of about 25 vehicles and 55 animals — horses and mules that had to carry food and ammunition over the last and most difficult stage of their journey to the front line.

Towards the end of the war, a division's artillery was organised into two field artillery brigades, each with four 6-gun batteries — three 18-pounder batteries and the fourth, a battery of 4½ inch howitzers.

The divisional ammunition column was responsible for the supply of small arms ammunition and grenades to the infantry, but mainly devoted to keeping the artillery supplied with the large amounts of ammunition that it required. Some 2000 animals and 280 vehicles were used for this purpose.

By 1917, a machine gun company was added to each division. In 1918, the four machine gun companies formed a divisional machine gun battalion with a strength of about 50 officers and 870 other ranks, equipped with 64 Vickers machine guns.

The divisional engineers were trained in all aspects of infantry work, but included men from different trades who acted as the handymen of the division. The divisional signal company not only provided telegraphy, telephony, wireless and visual signalling, it also provided a despatch rider letter service — motorcyclists who handled the division's written correspondence.

The divisional medical service included three field ambulances each with ten officers and 250 other ranks — each being a complete medical unit. About 150 of the personnel of the field ambulance were trained as stretcher-bearers, with most of the remainder constituting the nursing service of the ambulance. The ambulance was, thus, a field depot where the casualties were collected, treated and held until they could be evacuated to a casualty clearing station. The transport of the field ambulance included 50 horses and twenty vehicles, including seven motor ambulances and three horse-drawn ambulances. There were twenty regimental medical officers who lived permanently with the division, attending to sick parades, sanitation and accompanying it into action.

The divisional sanitary section was a separate medical unit of one officer and 27 other ranks, responsible for the sanitation of the divisional area.

The divisional train was not a railway train, but a transport and supply operation responsible to carry all the food and forage required by the division from supply dumps to brigade refilling points in horse-drawn vehicles, whence the first line transport units could collect them and carry them forward. The divisional train was also responsible for transporting the blankets, kit and other baggage of the division from place to place. In its spare time, the divisional train attended to the division's other transport requirements, such as transporting gravel to make or repair roads, or timber for use in engineering or construction.

Each division also had a mechanical transport unit to carry supplies from the railhead to the refilling point, whence they could be collected by the divisional train. At the end of the war a divisional mechanical transport company consisted of nine officers and 350 other ranks organised in five sections, each with sixteen lorries, complete with a workshop and a staff of motor mechanics responsible for repairing all the division's lorries, cars and motorcycles.

Just as each division had its own mechanics, each division also had its own veterinary staff of five officers and 40 other ranks. The mobile veterinary section, consisting of one officer and twenty other ranks, was a veterinary field ambulance, responsible for receiving and treating the battle casualties among the animals, and arranging for their evacuation to a base veterinary hospital.

There was a provost corps, which was responsible for policing the divisional area, and for the control of traffic through the area; a divisional salvage unit responsible for collecting from the battlefield all abandoned material and stores of military value; and a divisional paymaster who had a staff of about twenty sergeants who acted as pay sergeants, in addition to their normal duties.

The divisional canteen became a large operation, turning over many thousands of francs per day selling otherwise unprocurable items to the troops. There were five depot units of supply, a field bakery and a field butchery. And spiritual needs were accommodated by a staff of about twelve chaplains of various religious denominations.

For recreation, the divisional concert party of around twenty men provided entertainment for the troops, whilst the Australian Comforts Fund and the YMCA provided cinemas, which the division staffed and managed.

The divisional baths officer and his staff established baths throughout the divisional area and superintended the changing of underclothing. He also had command of the divisional laundry.

When a division marched along a road, the column extended 15 to 20 miles, and took five hours to pass a single point. It took 25 railway

Diggers of the 5th Division luxuriate in the divisional showers.
AWM E02314

trains, each with twenty horse trucks carrying eight horses each, to shift the animals of a division; 30 passenger trains to shift the officers and men of a division; and a further 25 goods trains to shift its general service, limbered wagons[4] and its guns.

The general officer commanding a division was assisted by an intelligence staff; a general staff, responsible for the battle training of the troops; by an adjutant-general's staff, responsible for personnel issues; and by a quartermaster-general's staff, responsible for supplies, transport and accommodation.

With a division being such a complex organisation, it was a formidable task to form two entirely new Divisions from the existing Australian Divisions. General White took the burden of the reorganisation. He began by issuing orders for the creation of new infantry brigades and new divisions. Over a six-week period in February and March 1916, he issued 51 'Circular Memoranda'. Those memoranda:

… prescribed the method of forming the new artillery, the field ambulances, the companies of engineers, signallers, and train, the pioneer battalions, the sanitary sections, the railway supply detachments, bakeries, butcheries, and other 'supply' units on lines of communication, the machine gun companies, the ordnance corps, postal services, cyclist companies, veterinary units, and corps of military police. They ended with two memoranda establishing the Anzac Mounted Division and the dépôt units in which reinforcements for the AIF were henceforward to be trained.[5]

The new divisions were formed by splitting most of the old brigades and battalions, and using the reinforcements to make up the full strength of each unit. In this way, each new unit had its share of experienced men, who could impart the benefit of their experience to the reinforcements.

Care was taken that the split was fair.[6] In some cases, the old commander divided the men into two groups and asked the new commander to choose which group he preferred.★ Whatever technique was followed, the separation was a wrench for the men. Lieutenant Rule described what happened when the 14th Battalion was split:

> At the time of the reshuffle, Bert Jacka was our company sergeant-major, and it was his duty to draw up a list of men who were to be transferred to the new battalion. The duty was an invidious one. I have no doubt that Bert endeavoured to be perfectly fair to both battalions, but for a few days, our lines were a seething mass of discontent. Men gathered together and cursed those who saw fit to separate brother from brother.[7]

★ This was the solution the Pope adopted when the Kings of Spain and Portugal asked him to arbitrate the dispute as to how they should divide the New World between one another. It is also sometimes used in the more competitive levels of backyard cricket.

Albert Jacka was the first Australian in the Great War to win the Victoria Cross. He was a tough disciplinarian, who told his men, 'I won't crime you.[8] I'll give you a punch on the bloody nose.'[9] He resented the separation as much as the rest of the men, yet he held to the unpleasant task of naming those who would have to leave the company. Lieutenant Rule wrote: 'A few days later we were drawn up on parade, and the final stage of the great separation began. I can still see Jacka standing in front of the company, his heels together, and disgust and rebellion written all over his face, as he called out: "The following sergeants will fall out on the right …"'[10]

But in the end, regardless of the manner in which the separation was carried out, a connection remained between the 'old' formations and the 'new'. As Rule said, 'Half of our battalion had to leave us to form a new battalion, the 14th's daughter, the 46th[11] The permanent loss of so many veterans was a great blow to the battalion,[12] yet bonds such as those between the 14th and the 46th Battalions lasted throughout the war.[13]

It was initially hoped to form an Australasian Army, but it was finally resolved to form two army corps, to be called 'I and II Anzac Corps'. The 1st and 2nd Australian Divisions and the New Zealand Division would make up I Anzac Corps. General Birdwood would be its commander. The 4th and 5th Australian Divisions would make up II Anzac Corps. General Godley would be its commander.[14]

With the doubling came the appointment of new commanders. Names that would later become famous came to the fore at this time, with White, Legge, Chauvel, M'Cay, Monash and Holmes emerging as contenders for divisional command, and Glasgow, Glasfurd, Gellibrand and Elliott emerging as brigadiers.[15]

Artillery was a problem. The Australian divisions had around half the artillery that was provided to a typical division on the western front. An Australian division had three brigades each with three batteries of field guns, and no howitzers, whereas a British division on the western front had three brigades, each with four batteries of field guns and one brigade of howitzers.[16]

To double the Australian divisions and, at the same time, bring their artillery strength up to that of the British divisions would require quadruplication, not duplication, of the existing artillery. Generals Birdwood and White agreed that doubling was the most that could be achieved.[17]

By February 1916, it was becoming apparent that the diggers' next destination would be the western front. Only one thing held back the move: the 'extreme indiscipline and inordinate vanity of the Australians'.[18]

General Murray, then in command of the forces in Egypt, was so concerned that he drafted a letter to General Robertson, the Chief of the Imperial General Staff, complaining that the Australians dressed untidily, lounged on the footpaths, cantered their horses and rode on horse-drawn wagons, in breach of military discipline. Worse, they failed to salute General Murray as he passed on horse or in his car.[19]

General Cox, who was in charge of training the new 4th and 5th Divisions, shared General Murray's views. He thought that saluting officers was the outward and visible sign of the subordination and readiness to obey that were the first essentials in war.[20]

It is uncertain whether General Murray's draft letter was ever sent, but it was circulated to Generals Birdwood, White and Godley, and by them to their subordinates.[21] If it was sent to Robertson, it may explain Robertson's reluctance to continue Birdwood's role as the 'Australian' commander. When Lord Hankey, the British Cabinet Secretary, visited Robertson on 16 March 1916, and found the normally unflappable Robertson upset, it transpired that Robertson had 'had a bad morning with Hughes [the Australian Prime Minister], who had insisted that Birdwood should command the Australian Corps coming to France'.[22] As late as February 1918, General Haig was still blaming Birdwood for the slackness of the Australian troops.[23]

In deference to the British way of doing things, some Australian officers instituted saluting drills and saluting schemes to teach the men to salute officers, and to punish those who would not.[24] Not everyone was impressed by the British insistence on saluting. Many Australians found it humiliating. The French did not enforce it either.[25] General Monash went so far as to describe General Cox as 'one of those crotchety, peppery, livery old Indian officers'.[26]

The diggers themselves loved their larrikin image. Joe Maxwell was a lance-corporal in No.8 Platoon of B Company of the 18th Battalion during this interlude:

After each day's march, while other troops were resting, No.8 platoon played football with a tin. We were certainly a happy family and one of the many ditties I recollect (sung to the tune of Greenland's Icy Mountains) was:

We are the ragtime army
The A.N.Z.A.C.
We cannot shoot, we won't salute
What [expletive] use are we?
And when we get to Berlin
The Kaiser he will say
Hoch! Hoch! Mein Gott,
What an [expletive] rotten lot
Are the A.N.Z.A.C.[27]

The qualities of independence and initiative that had brought the Australians success at Gallipoli were precisely the qualities that caused them to reject the notion that saluting was 'an honour paid to the King's uniform'.[28] For the Australians, it was not the uniform that counted; it was the man wearing it.

Captain Chaplain Tighe, a Jesuit priest who served in Egypt and France, explained the attitude of the men to a meeting in North Sydney on his return to Australia in March 1917:

The English cannot understand the apparent freedom and want of discipline of the Australian. The Australian is full of initiative, he has been accustomed to look after himself from his earliest years and therefore the style of discipline differs from that in the English Army, hence we have many amusing experiences of which you have heard.

… one day there was a weary Australian, he was born tired, leaning against a post and an English Officer came along on horseback. Now of course every soldier is supposed to mind the horse of an Officer when that Officer is on business, but the Australian Officer knows how to ask an Australian soldier to do so, and never gets anything but the readiest acceptance. The English Officer called out, 'Hi! Hi!' Well, our friend steps across, 'Yes sir'. 'Hold my horse'. The man looked at the horse and he looked at the Officer and said, 'Is he a wicked horse?' 'No man, the horse is alright'. 'But would he bite me if I touched him?' 'No! No! The horse is alright'. 'Well is he hard to hold — can one man hold him?' 'Of course one man can hold him'. 'Well hold him yourself'. The Australian disappeared around the corner and the Officer was left.[29]

Discipline could not be forced on men like this. Sergeant Denning's company of sappers had been so critical of the cook that the cook asked to be relieved:

The Sergeant Major, after giving us a lecture on discipline … called a parade, 'Now you men, you know how hard it is to get a cook, and none of you will volunteer for the job. The cook wants to be relieved. He says some of you chaps have passed disparaging remarks about his pedigree. He is insulted and fed up. I'd like the man who called the cook a bastard to step out and apologise to him so that he will carry on.'

Atwell stepped out.

'Oh it was you, Sapper Atwell?'

'No, Sir, I never called the cook a bastard, but what we all want to know is: who called the bastard a cook?' A broad grin slashed across the SM's face as he said, 'Parade dismiss.'[30]★

If General Murray seriously thought that the diggers' reluctance to salute disqualified them from risking their lives on the western front, he changed his mind fast when the Germans attacked the French fortress of Verdun on 21 February 1916.

The success of the German attack focused British minds on the essentials. They needed effective fighting troops in France as soon as possible. When General Murray offered to send troops from Egypt, with the British divisions to come first, complaints about Australian indiscipline were soon forgotten:

> Things at Verdun [are] going none too well … We must accordingly be prepared to risk something in Egypt … Originally it was intended by you and us that the Australians should come (to France) first, but they have gradually taken fourth place … you should generally work on the principle that three Australian divisions in France in April may be worth six at a later date.[31]

On 29 February 1916, General Murray warned General Birdwood that I Anzac Corps would begin moving to France in a fortnight. II Anzac Corps would remain in Egypt for the time being.[32]

Artillery, the old problem, surfaced once again. The 1st and 2nd Divisions would need a full complement of artillery when they arrived in France. This could only be supplied by stripping the 4th and 5th Divisions of their artillery. This was done. The decision brought the 1st and 2nd Divisions up to strength for their arrival in France, but left the 4th and 5th Divisions in Egypt to raise their own artillery from untrained officers and men.[33]

★   This may be an apocryphal story, but it is too good to exclude on that account alone.

In only two and a half months since its return from Gallipoli, the Australian and New Zealand divisions had undergone complete reorganisation. They were now equipped to fight alongside British divisions in France. In the process of the reorganisation, they had assimilated enough new recruits to double the size of the force that had fought so well at Anzac. The Australian force now numbered nearly 100 000 men.[34]

The reorganisation was not only finished on time, it was judged a complete success, for which General White was given the credit. Monash, then in command of the 4th Brigade, said that White was 'far and away the ablest soldier Australia had ever turned out'. Bean said that this opinion was universal among Australian leaders and staffs.[35]

General White now left for France as General Birdwood's chief of staff. I Anzac Corps would be the first of the diggers on the western front — the first to confront the might and power of the German Army.

CHAPTER THREE

ARRIVAL IN FRANCE

I Anzac Corps began the march from its desert camps to the ports where they would embark for Marseilles on 5 March 1916.

As the men assembled, General Birdwood addressed them, reminding them of the need to uphold the good name of Australia among the people of France. He told them that, when they arrived in the French countryside, they would find that most of the young French men were already fighting for their country, leaving the old men, women and children behind. He warned the diggers to behave honourably towards them.[1]

The troops were not sorry to be leaving Egypt. Sergeant Campbell wrote to his parents:

We weighed anchor and steamed out of port at 4pm. Thank God we were able to say good-bye to that Cursed Egypt, the Land of Deserts & the home of the Coon or Gyppo.

All went well on our voyage till about midnight on the Sunday, when we got the alarm signal & heaved hard to port. We were then passing the 'Meniopolis' and the 'Suffolk', which were torpedoed at the same time. So we steered clear of Malta & headed for Toulon.[2]

A German submarine had torpedoed the *Minneapolis*. Fortunately, this happened when she was returning empty from Marseilles to Egypt to collect more troops. She sank near Malta.[3]

Private Bishop travelled in the *Caledonia*. She anchored in St Paul's Bay, Malta. It transpired that Malta was the home of the parents of one of the diggers travelling on the ship.

'My people, my momma, my poppa, they live just there,' and he pointed out a cluster of cottages among the fortifications.

He got more and more excited. Someone told him to swim it.

No, no, too far, I poor swimmer, and ship might go. He was close to crying.

An officer had been watching and listening nearby. He quietly stole away. In a moment he was back, accompanied by our colonel and a high ship-ranker.

The Maltese was pushed towards them. The ship's officer, well-travelled, could converse easily with our man. He told our colonel all about it.

'We're not getting under way till dark. If you wish, it is OK as far as the ship is concerned.'

Away went the ship's officer. In a moment or two a boat swung out, dropped into the water. A rope ladder fell down into the boat. Four crewmen slithered down the ladder, bringing the boat hard up against the ladder. The Maltese, almost jumping out of his skin with excitement, sprawled down to the boat, and away they went. The seaman in charge had his orders, one hour ashore, straight back.

The Maltese saw his family, returned to the boat. They got a great cheer on returning.

A chap nearby turned to me.

'Wasn't that a wonderful thing to happen? Humanity isn't completely dead.'[4]

The navy took every precaution against the risk of submarine attack. The troops wore life jackets during the day. They used them as pillows at night. Lookouts were posted. Their job was to search for periscopes. They were armed with rifles. The idea was that, if they saw a periscope, they would fire at it in the hope that the splash of the bullets would obscure the view of the submarine commander.[5]

The authorities in Marseilles were apprehensive about the arrival of the Australians. Their first concern was the introduction of disease. The men were vaccinated, disinfected and inspected for venereal disease — 'Short Arm inspection', as Sergeant Lawrence called it.[6] It was considered important that, if the diggers were going to kill Germans, they should be free of sexually-transmitted disease. The process was as brutal as it was public: 'Had a pretty rough medical inspection before dinner. The doctor just walked down our line as we stood completely naked. It seems its chief purpose was to discover cases of VD. One poor red-faced lad was singled out to report to the medical quarters amid much cheering.[7] The second concern was riotous behaviour. The transit through Marseilles was planned to be rapid, to avoid the risk of misadventure.[8]

The men eagerly anticipated their arrival. Marseilles gave an exotic introduction to France. The port was busy. It was surrounded by rocky islands and cliffs, dominated by Château d'If, made famous in the *Count of Monte Cristo*.[9]

As the troops marched from the docks through Marseilles, regimental bands played 'Australia Will be There'[10] and the 'Marseillaise' — 'the most inspiring martial music ... but to hear it in such a setting and feel it in one's bones — well, it's the most thrilling experience I have ever had'.[11] The men cheered. The French citizens cheered. Some even showered the men with rose petals.[12]

The diggers saw German prisoners of war working on the quays under the guard of French Territorials, who were wearing kepis and red trousers.[13] The prisoners were members of the 'once proud Prussian Guard' whose regiments the Australians would later come to respect as hard-fighting foes.[14]

Sergeant Lawrence commented on the free and easy continental customs:

> The thing that I first noticed as being so different from our mode of doing things was the urinals. I have often been told that in these matters on the continent they are extremely free and easy and here I had the proof. In the corners of wall buttresses I noticed a small stream of water trickling down which at first I could not understand until I saw a man stroll up, relieve himself and walk away again quite unconcerned, and although an electric tram with any amount of ladies aboard had pulled up not 6 yards from him no one took any notice.[15]

The first men to arrive in Marseilles marched to a camp at Château Santi, overlooking the harbour. They were due to depart by train the next day. As more shiploads arrived, the men would be kept under guard, locked at the docks until they could be marched direct to the train station for the train journey north. Some battalions marched through the town during the day — these were cheered by the inhabitants — but most battalions passed through the town, unnoticed, at night.[16] Artillerymen, who had to lead their horses through the town two at a time, found that their horses shied at the trams.[17]

For most men, this was their first sight of Europe, and they were keen to explore. Lieutenant Rule recalled that, 'Naturally on this day, the men were possessed by an intense longing to get ashore and have a look around. The number who had dying mothers or fathers, who imperatively must be cabled to, was countless. But our military chiefs knew their jobs, and were taking no risks.'[18]

The riotous behaviour that the authorities had feared did not eventuate. Contrary to their reputation, the Australians gave little trouble, to the point that the British commandant in Marseilles wrote to

General M'Cay congratulating him on the behaviour of the 5th Division: 'Notwithstanding the many and varied attractions and temptations of this huge seaport, I am glad to say that not a single case of misbehaviour or lack of discipline has been brought to my notice.'[19]

The journey from Marseilles to the front was about 600 miles. The train took 58 hours to cover the distance — an average speed of around ten miles an hour.[20] Slow train travel and frequent stops were facts of life in wartime France, especially near the front, where the railways became congested with military traffic.

The officers travelled in first class carriages. The men travelled third class, eight to a compartment with rifles and full marching kit.[21] The horses travelled in covered wagons, eight to a wagon.[22] The wagons were marked 'Hommes 40, Chevaux 8'.[23] Later in the war, the Australians would experience the use of these same wagons to carry human cargo — the diggers themselves. On this journey, the horses were carried four at each end, heads inwards, with the men in charge of them riding in the middle.[24]

The logistics involved in the move were huge. Thirty trains were needed to carry the 5th Division. Each train carried four days' supplies.[25] Sergeant Lawrence's train had 42 carriages and eight vans full of gear and provisions.[26]

The trains travelled up the valley of the Rhone, with spectacular views of the Alps to the east. The Australians received an enthusiastic welcome on their slow progress through the countryside. Three times a day, they stopped for an hour to allow the men to stretch their legs and have tea or coffee. At each stop, the citizens cheered the Australians, shouting 'Vive l'Australie'.[27] They gave the men gifts of fruit and wine.

For many diggers, this was their first contact with the French people. From the outset, they felt an affinity with the French.[27] Sergeant Clay wrote to his family:

We got a great reception all along the route from the farms, etc. There wasn't a man of military age to be seen anywhere. In every place there were old men of all ages up to seventy or so and young boys, girls and women of all ages working. It seemed hard to see women and girls hoeing vegetables, etc; tying up vines and thinning them, raking up hay, stooking and, in many case, forking it on to wagons; saw one old lady on top of a great load, building it in fine style; she must have been quite sixty, and another one driving a reaper. The old men waved their hats, the girls and women threw kisses, etc, and old grandmothers stood at the doors with tears in their eyes and waved too.[29]

Just short of Paris, the trains veered off to the west, skirting the city and passing through Versailles before heading north almost to Calais, where, eventually, they turned east to their final destinations.[30]

The 25th Battalion was among the first to arrive at the front. As the battalion made its way to its billets on 24 March 1916, the weather turned sour. It began to snow — the first time many of the Australians had seen snow. The thrill of seeing the snow soon gave way to dismay when the troops, accustomed to the hot sun of Egypt, remembered they had only one blanket each.[31]

Sir Douglas Haig, the austere British Commander-in-Chief, inspected men from the 5th and 6th Brigades and the 2nd Divisional Artillery. He told them: 'Well boys, I am glad to welcome you in France. If you uphold your reputation gained on Gallipoli, you will be loved by everyone but the Germans.'[32]

The troops, many of them raised on farms, had been impressed by the French farms they had seen on the trip north. They were looking forward to being billeted in farmhouses at the front. It would be the first time they had lived among civilians since leaving Australia. But if they were looking forward to the luxury of a warm bed and clean sheets, they were about to be disappointed.

On each farm, the officers and NCOs took the rooms in the main house, whilst the men shared the hay in the barn with the hens and the rats:[33]

The men are sleeping up in the hay loft, whilst we sergeants have a large kitchen and two bedrooms with double beds. Solid oak structures that would cost two pounds in Australia. This farm is quite an enormous structure. Two-storeyed with red tiled gable roofs. The building being on the square with a great courtyard affair in the centre. Each side must be at least 160 feet long. Completely surrounding the building is a moat (all farms have them here) about 5 feet deep and 8 feet wide. They have no carpet on the floors, simply the stone flags. They are none too warm I can tell you …

[The farms] are always brick being rectangular with a kind of courtyard in the centre into which all the manure, from the stables which surround it, is dumped. This pit gradually gets full of water which is then cleaned out and thrown on the land as manure, stink, gee, it's just some humdinger.[34]

Diggers share the hay with hens and rats, keeping their boots on and rifles and gas-masks close at hand. AWM E02176

The Australians were thrilled to be part of a family once again. Bean described the scene:

> The soldiers played with the children, attempted to flirt with the girls — a few tags of bad French and broken English being amply sufficient — and occasionally sipped coffee and rum with 'grandpa' at night over the stove in the living room. But it was above all to 'Madame', who sold them beer and eggs at not unreasonable prices, and who often grew to care for them and tend them like a mother, that the Australians' affections went out. Naturally the men of the transport, the artillery, and the more stationary units came to know them best. The infantry were moving, and only occasionally returned to billets which they had occupied before. But even they made firm friends of these homely and kindly people.[35]

Sergeant Lawrence enjoyed the new arrangements:

> Last night we were having tea and in came an old dame with a glass of beer each. Of course we wanted to pay, but, Oh, no! Then again later in came Madame with her husband with coffee and they sat and yarned to us ... This is the first time that any of us have slept in a real house since leaving home and we certainly have never been treated as though we belonged to the family before, and I think we all felt it a little. We had about 7 rounds of coffee and cognac tonight and I have laughed more than I have done for ages it seems.[36]

The next day, he wrote that he had 'spent most of [the day] playing with the kiddies. Golly it's just like being at home again.'[37]

Lieutenant Joseph Maxwell was also enjoying himself:

> No. 8 platoon was billeted in a barn. Our lodging adjoined a pigsty, but even these neighbours were pleasant after the dust and fire and stinks of Egypt. Heidsiech champagne was but five francs a bottle. All

was right with the world. A run of pleasant days and pleasant associations, such domestic pictures as hens and eggs and plump pink pigs, and hardened diggers cooing infants while Madame cooked eggs and chips. Back flooded memories of home.[38]

Few of the diggers spoke French. They had to learn by trial and error. Sergeant Denning described how he and his mates — Nuggett, Fatty and Perce — learned the ropes when they visited a local café:

A dainty young miss was leaning on a small counter, her attitude to us one of disdain … Quite a few minutes passed before we were composed enough to speak, then Perce said, 'Ask her for eurfs Fatty, that's French for eggs.'

'Ask her yourself, you seem to know all about French.'

'You then Roy.'

'Not on your sweet life. I'm not going spluttering eurfs to her,' Perce said.

'How many do we want? Two each? What's that in French?'

'Try her in English, she may understand a little and we can semaphore the rest.'

Perce stood up and with a great effort gurgled forth, 'Er, any eurfs Mademoiselle?'

'Yes, how many do you want?' she chirped with a giggle.[39]

The French families living close to the front had already endured two years of war before the diggers arrived. The fathers and sons of military age were away fighting or, in many cases, dead.[40] With so many young Australian men in France, there was a similar shortage of men at home. Sergeant Harold Campbell wrote to his mother in Wellington, New South Wales:

Well, I don't suppose Dad will be able to crop much of the old farm this year as labour will be so scarce. You will have to do like the

French women — let the girls go and work the farm. One can see them ploughing, digging spuds & turnips, pruning fruit trees and vines, working threshing machines, etc. As I said before, very rarely will you see a young man at work.[41]

The billets were so close to the front that the men could hear the guns by day, and see the muzzle flashes and the flares by night. As Lawrence wrote in his diary, 'We are not at the war yet but we are very near it. Aeroplanes are buzzing about overhead all day. It is just one ceaseless hum and the bang bang bang of the anti-aircraft guns. These are mobile batteries, as a rule 13-pounder guns on naval mountings fitted on special cars.' Later, he paused to write, 'Whoof, whoof. Christ, someone's copping hell.'[42]

The Australians did not always live up to Birdwood's strictures of good behaviour, and English distaste for the Colonial presence was never far below the surface. Siegfried Sassoon's wonderfully disdainful description in his semi-autobiographical *Memoirs of an Infantry Officer* is a case in point:

Some Australians had been in the billets at La Chaussée, and (if they will pardon me for saying so) had left them in a very bad state. Sanitation had been neglected, and the inhabitants were complaining furiously that their furniture had been used for firewood. Did the Australians leave anything else behind them, I wonder? For some of them had been in Gallipoli, and it is possible that dysentery germs were part of the legacy they left with us.[43]

The diggers were sent on route marches covering fifteen or twenty miles a day. At night, they relaxed:

The *estaminets* were patronised freely at night when the training was done, and the euphonious French word quickly superseded 'pub' in the men's vocabulary. *Vin rouge, vin blanc,*[44] generally diluted with *grenadine* (which is pomegranate syrup) and the light, innocuous beers of the country, were consumed with avidity, the healthy, vigorous life guaranteeing immunity from the after effects.[45]

The veterans of Anzac found their first experience of the western front relatively easy. Sergeant Lawrence observed:

> To men who went through Anzac this scrap is fine. There, there was no escape from shells and bullets, you were in it every minute day and night, and although [Anzac] is pretty country and the view of the Mediterranean was fine, it palled on one awfully. Here, except for artillery fire, if you are not on duty you can get back into towns and villages, buy what you like and enjoy a certain amount of civilization, for the women and children live right up almost into the firing line itself and only leave when they are blown out. Then again the trenches in our area, the nearest they approach each other

Madame pours coffee for Australian and Scottish soldiers. Astoundingly, her estaminet was within 800 yards of the front line. AWM EZ0032

is 200 yards and it is more often 400, whilst at Anzac 5 yards was the distance and 200 yards the extreme.[46]

As Sergeant Denning said, 'There were no girls at all to talk to on Gallipoli, and no beer, or white or red wine.'[47]

When General Monash arrived in France, he was surprised to find a vibrant, civilian community close to the front. The headquarters of his 4th Brigade were in the town of Erquinghem, near Armentières on the Belgian border. In a letter home, he wrote:

This town is a truly astonishing place. It is within seven kilometres of our front trenches. Our artillery is on its eastern outskirts. When our guns are not making a noise we can hear the Boche guns quite plainly. Aeroplanes, both ours and enemy's, often fly overhead (there was quite a pretty though inconclusive airfight this afternoon). Yet in spite of all this the town is in full swing and teeming with life, except that one sees nothing but women and children and old men and British and French soldiers and motor lorries and automobiles … The town is replete with every comfort, a plenitude of fresh eggs and butter, fruit, vegetables, fresh fish, poultry, cheese, still and sparkling wines, delicatessen of all kinds; while in the shops, there is nothing you can think of that you cannot buy, from Maltese or Honiton lace to a kit of carpenter's tools. And if by chance you can think of anything the shops haven't got, they'll understand and get it for you from London or Paris in forty-eight hours. I came here expecting to find a ruined devastated country, without population, with farms and fields laid waste, buildings and churches in ruins and a population of refugees living in misery. Yet here, within four and a half miles of the German Army, I find a peaceful, prosperous, medieval Flemish (once Spanish) town, full of life … replete with the most up-to-date civilized comforts, and a people calm, sedate, confident, and utterly unconcerned as to the terrible slaughter going on within earshot.[48]

'On 25 April 1916, the diggers celebrated the first Anzac Day. In London (where the occasion was celebrated as 'Gallipoli Day'), the King and Queen, the Australian Prime Minister, WM Hughes, Lord Kitchener, General Birdwood, the High Commissioners and Agents-Generals for the Dominions and Colonies, and a large contingent of diggers attended a service in Westminster Abbey. Birdwood wrote that, 'After the service, the men surrounded the car in which my wife and I were seated, and for quite ten minutes refused to let us move. They kept up a continuous roar of cheering which affected us both very much, though I felt it an embarrassing thing to happen in the London streets.'[49]

In France, the diggers marked the anniversary 'as fittingly as the place and conditions would allow, and the toast of "fallen comrades" was drunk in silent remembrance of good pals. Most of the veterans of this day a year ago had clung together in little groups, and the "reinforcement" who was admitted into the comradeship of their circle felt honoured indeed.'[50]

In the 4th Battalion, Major Mackay ordered that every man be given a half-pound fruit cake to mark Anzac Day.* Shortly after eating his cake, Private Gibbs, of D Company, was killed by a sniper's bullet. It seemed impossible that this could happen so far from the front.[51]

Preparations for war on the western front began in earnest. The diggers could not help but be impressed by the scale of the enterprise of warfare. When the diggers arrived on the western front in 1916, the Allied front line was held with 160 divisions, facing 120 German divisions.[52] The five Australian divisions were, therefore, less than 2 per cent of the whole.

The British Expeditionary Force consisted of four armies. An army was generally four corps. A corps had between two and four divisions. Corps commanders were responsible to army commanders for the tactical defence of the corps area. Their task was to create and maintain

---

* Major (later General Sir Iven) Mackay was the first of my father's (three) fathers in law.

the entire system of field defences covering their frontage of the line. These included successive zones of trench systems, field fortifications, preparations for the possibility of a forced withdrawal and planning to advance into enemy territory when the opportunity presented itself.

The corps commander controlled all local and geographic functions in his area. He maintained the roads, railways, canals,[53] telegraphs, telephones, traffic, billeting and quartering, all means of transport and the distribution of supplies — food, water, forage, munitions, engineering and construction materials. He controlled sanitation, medical and veterinary services, evacuation of the sick and wounded, workshops for general engineering and ordnance purposes, laundries, bathing establishments, rest camps, entertainment and recreation facilities and schools for military training and education.

The corps headquarters staff included the staff officers, clerks, orderlies, draughtsmen, drivers, grooms, batmen, cooks and general

Outside the 4th Division signal office a pipe-smoking despatch rider prepares to take a basket of carrier pigeons back to the trenches.
AWM E00646

helpers. The corps cavalry included not only the light horse, but also a cyclist battalion, used for reconnaissance, escort and despatch rider duty.

Signallers had to adapt to conditions, communicating by telegraph, telephone, wireless, carrier pigeons, messenger dogs, aeroplane and despatch rider. Their personnel included sections responsible for laying out and maintaining hundreds of miles of overhead wires and underground cables within the corps area.

By far the majority of the corps troops were in fighting units: artillery, heavy trench mortar, air squadrons and tanks. The artillery was divided into two parts: light, or field artillery, and heavy, or siege, artillery. The light, or field, artillery were guns and howitzers of 4½ inches bore or less. The heavy, or siege, artillery were of guns and howitzers of greater bore, up to 15 inches. Some artillery, notably the versatile 60-pounder, was horse-drawn. Larger ordnance was tractor-drawn, whilst the largest were mounted on railway trains and hauled by steam locomotive.

Artillery might be used for barrage or harassing fire, for bombardment, for counter-battery fighting or for anti-aircraft purposes. By 1918, as many as 1200 guns of all natures and calibres were under the orders of the Australian Army Corps.

The tactical role of the aeroplane was developing. Some squadrons specialised in reconnaissance and aerial photography; others worked in conjunction with the artillery, directing fire; others acted as longer range bombers;★ and others were fighter planes, whose role it was to drive off enemy planes or to pursue enemy infantry or transport.

There was a captive balloon service, providing balloons with a basket attached in which artillery observers could be raised to a height of 2000 to 3000 feet on anchor cables to observe the enemy through binoculars or telescopes, and report on their movements by telephone lines woven into the anchor cables.

★   The range of German bombers was sufficient to bomb London, and this
      commonly occurred.

The tank was in the first stages of its development. By 1918, the standard of the tanks themselves, and the skill of their crews, had improved, with the consequence that they were able to play a decisive role in some of the battles of 1918. In 1916, their capabilities were unknown.

The system for supplying food, forage, ammunition and other supplies had been streamlined after the front became stationary. By 1916, when the diggers arrived, there had been time to devise and build a complex railway system running from the Channel ports to the front. Each day, around 8500 tons of supplies, ammunition, food, forage, mail and other equipment were transported from the ports to 46 different railheads serving the front. New units, reinforcements and remounts made the same journey by rail.[54]

Each division received a standard 'pack' of food each day. A pack consisted of approximately two trucks of bread, two of groceries, one of meat, four of hay, five of oats and one of petrol.[55] It says a lot about

Stretcher bearers load wounded men onto the light rail during the Battle of the Somme. AWM E00249

warfare and the wartime supply system that each pack contained nine truckloads of food for the horses, and only five truckloads of food for the men.

There was also an extensive system of light rail and tramways that operated near the front. The Third Army had the following order of priority for use of the light rail: '(a) siege and heavy ammunition; (b) light ammunition; (c) engineer materials; (d) rations; (e) empty ammunition boxes, cartridge cases, etc.; and lastly other stores, such as ordnance stores, salvage, coal, etc.; wounded men returning from the front were to be carried in preference to other traffic'.[56]

Only a limited number of horses made the trip from Egypt to France. When the 5th Division came to France in June 1916, it left most of its horses behind, bringing mainly officers' chargers and heavy draught horses of the divisional train and other units.

When an Australian division arrived at the front, its shortage of horses was made up mainly with mules. Far from being disappointed with the mules, the men loved them. According to an Australian veterinary officer, Lieutenant-Colonel Henry, the mules were, 'Hardy, economical to feed, resistant to disease, patient and long-suffering, with powers of haulage apparently out of all proportion to their size and weight, no better animal could have been provided for an army entering the horrors of the winter of 1916–17.'[57]

There was good equality in the weapons the opposing sides had available. The weapons included knives, pistols, rifles, bayonets, grenades, machine guns, trench mortars, field guns, heavy guns, howitzers,[58] gas and tanks. The British led the way with the development of the tank, but with that exception, and the less significant exception of the flamethrower, which the Germans first developed, the full suite of weaponry was equally available to both sides.

The standard rifle of the British Army was the .303-inch Lee Enfield short magazine rifle. This was a bolt-action rifle which fired .303 inch calibre bullets. Its magazine held ten rounds. Vickers and Lewis machine guns used the same ammunition.

Whilst artillery had played a major role in the American Civil War (producing huge casualty lists which foreboded those of the Great War), artillery, particularly the guns of larger calibre, had not played so prominent a part in the Franco-Prussian War of 1870–71, the Boer War of 1899–1902 or the Russo-Japanese War of 1904–05. In those wars, guns of smaller calibre had been used in more mobile roles that would not commonly be seen on the western front. The stationary front allowed large guns to be sited in virtually permanent positions near the front, ranged to local landmarks, and brought to bear with devastating effect.

An infantryman on either side might arm himself with a portable arsenal, including a rifle, a bayonet, a knife, a pistol and hand bombs. The Mills bomb was the most effective of the hand bombs on the Allied side.

Artillery designs have become more versatile since but, in the Great War, guns fired on a relatively flat trajectory, and howitzers and mortars lobbed shells at high angles to land behind an obstacle, or in a trench. The Stokes gun was one of the best trench mortars used by the British.[59]

Shrapnel shells spread fragments of metal over a broad radius. They were efficient at killing soldiers, but inefficient at destroying barbed-wire entanglements or blowing up fortified positions. High explosive shells were better adapted to these tasks.[60]

The Germans saw the machine gun as an ideal defensive weapon. Early in the war, they favoured large, fixed machine guns, not because they could pick off individual soldiers in an attack, but because they could be sited in defensive positions to create enfilade fields of fire,[61] called beaten zones, in which the guns sprayed a lethal rain of bullets in the zones where the attacking force would have to make its advance. Later in the war, the development of lighter machine guns, notably the Lewis gun, would make the machine gun portable, allowing it to be used as an offensive weapon as well.

The French were the first to use gas — a variety of tear gas. The Germans took to the use of gas with enthusiasm. They used chlorine gas at Second Ypres on 22 April 1915.[62] Later, phosgene gas was used; then 'white star', a mixture of chlorine and phosgene; then mustard gas, which was sometimes called 'Yperite'; as well as a variety of other compounds.[63]

The Germans were more sophisticated than the British in the construction of defensive lines. They dug deep bunkers. They reinforced the bunkers with timber, steel and concrete. The British, by contrast, were prepared to make do with more temporary fortifications that were often not trenches, but only parapets and parados,[64] raised above ground level, with walls made of sandbags. For British troops, one of the rewards of a successful advance was often the opportunity to occupy a German dugout, even if its entrance did face the wrong way — towards the Germans. For the British, this was a serious issue, since it allowed German shells to land through the main entrance.

The 1st Division's first indent for stores in Calais was for:

20 000 blankets
8000 woollen vests
8000 woollen drawers
5000 cardigan jackets
40 000 gas helmets
21 000 gas satchels
20 000 anti-gas goggles
14 000 steel helmets[65]

The indent reflected three of the unpleasantries that the diggers would face on the western front: the cold; the gas; and the artillery.

Gas was a new experience. The men had to learn the discipline of using gas helmets. For that, they were sent to gas schools. They practised their new skills by walking through trenches filled with asphyxiating gas.[66]

In a testament to the extent to which the British had underestimated the effect of the artillery in prewar planning, the British first sent their men to war wearing cloth forage hats. The diggers had not been issued with steel helmets at Gallipoli, and they had only recently become standard issue on the western front. The 1st Division was only now catching up with the fashion.

I Anzac Corps first went into the line near Armentières in April 1916. This was a 'nursery' sector, intended as an easy introduction to the rigours of life in the trenches of the western front. Accoding to Bean, this was the diggers' 'outstanding experience of trench warfare in its most settled form':

> About half the troops had learnt trench warfare in Gallipoli, but here in Flanders it was less tense and more comfortable. Food, brought up on the tramways by nightly ration parties was more varied; water was 'laid on' through pipes. Instead of steep, dusty paths leading almost immediately down to the sea lapping the shingles, there was an approach through mile-long communication trenches, winding through green fields and hedgerows. Behind these were country roads, farms and villages to which the battalions and brigades were regularly withdrawn for rest. There were shops in the villages, and *estaminets* selling Flemish beer and cheap wine — at least one of them [Spy Farm] within 800 yards of the firing line; men hopped out of a communication trench to go across the fields to it.[67]

Gunner Howell was a signaller with the 1st Australian Field Artillery Brigade. He went into the line on 11 April 1916:

> We left the billets this morning at 9am. Rode in motor buses which on the slippery roads threatened to overturn every minute. Rained all the time. Arrived at an old farmhouse near the line at 1.30 am. Passed through St Eloi and the outskirts of Armentières...
>
> Our dugout will be quite comfortable when it is installed. The place is only about six feet by five with a table in one corner on

which is the telephone and the switchboard. A sandbag seat on the opposite side and a few cuttings from illustrated journals adorning the walls. Some nails which serve as hat and coat hangers and a chair about completes the furnishings ...

Enemy aircraft are very busy this morning and the 'ping' of shrapnel pellets on the dugout roof can be heard frequently.[68]

Gunner Howell went about his business repairing the telephone lines, often in appalling weather. This took him far and wide across the battlefield. He saw a tree that had been blown down by artillery, killing a cow. He 'came across a sparrow in a shell hole. Examining it to see why it couldn't fly we discovered that it had been hit by a shell fragment.' When not on duty, Howell 'went into Laventie and bought some handworked post cards to send home, also had a feed of eggs and chipped potatoes'.[69]

Captain Woodward, of the 1st Australian Tunnelling Company, went from Armentières to the front by motor car. He found that the trenches were often sandbag revetments — shallow trenches topped with walls made of sandbags. Trenches dug too deeply into the ground soon became waterlogged.

Woodward's dugout was 'a splinter-proof shelter formed by driving a length of trench and enlarging the end to give an excavation 8 ft by 6 ft and 6 ft 6 in deep. Walls of 9 in by 3 in Oregon timber were placed round the excavation and if lucky a few railway irons supported a timber roof over which sandbags and layers of brick were laced'.[70]

On his first visit to the front line, Private Bishop found a man standing on the firing step holding a long metal gadget with mirrors. The man offered the gadget to Bishop:

I gently slid it up till in the bottom mirror I saw the reflection from the top mirror of no-man's-land. A little higher and I was looking at the German front line. The scene was more like a garbage tip, weeds and rubbish everywhere, masses of barbed wire sprawling in front of both our own and the German line. Everything was quiet, nothing moved.

'This is the world-renowned western front,' I said, 'and there's no war at all.'[71]

This feeling of remoteness from the enemy was common. Siegfried Sassoon described the false world of patrolling in no-man's land:

He [the enemy] patrolled and we patrolled. Often, when I was crawling about on my belly, I imagined a clod of earth to be a hostile head and shoulders watching me from a shell-hole. But patrols had a sensible habit of avoiding personal contact with one another. Men in the Tunnelling Company who emerged, blinking and dusty white, from the mine shafts, had heard the enemy digging deep underground. They may even have heard the muffled mutter of German voices. But, apart from the projectiles he sent us, the enemy was, as far as we were concerned, an unknown quantity. The Staff were the people who knew all about them ...[72]

Later, in another quiet sector, Ploegsteert Wood, Captain Woodward saw a Stokes gun officer setting up his gun. When Woodward asked what he was doing, the officer replied:

'Oh just going to shoot up the Hun'. I wished him success. He located a position not far from my dugout and when ready to fire his presence was noticed by the Company Commander in that Section of the line. The Captain's query received the same answer as had mine, but in this case the Captain forcibly replied, 'Oh, are you? Get to hell out of here'.[73]

That was no way to behave in a quiet sector.

Most soldiers commented on the smell of the trenches. Often enough, the smell was from decomposing bodies, but, other smells were more constant, and also unpleasant. Special care had to be paid to sanitation. A British Naval division was serving in the trenches under the command, not of an admiral, but of a stern general named General Shute. When the general inspected the trenches, he found sanitation a problem, whereupon the following poem was composed, reputedly by A P Herbert:

> *The General inspecting the trenches*
> *Exclaimed with a horrified shout*
> *'I refuse to command a division*
> *Which leaves its excreta about'.*
>
> *But nobody took any notice*
> *No one was prepared to refute*
> *That the presence of shit was congenial*
> *Compared to the presence of Shute.*
>
> *And certain responsible critics*
> *Made haste to reply to his words,*
> *Observing that his staff advisers*
> *Consisted entirely of turds.*
>
> *For shit may be shot at odd corners*
> *And paper supplied there to suit,*
> *But a shit would be shot without mourners*
> *If somebody shot that shit Shute.*[74]

The diggers did come under long-range artillery fire, even in quiet sectors. The fire was so accurate that the diggers suspected that their positions were being given away by spies. 'Many poor old French women were accused of signalling to Huns whenever they hung out their washing. Cows in certain fields, and lights at night, also came in for comment.'[75]

Eventually the penny dropped that it was not spies, but the diggers' own carelessness that was to blame. The Germans kept the diggers under constant observation, ready to pounce when they gave themselves away 'by hanging out their washing on the side of the farm exposed to the enemy's view, or themselves lounging there, or lighting fires which smoked, or crowding to the skyline to watch an aeroplane dodge the enemy's shells'.[76]

Sometimes Allied artillery mistakenly dropped short, landing in the Allied trenches. Captain Knyvett described the following incident:

> We soon discovered that the shells that were bursting among us were many of them coming from behind. This made us very uncomfortable, for we were not protected against our own infantry fire ... Our first message over the phone was very polite. 'We preferred to be killed by the Germans, thank you', was all we said to the battery commander. But as his remarks continued to come to us through the air, accompanied by a charge of explosive, and two of our officers being killed, our next message was worded very differently, and we told him that 'if he fired again we would turn the machine-guns on to them'.[77]

In June 1916, the Australians were ordered to undertake trench raids. In the first raid, Captain Foss led a group of men across the wire and entered the enemy's trench, killing some of the occupants, and taking prisoners.[78]

Captain Murray, of the 14th Battalion, saw his first German soldier whilst patrolling alone and unarmed:

> I determined to take him prisoner, he had not seen me. It was getting darker. He had his rifle slung from one shoulder only. I, crouching so as not to get on the skyline, felt about and picked up a piece of black mud that had dried very hard. I intended to bash him in the face with it and take his rifle from him. When about six feet

from him and on his right side, I said in a savage voice 'hands up!'
He dropped his rifle and put up his hands. What a wonderful feeling
of relief it was to get it.[79]

Whilst the Australians were learning some of the tricks of trench
warfare, western front style, planning was under way for the major
British offensive of 1916, an attack in force on either side of the River
Somme, 50 miles south of the Australian positions at Armentières.

CHAPTER FOUR

THE BATTLE OF
THE SOMME

General Haig originally conceived the Battle of the Somme as a massive attack; he planned to use 39 French divisions and 25 British. As planning for the battle progressed, the attacking force was whittled down to six French divisions and thirteen British.[1] They were to advance on a front of six miles.

In his despatch after the battle, General Haig claimed he had three objectives for the battle. The first was to relieve the pressure on Verdun, where the Germans had been concentrating a huge attack on the French for some months. The second was to assist the Allies by stopping the Germans diverting troops from the western front to other fronts. The third was to 'wear down the strength of the forces opposed to us'.[2]

If this report after the battle is to be believed, it was not General Haig's objective to drive back the Germans from the positions they held, nor to advance the front. Before the battle, however, a physical objective of the battle was stated. It was the Bapaume ridge — an objective that was never attained.

All of Haig's despatches are elaborate and professional productions, designed to cast his own performance in the most favourable light. It is difficult to resist the conclusion that Haig omitted reference to the physical objective of the battle for fear of highlighting the failure to achieve it. Could he seriously claim that it was not an objective to advance the front?

General Haig claimed that preparations for the battle were meticulous:

> Vast stocks of ammunition and stores of all kinds had to be accumulated beforehand within a convenient distance of our front. To deal with these, many miles of new railways — both standard and narrow gauge — and trench tramways were laid. All available roads were improved, many others were made, and long causeways were built over marshy valleys.
>
> Many additional dug-outs had to be provided as shelter for the troops, for use as dressing stations for the wounded, and as magazines for storing ammunition, food, water, and engineering material. Scores of miles of deep communication trenches had to be dug, as well as trenches for telephone wires, assembly and assault trenches, and numerous gun-emplacements and observation posts.
>
> Important mining operations were undertaken, and charges were laid at various points beneath the enemy's lines.
>
> … wells and bores were sunk, and over one hundred [water] pumping plants were installed. More than one hundred and twenty miles of water mains were laid, and everything was got ready to ensure an adequate water supply as our troops advanced.[3]

On the railways, those planning the battle had worked out precisely the number of trains that would be needed each day to carry in supplies and take out the wounded:[4]

Item	Third Army quantity	Third Army trains required	Fourth Army quantity	Fourth Army trains required
Supplies for	21 or 22 divs	11	21 divs	11
Ammunition	4250 tons	11	5250 tons	14
Reinforcements	3000	2	3000	2
Remounts	720 animals	2	720 animals	2
Engineer stores and spare parts	2 train loads	2	2 train loads	2
Permanent ambulance trains		12		18
Temporary ambulance trains		12		15
Returning supply trains		6		6
Total		58		70

Preparations as vast and time-consuming as these could only be contemplated on a stationary front. Nor could they be disguised. The Germans knew that an attack was coming.

It was just as well the Allied preparations were meticulous, because the Germans had taken equal care in selecting and preparing their defensive positions, and Haig knew it. Haig himself reported:

During nearly two years' preparation [the Germans] had spared no pains to render these defences impregnable. The first and second systems each consisted of several lines of deep trenches, well provided with bomb-proof shelters and with numerous communications trenches connecting them. The front of the trenches in each system was protected by wire entanglements, many of them in two belts forty yards broad, built of iron stakes interlaced with barbed wire, often almost as thick as a man's finger.

The numerous woods and villages in and between these systems of defence had been turned into veritable fortresses. These deep cellars usually to be found in the villages, and the numerous pits and quarries common to a chalk country, were used to provide cover for machine guns and trench mortars.

The existing cellars were supplemented by elaborate dug-outs, sometimes in two stories, and these were connected up by passages as much as thirty feet below the surface of the ground. The salients in the enemy's lines, from which he could bring enfilade fire across his front, were made into self-contained forts, and often protected by mine fields; whilst strong redoubts and concrete machine gun emplacements had been constructed in positions from which he could sweep his own trenches should these be taken. The ground lent itself to good artillery observation on the enemy's part, and he had skilfully arranged for cross fire by his guns.[5]

Churchill was scathing of Haig's decision to launch his attack at enemy strong points. How could such well-prepared positions be a suitable field for an offensive? The best Churchill could say about the decision to attack there was that, 'if the enemy were defeated here, he would be more disheartened than by being overcome upon some easier battleground'.[6]

Churchill was not alone in his criticisms of the plan. The Cabinet Secretary, Maurice Hankey wrote:

The critics of [the Somme battle] plan were frankly derisive. They said it had really been tried before by both sides without success. Even the German attack at Verdun, terrible as it was for France, was proving no less costly to Germany. The initial stages were too difficult. It might be possible, they admitted, at great cost to break through the first line of the enemy defences. But the range of the guns was not sufficient to ensure the destruction of the successive lines of any one section of these defences, which were constructed in depth. While our guns were being moved forward over the broken and pitted lines of our first advance in order to prepare the attack on the next position, the enemy's reinforcements and reserves would be coming up. Fresh trenches would be constructed and the battle would have to begin all over again. Even if, *per impossible* a gap were made in the enemy's line, he had ample reserves wherewith to form an 'army of manoeuvre' to deal with the 'army of pursuit'. There were some who continued to believe that for the present our best plan was to limit ourselves to a series of operations of a comparatively limited scope.[7]

The bombardment preceding the battle began on 24 June 1916. It continued until 7.30 am on 1 July 1916. The start of the infantry attack was marked by the explosion of seventeen underground mines beneath the German positions.

Churchill quoted a brilliant German account of the first day of the Battle of the Somme:

The intense bombardment was realized by all to be a prelude to the infantry assault at last. The men in the dug-outs therefore waited ready, a belt full of hand grenades around them, gripping their rifles and listening for the bombardment to lift from the front defence zone in to the rear defences.

It was of vital importance not to lose a second in taking up position in the open to meet the British infantry who would be advancing immediately behind the artillery barrage.

Looking towards the British trenches through the long trench periscopes held up out of the dugout entrances, there could be seen a mass of steel helmets above their parapet showing that their storm troops were ready for the assault.

At 7.30 am the hurricane of shells ceased as suddenly as it had begun. Our men at once clambered up the steep shafts leading from the dugouts to daylight and ran singly or in groups to the nearest shell craters. The machine guns were pulled out of the dugouts and hurriedly placed into position, their crews dragging the heavy ammunition boxes up the steps and out to the guns. A rough firing line was thus rapidly established.

As soon as in position, a series of extended lines of British infantry were seen moving from the British trenches. The first line appeared to continue without end to right and left. It was quickly followed by a second line, then a third and a fourth.

They came on at a steady even pace as if expecting to find nothing alive in our front trenches …

The front line, preceded by a thin line of skirmishers and bombers, was now half way across No-man's-land. 'Get Ready!' was passed along our front from crater to crater, and heads appeared over the crater edges as final positions were taken up for the best view and machine guns mounted firmly in place.

A few minutes later, when the leading British line was within 100 yards, the rattle of machine gun and rifle fire broke out from along the whole line of craters. Some fired kneeling so as to get a better target over the broken ground, while others in the excitement of the moment, stood up regardless of their own safety to fire into the crowd of men in front of them.

Red rockets sped up into the blue sky as a signal to the artillery, and immediately afterwards a mass of shells from the German batteries in rear tore through the air and burst among the advancing lines.

Whole sections seemed to fall, and the rear formations, moving in close order, quickly scattered. The advance rapidly crumpled under this hail of shells and bullets. All along the line men could be seen throwing their arms into the air and collapsing never to move again. Badly wounded rolled about in their agony, and others less severely injured crawled to the nearest shell hole for shelter.

The British soldier, however, has no lack of courage, and once his hand is set to the plough he is not easily turned from his purpose. The extended lines, though badly shaken and with many gaps, now came on all the faster. Instead of a leisurely walk they covered the ground in short rushes at the double.

Within a few minutes the leading troops had reached within a stone's throw of our front trench, and while some of us continued to fire at point blank range, others threw hand grenades among them. The British bombers answered back, while the infantry rushed forward with fixed bayonets.

The noise of battle became indescribable. The shouting of orders and the shrill British cheers as they charged forward could be heard above the violent and intense fusillade of machine guns and rifles and the bursting bombs, and above the deep thunderings of the artillery and shell explosions. With all this were mingled the moans and groans of the wounded, the cries for help and the last screams of death.

Again and again, the extended lines of British infantry broke against the German defence like waves against a cliff, only to be beaten back.

It was an amazing spectacle of unexampled gallantry, courage and bull-dog determination on both sides.[8]

The day was an unmitigated disaster for the British Army.[9] Almost 60 000 British troops were killed, wounded or captured.

The first phase of the battle continued for five days, with casualties reaching almost 100 000 men. In his despatch, General Haig wrote, 'To sum up the results of the fighting of these five days, on a front of over six miles … our troops had swept over the whole of the enemy's first and strongest system of defence, which he had done his utmost to render impregnable. They had driven him back over a distance of more than a mile, and had carried four elaborately fortified villages.'[10]

If this was 'wearing down', it was difficult to judge which side had been worn down more. If this was taking a punch to land a punch, General Haig or, more correctly, the men in his command, took many more punches than they landed.

The Australians were not involved in the first phase of the battle. II Anzac Corps, which had now taken over the nursery trenches at Armentières, was, however, asked to support the main offensive by conducting trench raids at Armentières.[11] General Godley, commanding II Anzac Corps, explained the justification for making such attacks:

> It is imperative that raids and all possible offensive should be undertaken at once by both divisions of the corps in order to make a certainty of holding on our front such German troops as may now be there.
>
> Raids must therefore take place immediately and must be on a larger scale than has hitherto been attempted — about 200 men or a company. The Corps Commander wishes to impress on divisional commanders, and begs them to impress it on their subordinates that we must fight now, at once, in order to give help to our comrades fighting desperately in the south, and that, however little we may be ready, or however difficult it may be, we should never forgive ourselves if we did not make the necessary effort, and, if necessary, sacrifice, to help them.[12]

The notion was that the trench raids would pin down German divisions, and prevent their being moved to reinforce the Somme.

The 14th Battalion, part of the 4th Division, carried out one such raid at Bois Grenier, north of the main Somme battlefield, on the night of 2 July 1916.[13] The raiding party was organised in two groups. The assault party had four officers and 56 men, in turn split into two parties. Members of each party were detailed to act as bombers, trench raiders, stretcher-bearers and, a gesture of hope, as prisoners' escort. There was also an intelligence non-commissioned officer, an engineer and a machine gunner. The second group was a covering party, to act as reserves, and to cover the raiders as they returned to their own trenches.

The raiders were armed with rifles, revolvers, bayonets, bombs, and knob-kerries — vicious weapons consisting of an entrenching tool handle with iron cog-wheels on the end.[14]

The raiding parties had trained for ten days. They stood ready for the raid, their faces blackened with cork. A three-minute artillery barrage preceded the attack. The purpose of the barrage was to box in the area to be raided, and to discourage enemy supports from coming up. The trench mortars also supported the attack. Only ten minutes were allowed to complete the raid. After that, the artillery would resume the barrage on the German trenches.

This was to be a short, sharp raid. Following the shock of the bombardment, the diggers would rush headlong into the enemy trenches, ready with bayonets and clubs to kill the enemy in a vicious hand-to-hand fight. It was a premeditated, desperate and violent attack.

The raiding party rushed the wire protecting the German positions, crossed it, entered the German trenches and bombed the occupants. The Germans responded with machine guns and artillery. Flares lit up no-man's land. Machine guns raked the area. The artillery bombed it. The raiding party had to retire pell-mell. The covering party had to do its best to give protection. Men wounded in the attack were wounded a second or a third time as they attempted to return to the trenches. Their comrades were wounded when they stopped to help them.

Five members of the raiding party were killed. Three more died of wounds. Thirty-six were wounded. At the time, the 14th Battalion estimated that the Germans had suffered a minimum of 51 casualties, but this was thought to be an overestimate. After the war, the German account of the raid gave the German casualties as six dead and 47 wounded, so the estimate was accurate enough. No prisoners were taken.[15]

Compared with the attacks taking place on the Somme, this raid was strictly small beer. There is no way of knowing if the raid succeeded in holding at Bois Grenier German troops who would otherwise have been sent to the Somme. There was no doubt that the men of 14th

Battalion had made a heavy sacrifice in the name of helping their comrades on the Somme, and possibly to no avail.

It was not long before the Australians would be called on to make a greater sacrifice in the same cause. This doubtful privilege would fall to the 5th Australian Division. ⫯

CHAPTER FIVE

FROMELLES

In the valley below the town of Fromelles lay a section of the German line known as the Sugar Loaf salient. The salient was a point where the German front line bulged into the Allied front line. The disadvantage of a salient was that it permitted the Germans occupying the salient to fire enfilade fire into the Allied trenches on either side of the salient.

The salient lay to the south of the II Anzac Corps line at Armentières, and 50 miles north of the Somme battlefield.[1] The Sugar Loaf was a small hill in the centre of the salient. It was fortified with concrete machine gun posts.

General Haking, who was a close friend of General Haig, had conceived the idea of attacking Sugar Loaf salient. He was a proponent of an offensive approach to military tactics, believing that an attacking force, imbued with the offensive spirit, would overcome a defending force 'as sure as there is a sun in the heavens'.[2]

General Haking had originally suggested an attack on the Sugar Loaf in June, as part of a program of applying pressure to the Germans in anticipation of the attack at the Somme. Now that the Somme battle had begun, he revived the suggestion that an attack be made as a means of stopping the Germans diverting troops from the area of the Sugar Loaf to the Somme. The attack was originally planned as an artillery demonstration only.

Haking's plan was that the bombardment would begin on 14 July 1916 and the attack would take place on 17 July 1916. General M'Cay, commanding the 5th Division, was not told that his division would be involved in the attack until 13 July 1916.

Begun on such short notice, the planning for the attack had a chequered history, as Bean noted:

> Suggested first by Haking as a feint attack; then by Plumer as part of a victorious advance; rejected by Monro in favour of attack elsewhere; put forward again by GHQ as a 'purely artillery' demonstration; ordered as a demonstration but with an infantry operation added, according to Haking's plan and through his emphatic advocacy; almost cancelled — through weather and the doubts of GHQ — and finally reinstated by Haig, apparently as an urgent demonstration — such were the changes of form through which this ill-fated operation had successively passed.[3]

This series of hesitations suggests that there were real doubts as to whether an attack was justified at all. Generals Birdwood and White, who had handed over the Armentières sector to II Anzac Corps, were opposed to the attack and 'made no secret of their opinion' of it.[4]

General Elliott, commanding the 15th Brigade, which was to take part in the attack, also opposed the attack. At the point where the 15th Brigade would have to attack, the trenches were between 350 and 420 yards apart. The British high command had recently issued a circular advising that 200 yards was the maximum advance that should be attempted.[5] Elliott confided his reservations to an officer from GHQ, Major H C L Howard. Howard agreed with Elliott. He thought the attack would be 'a bloody holocaust'.[6]

A similar but smaller attack, made on General Haking's orders three weeks previously at the nearby Boar's Head salient, had failed disastrously.[7]

Yet General Haking continued to push for the offensive to be made. His plan was to attack and occupy the first and second lines of the German trenches. He was optimistic that the attack might succeed in taking the village of Fromelles that lay on the crest of Aubers ridge, a ridge 40 yards high and two miles behind the trenches, but General Haig had restricted the attack to the more limited objective of the trenches.[8]

Initially, General Haig and the GHQ were not anxious for the attack to be made. Haig approved an infantry attack only if there was an adequate supply of guns and ammunition. On 16 July 1916, the assessment of the GHQ was that the information it had about the threat of transfer of German reserves 'did not impose the necessity for the attack to take place tomorrow, 17th, as originally arranged'.[9]

Still General Haking continued to push for the offensive. At a conference on 16 July 1916, he 'was most emphatic that he was quite satisfied with the resources at his disposal; he was quite confident of the success of the operation, and considered that the ammunition at his disposal was ample to put the infantry in and keep them there'. When the GHQ said that the attack was no longer urgent, Haking argued strongly against its postponement.[10]

At the front, the limited notice meant that preparations for the battle were undertaken in haste. Things were ready by the day of the battle, but at the time the bombardment was due to begin, there was a heavy mist over the battlefield. This caused the battle to be postponed.[11]

The postponement of the battle fuelled more doubts as to the value it offered. General Monro, General Haking's superior in command of the First British Army, decided to cancel the whole operation. When Monro informed Haig that he proposed to cancel the attack, Haig replied with an equivocally worded telegram:

The Commander-in-Chief wishes the special operation ... to be carried out as soon as possible, weather permitting, provided always that General Sir Charles Monro is satisfied that the conditions are favourable, and that the resources at his disposal, including ammunition, are adequate both for the preparation and execution of the enterprise.[12]

General Haig may have had some new reason to be concerned that German troops might be diverted from Armentières to the Somme,[13] but his telegram was so hedged about with qualifications that it indicated, at the least, that he did not regard the attack as vital. Certainly, if it was intended to be an order to attack, the telegram lacked the precision that would normally be expected.

Despite this uncertainty, the attack was fixed for 19 July 1916. On 18 July 1916, General Haking published the following order:

As you know we were going to have a fight on Monday, but the weather was so thick that our artillery could not see well enough to produce the very accurate shooting we require for the success of our plan. So I had to put it off and GHQ said do it as soon as you can. I have fixed Zero for Wednesday and I know you will do your best for the sake of the lads who are fighting down south.[14]

The bombardment began at 11.00 am. It was intended to give the impression that another large attack was about to take place, but the attack would be made by only two divisions, the 5th Australian Division and the 61st British Division.[15] The bombardment lasted seven hours. The attack began in broad daylight, at 6.00 pm.

The plans for the 5th Division's attack were simple. Three brigades, the 15th, 14th and 8th, would each attack on a two-battalion frontage. The third battalion in each brigade would carry stores to the attacking troops and garrison the front line after the first two battalions had advanced. The fourth battalion in each brigade was held in reserve. The assaulting troops went over in four waves about 100 yards apart.[16]

A member of the 8th Brigade, on the left of the front, gave this description of the attack:

As the men of the 30th move up they pass the colonel. He looks cool, calm and collected, a gloved hand grasps his cane … Ten yards ahead the trench is blown in and a human shriek is heard. From underneath the debris two figures crawl out and one staggers to his feet. He has lost half his head — nose, jaws and mouth — and his bloody tongue hangs down on his chest. Turning right into a bay, they find it blocked by two men who are trying to get a casualty around a corner on a duckboard. The wounded man's leg is hanging off, but he shouts 'Good luck lads!' as they climb over the parapet.

God! What sights they see out there. Huddled and stretched out bodies, khaki heaps that were once men — some of A company digging a trench — others, like themselves, making short crouching runs and flinging themselves down before anything that will afford the slightest cover.[17]

Sergeant William Mair, in the 14th Brigade in the centre of the front, wrote home the following account of the attack:

I had bad luck myself to run against a bursting shell and still I think I am the luckiest man to be alive today, for out of 64 men that were in 14 Platoon, there is only 14 left …

I'll never forget it, for when we leapt over the parapet at the order to charge we were met with such a deluge of shells and machine gun fire it seemed almost impossible for human beings to have the nerve to face such a fearful blast, but we did, and got over right in amongst the 'Boches'.

How I reached there I hardly remember, but there are two things I distinctly recollect: a hare jumping up and running across our front; and someone singing out, 'At 'em, boys! Stick 'em! Stick 'em! Down 'em!' and then I know I jumped — or rather, fell — down amongst the Germans. I think they were too thunderstruck to bayonet me, but they were glad to be taken.

They were mere boys and some of them were sitting in the dugouts crying, but it was in the 2nd line of their trenches where we had the trouble. They were all big Prussians and Brandenburgers.[18] Their officers were singing out 'Vorwarts! Vorwarts!' (which means 'forwards') but the boys gave them 'Vorwarts'!!

Then the Germans turned their guns on the whole lot of us, and it will give you an idea what inhuman brutes they are. They will kill their own men if they thought that by doing so they were killing their enemies.

That was when I was bowled over, and Ellen, the man that carried me back to the rear was Dan Ryan from Cootamundra, and he had half the side of his face shot away. I will always say that Dan Ryan saved my life, because you know I would have laid there all through the night, and would surely have been blown to pieces. The stretcher-bearers were all killed or wounded so you can see I am a lucky man.[19]

Things were worst on the right of the line, where the 15th Brigade attacked. Here, the distance to the German trenches was greatest. Moreover, if the 61st British Division, attacking on the right of the 15th Brigade, did not take the Sugar Loaf, the 15th Brigade would be exposed to a murderous enfilade fire from the machine gun nests situated there.

The 15th Brigade was not relying solely on the 61st Division. The bombardment was supposed to have cleared the way for the attacking .troops. As General Elliott told his men as they waited to attack, 'Boys, you won't find a German in the trenches when you get there.'[20]

The upbeat nature of Elliott's exhortation is reminiscent of the difference between a surgeon and an airline pilot. Whilst both encourage others to undertake risky activities, the fact that the pilot shares the fate of the passengers generally means that flying is safer than surgery. It says something about the disaster at Fromelles that General Elliott was cast in the role of surgeon, not pilot.

Captain Alex Ellis recounted what actually happened:

[On] the entire front of the 15th Brigade within half an hour from the time of the assault it was apparent that the 61st Division had failed to take the Sugar Loaf, and that it was beyond human power to cross so wide a No-man's-land in the face of the machine gun fire that streamed continuously from it.[21]

The bombardment had been long enough to remove any element of surprise, but not long enough to do any lasting damage to the German trenches, nor the troops occupying them. At 7.18 pm, General Elliott sent a note to M'Cay: 'The trenches are full of the enemy. Every man who rises is shot down. Reports from the wounded indicate that the attack is failing for want of support.'

The 15th Brigade fell short of its objective. The men had no alternative but to dig in as close as possible to the enemy parapet and hold on as best they could.[22]

In the centre and on the left, the attack fared better:

The troops of the centre and left brigades, although they had suffered heavily under the preliminary bombardment, experienced in their assault a vastly different fortune. Immune from the fatal enfilade of the Sugar Loaf, the 53rd and 54th Battalions completed their deployment with comparatively slight additional casualties and, as the barrage lifted, the leading waves dashed into the enemy front lines. The enemy was caught in the act of manning his parapets and some bitter hand to hand fighting followed. It terminated, as all such hand to hand fighting terminated throughout the war, in the absolute triumph of the Australians and the execution or capitulation of the Germans.[23]

This was to be about the only triumph the Australians would enjoy. By 7.30 pm, it was apparent that the attack had failed on the right, but had succeeded in the centre and on the left.[24] The 61st Division, meanwhile, had failed to take the Sugar Loaf. In the face of this failure, the troops of the 61st Division who had succeeded in reaching the enemy trenches were withdrawn. The exhausted men regained their own trenches as dusk fell at 9.00 pm.[25] This left General Elliott with no option but to withdraw his men. Ellis continued:

> The Brigade had failed — failed magnificently in a sublime attempt to achieve the impossible. The ground was covered with its dead and dying, among whom the wounded dragged themselves painfully, seeking the fearful security of a shell-hole or a mound that might give some protection from the machine gun fire that still enveloped them. Some few, preserved by a miracle from either wounds or death, did what was in their power to assist the wounded, and even to patch up some form of defensive line; but the fruitlessness of further sacrifice was now apparent to all.[26]

The position on the left and in the centre was not as desperate, but the collapse of the right flank left the 8th and 14th Brigades in a precarious position. Not only was their right flank exposed, but the line they held was not continuous, and communication between parts of the line were irregular and uncertain.[27]

The 8th Brigade, on the left, fell back early on the morning of 20 July 1916, followed by the 14th Brigade.[28] The battle ended by 9.20 am.[29] The disaster was complete. In one night, the 5th Division had lost 5533 men. 1701 were killed in action, 216 died of wounds, 470 were taken prisoner and 3146 were wounded in action.[30] Captain Knyvett described the scene:

> The sight of our trenches that next morning is burned into my brain. Here and there a man could stand upright, but in most places if you did not wish to be exposed to a sniper's bullet you had to

progress on your hands and knees. In places the parapet was repaired with bodies — bodies that but yesterday had housed the personality of a friend by whom we had warmed ourselves. If you had gathered the stock of a thousand butcher shops, cut it into small pieces and strewn it about, it would give you a faint conception of the shambles those trenches were.

One did not ask the whereabouts of brother or chum. If we did not see him, then it were best to hope that he were of the dead.[31]

General Elliott was devastated. He did his best to comfort his men, but he was weeping pitifully at the senseless slaughter.[32] Lieutenant Freeman wrote that, 'I ... will always have before my eyes the picture of Pompey [Elliott] ... the morning after Fromelles, tears streaming down his face, shaking hands with the pitiful remnant of his brigade.'[33]

Bean reported that, 'In the Australian trenches the scene was such that General Tivey [the commander of the 8th Brigade], who, always solicitous for his men, had hurried thither on hearing of the retirement, could not hold back his tears.'[34]

Sergeant Downing wrote: 'And the sandbags were splashed with red, and red were the firesteps, the duckboards, the bays. And the stench of stagnant pools of the blood of heroes is in our nostrils even now.'[35]

The field was strewn with wounded. The bearers of the field ambulances, the medical officers and the regimental stretcher-bearers worked all night, and on through the day of 20 July 1916. Thousands of wounded were evacuated. Ellis again:

Stretcher-bearers, their knuckles bleeding from repeated knocking against the sides of the narrow trench, struggled hard to get their burdens back to the dressing stations ... Trolley lines in the front trench were repaired and the bodies of the dead were placed on them and conveyed back to one of the cemeteries in the rear. Here graves had been dug and chaplains were busy officiating at their sorrowful duty.[36]

General Haig cabled his congratulations:

> Please convey to the troops engaged last night my appreciation of
> their gallant efforts and of the careful and thorough preparation
> made for it. I wish them to realise that their enterprise has not been
> by any means in vain, and that the gallantry with which they carried
> out the attack is fully recognised.[37]

General White's appreciation was more to the point. For all it had cost
in lives, the attack had not diverted any troops from the Somme:

> I hate these unprepared little shows … What do we do? We may
> deceive the enemy for two days; and after that, he knows perfectly
> well that it is not a big attack, and that we are not in earnest there.
> We don't get anything that does us any good — the trenches are
> hard to keep, and it would mean the breaking up (i.e. the smashing)
> of two divisions.[38] *

The disaster was covered up. The official communiqué stated only:
'Yesterday evening, south of Armentières, we carried out some
important raids on a front of about two miles in which Australian
troops took part. About 140 German prisoners were captured.'[39]

General Haking, the architect of the disaster, was quite unmoved.
The failure was not his fault. He blamed it on the troops under his
command. He wrote:

> The Australian infantry attacked in the most gallant manner and
> gained the enemy's position, but they were not sufficiently trained to
> consolidate the ground gained. They were eventually compelled to
> withdraw and lost heavily in doing so.
>
> The 61st Division were not sufficiently imbued with the
> offensive spirit to go in like one man at the appointed time. Some
> parts of the attack were late deploying.

With two trained divisions the positions would have been a gift after the artillery bombardment.[40]

The justification for the Battle of Fromelles — that it would prevent troops being diverted from the Sugar Loaf to the Somme — was always dubious. The intelligence that it was likely that troops would be diverted by the attack was equivocal. Further, as General White said, an 'unprepared little show' like Fromelles would not deceive the Germans for more than a couple of days, so that the troops would ultimately be diverted in any event.

The planning of the attack was rushed. The 5th Division was given only a few days to prepare for the attack. The undue haste was particularly regrettable given that the troops making the attack were new to the front, and would require as much training as possible for a difficult task.

Generals Birdwood and White had expressed reservations about the attack. The earlier attack at Boar's Head had failed. General Elliott had taken his concerns to Major Howard of the GHQ, who had agreed with his views. General Monro had been prepared to cancel the attack altogether. In the haste to call on the attack, no time was taken to weigh in balance these reservations. Alarm bells should have been ringing.

The bombardment sacrificed surprise, without destroying the enemy positions. At the Somme, a bombardment of seven days had not destroyed the enemy positions. There was no way a bombardment of seven hours would destroy the enemy positions at the Sugar Loaf. General Haig had specifically said that the attack should only take place if there was adequate artillery support.

In giving way to General Haking's urgings, the lessons of earlier battles were ignored. The Battle of the Somme had demonstrated the folly of attacking known strong points — here the attack was on concrete machine gun nests. GHQ had circulated a memorandum advising that advances across no-man's-land should not exceed 200 yards — here 15th Brigade was ordered to advance over 400 yards.

Having suffered the loss of 5533 casualties, and a severe blow to its confidence, the 5th Division was out of offensive action for many months.[41] The British 61st Division had lost 1547 men. The German losses, on the other hand, were less than 1500 men.[42] Moreover, as Charles Bean commented, now that the Germans, 'knew the operation to be a mere feint, and if they had previously had any doubts about the wisdom of "milking"' that front for reserves for the Somme, the fight had actually dispelled those doubts'.[43]

The remorse shown by Generals Elliott and Tivey stands in marked contrast to General Haking's refusal to take responsibility for the failure of the attack. With the blood of a thousand butcher shops on his hands, General Haking had earned the name he would carry throughout the war: Butcher Haking.[44]

The Australian generals who fought at Fromelles learned, yet again, the tough, but obvious, lessons that they were responsible for the lives of the men in their command, and that it was their job, as commanders, to devise ways of winning battles which limited loss of life.

As the slaughter continued on the Somme, the generals must have despaired that this would be easier said than done.

CHAPTER SIX

POZIÈRES AND MOUQUET FARM

In July 1916, I Anzac Corps transferred from the nursery trenches near Armentières to positions behind the Somme front, near Amiens. Some marched the whole way.[1] Some went by train, travelling in the horse carriages. 'It wasn't very comfortable travelling in a stock train and we were very glad when we arrived,' a couple of diggers remembered.[2] The brass did rather better, according to the *Official History*:

> The Anzac headquarters, down to those of the brigades, having since their arrival in France been provided with fleets of powerful touring motor cars, made the move from the north by road, most officers travelling by car, clerks and orderlies following in lorries which brought the office furniture and stores.[3]

Once again, there was a striking contrast between conditions at the front and conditions only a few miles behind it:

> Amiens was then a miniature Paris, far beyond shell-range, practically undamaged, the important streets and boulevards

thronged with a bright population not visibly affected by the war; hotels, shops, cafés, *cabarets*, and newspaper kiosks carried on a brisk trade, the light blue uniforms of the French brightening the sombre crowds of black-coated civilians and khaki-clad British. From many of the rolling hill-slopes on which the Australians drilled, the faint blue-grey shape of the cathedral could be seen rising high above the mists of the valley. The surrounding region was largely rolling pasture land, much more open than the crowded agricultural lowlands of Flanders. The farmers lived chiefly in the villages, many of whose streets were bordered by barns with rough timber roof beams and cracked walls of white-washed mud and straw. The back gardens and orchards with their protecting hedges gave to each hamlet, from the distance, the appearance of a wood. The wheatfields were ripe, their edges brilliant with poppies and corn-flowers. The woods, which were few and small but well tended, were thick with their dark summer foliage.[4]

Marching east, towards the Somme, the Australians were pleased to find that their French was improving. Captain Thomas White wryly observed:

> Major Twynam distinguished himself by informing a demoiselle that one of her cows was leaving the yard. 'Le lait promenades,'[5] he told her. A Digger entered a new billet with 'Bongjou, madam.[6] You needn't reply, for that's all I know'. Another after listening to an excited Frenchman for a long time, asked, 'How does the chorus go?'[7]

The Australians also witnessed some of the results of the Somme offensive, which had been in progress for almost three weeks. Sergeant Denning recalled:

> Trains were rushing towards the front line crowded with soldiers. Hospital trains were rushing back with the wounded, and the roads

were choked with horse-drawn and motor traffic. Fit soldiers going in were trying to make way for walking wounded and weary Tommies coming out. These were 'old' young men with quivering lips and bloodshot eyes and sweat-matted hair, bloodstained uniforms and puttees dragging along behind them. Those not badly wounded were trying to help their more seriously injured mates. They [were] displaying blood-stained and dirty bandages on their legs, arms and heads — such a bedraggled lot. These men had to get out as best they could, as the casualties were out of all proportion to the preparations made to deal with them.[8]

On 19 July 1916, the leading troops of the 1st Division arrived in Albert, only a few miles from the front. They marched past the 'Leaning Virgin', a 30-foot-high statue on the top of the cathedral spire that had been hit by German artillery and was toppled over and leaning horizontally out from its tower.[9] The 2nd and 4th Divisions were marching close behind the 1st. I Anzac Corps was to join the Reserve Army. The commander of the Reserve Army, General Gough, had orders to 'carry out methodical operations against Pozières with a view to capturing that important position with as little delay as possible'.[10]

Whilst the 5th Division was decimated at Fromelles in an attack lasting less than 24 hours, I Anzac Corps was now to make sacrifices on a similar scale in a series of battles lasting 45 days, in which its three Divisions would take turns in mounting attack after attack — nineteen in all — in conditions as trying as any experienced in the entire Battle of the Somme.[11]

To the extent that General Haig had defined a geographic objective for the Somme attack, it was to take control of the Bapaume plateau to the north of the Somme. To reach the Bapaume plateau, it was first necessary to take the ridge that forms the watershed between the valley of the Somme in the south and Belgium to the north.[12] Being a methodical man, General Haig divided the Somme battle into three phases. The first phase consisted of the attack on 1 July 1916 and the attacks between 14 and 17 July 1916, by which the Allies had taken possession of the southern crest of the main plateau between Delville Wood and Bazentin-le-Petit.[13]

I Anzac Corps arrived at the front in time to join the second phase. According to Haig, in this phase, the enemy,

> now fully alive to his danger, put forth his utmost efforts to keep his hold on the main ridge. This stage of the battle constituted a prolonged and severe struggle for mastery between the contending armies, in which, although progress was slow and difficult, the confidence of our troops in their ability to win was never shaken. Their tenacity and determination proved more than equal to their task, and by the first week in September they had established a fighting superiority that has left its mark on the enemy, of which possession of the ridge was merely the visible proof.[14]

The third stage, which began on 15 September 1916, would see the advance pushed 'down the forward slopes of the ridge and further extended on both flanks, until, from Morval to Thiepval, the whole plateau and a good deal of ground beyond were in our possession'.[15]

When the 1st Division arrived in Albert, the British had gained a foothold on the plateau, between Delville Wood and Bazentin-le-Petit. Pozières lay directly to the north of this section. Mouquet Farm was one mile north of Pozières. Thiepval was half a mile west of Mouquet Farm. Pozières and Thiepval stood on the crest of the Pozières ridge. Mouquet Farm stood on the far side of the ridge.

Situated 'on the wide, open, slightly-swelling surface of the hill-top', Pozières formed a bastion, 'its strength arising from the fact that it lay on an open projecting plateau of the ridge, and consequently ... there existed a clear gently graded field of fire for many hundred yards in all directions'. The Germans called this area Hill 160.[16]

According to General Haig, his plan for this section of the front was simple:

West of Bazentin-le-Petit the villages of Pozières and Thiepval, together with the whole elaborate system of trenches round, between and on the main ridge behind them, had still to be carried. An advance further east would, however, eventually turn these defences, and all that was for the present required on the left flank for our attack was a steady, methodical, step by step advance as already ordered.[17]

Rather than a steady, methodical advance, General Gough had taken to heart the part of the order that asked him to take Pozières 'with as little delay as possible'.[18] Haste was his watchword. On 18 July 1916, before the 1st Division had reached Albert, he summoned its commanding officer, General Walker, to his headquarters. General Gough said, 'I want you to go into the line and attack Pozières tomorrow night.'[19] Unmoved by Gough's impetuosity, Walker was sufficiently senior to insist on deferring the attack until there was time to reconnoitre the ground and plan a structured attack. This he set out to do.

The line of march from Albert to Pozières lay through Sausage Valley, which was so crowded with men and materiel that it reminded the men of the beach at Anzac.[20] The ground conditions at Pozières were appalling:

The German front line was on a ridge, with the village of Pozières beyond (or what had once been a village), because all the Australians could see were heaps of brick, dust, and a few clumps of blasted tree trunks. Until recently, they were told, an occasional rat was seen slinking through the debris. Now, even the rats had given up. 'I find it hard to believe my eyes,' said Mackay, 'there is barely a square foot of soil that hasn't been torn about by high explosive'. Dawn disclosed bodies, half-bodies and smaller denominations of bodies sprawled all over the place. Chaplain McKenzie took his jacket off (and soon afterwards, his shirt) as he toiled with pick and shovel to bury the impatient dead — so many more British than German.

With a few words of comfort he would consign them to Glory. There were tens of thousands of craters. Every handful of earth contained a chunk of shrapnel.[21]

The surface of the ground was like a choppy sea. Two German trenches called OG1 and OG2 were supposed to be key landmarks. They were often so obscure as to be untraceable.[22] When Lieutenant Trotter arrived in the village, he asked a mate, 'Where is Pozières?' and was told 'We are standing in its main street.'[23]

The 1st and 3rd Brigades of 1st Division took over positions in the front line on 20 July 1916. At first, the plan was that they would attack on the night of 21 July 1916. The attack was now postponed until half an hour past midnight on the morning of 23 July 1916.[24] The idea of a night attack was to negate the effect of the enemy's machine guns.

The first objective of the attack was the German trench in front of the village. The second was a recently constructed trench skirting the orchards. The third was the southern side of the main road that ran through the village.[25]

The bombardment was spectacular in the night sky, and the attack was a success.[26] Sergeant Campbell described the comparative ease with which the objectives were taken:

At last No.1 party went over, led by Lt. Howie, and I gave the order for No.2 party to get ready.

'Forward, and follow me!', and away we went, 20 yards in arrear of No.1, through the hail of shrapnel. Brave lads they were, not a murmur. Gradually, we overtook No.1 party & we lost Lt. Howie, so I continued to press forward. By this time we were beyond the enemy's veil of shrapnel and his machine gun and rifle fire had practically ceased, so we formed up … and marched across in one long line until we got to within a few yards of the Third Line. But it really didn't need any taking — our Artillery had done its work, and what few Germans were left ran for dear life & were accounted for by our shrapnel.[27]

Major Mackay saw

> 'lots of dead Germans. Lots with their hands up, mumbling in a half-dazed way, 'Mercy, Kamerad!' Lots of them were racing back towards their second line, only to run into our artillery fire once more. Many of them remained in their dugouts, terrified, and had to be bombed or bayoneted out. Some never came out. A number of the Germans taken prisoner would not, through pure fright, cross No-man's-land. They had to be killed.[28]

Gunner Howell, manning an artillery observation post on the front line had to cross the battlefield to check and repair the wires on which the artillery's signallers depended:

> The country was strewn with dead and streams of wounded were to be seen on their way to the dressing stations, while long lines of men could be seen winding in and out of the shattered trenches on their way to relieve the men in the line, or to consolidate a part of the ground won last night. Casualty Corner was simply impassable … When we were passing the Chalk Pit … a flare went up from the line [and] I saw the most awful sight of the night. There were about fifty wounded men on stretchers waiting to be carried back and while I looked a German shell fell amongst them.[29]

At this spot, Lieutenant Henderson, a chaplain with the 12th Brigade, had to perform his first burial — that of a twenty-year-old stretcher-bearer:

> The little cemetery was on the right of the road, just before you go down to the chalk pits … Behind us cracked the field batteries, and

the heavier guns in 'Sausage Valley' ... I pulled out of my pocket a long surplice of very fine material made to roll up small, and a simple cloth stole, and, the comrades of the fallen man standing round, I began the service. They had only been relieved the night before, and had almost certainly not slept for several days. We all kept on our steel hats ... The service [drew] quickly to its close ... 'Fall in! C Section!' The speaker [was] a heavy-eyed, unshaven sergeant, in a blue sweater. The barrage [was] falling on the road up to the trenches, but the trumpets of God [were] calling His servants to duty and beyond.[30]

As Colonel Stevens and Major Mackay planned their next attack under severe artillery and machine gun fire, and 'amid dozens of corpses and moaning wounded, mainly Germans', a messenger appeared and handed them a note marked 'Urgent and Secret'. It was from General Gough himself — important orders, no doubt. Gough told them that, recently a number of men had failed to salute his car, despite the general's flag being prominently displayed on the bonnet. The order? 'This practice must cease.'[31]

Diggers bury a mate. AWM P00077.011

The only disappointment with the attack on 23 July 1916 was that a small section of trench on the right, part of the OG trench, was not taken. This allowed the Germans to fire into the open right flank of the Australians, but that did not prevent the Australians pressing into the village north of the road during the day of 23 July 1916, where they captured more Germans.[32] Preparations were in hand to take the rest of the village that afternoon.[33]

Working with his battery some distance behind the line, Gunner W J Duffell wrote to his family:

> Wounded infantry were walking back, many of them driving small batches of German prisoners before them, terrified humans who looked as though they had glimpsed hell. They were safe now except those who happened to be caught by their own shellfire. This often happened and many of those walking wounded succumbed to those same shells.
>
> Horse drawn ambulances slowly made their way along Sausage Gully bringing out the wounded that were unable to walk. Sometimes a shell would burst on the track close to the ambulances & often a whole team & party would be torn to pieces by the tearing flash of a bursting shell.[34]

Sausage Valley was, however, a legitimate target for the German artillery. According to Lieutenant Rule: 'By the number of guns all along it, it must have been the best hiding place for artillery in this part of the field. Nearly everyone describing the place said that the guns were "wheel to wheel" along it.'[35]

Meanwhile, at Pozières, three German counterattacks were driven back. The Germans resolved to wear down the Australian defenders by an artillery barrage. The barrage began at 7.00 am on 24 July 1916.[36] The German artillerymen worked 'slowly, regularly, methodically, at first. Then with growing intensity. Gradually leading with a terrifying ferocity to the worst bombardment ever experienced by the Australians', wrote I D Chapman.[37]

Despite the bombardment, General Gough urged the Australians to press on with their attack. He asked them to push on towards Mouquet Farm.

The German bombardment increased in intensity. It spread to include the approaches to Pozières, hindering the delivery of supplies of food, water and ammunition.[38] This disrupted the Australian attack on the night of 24 July 1916. Although a section of German trenches was taken, not all of it could be held.[39]

The German barrage lasted 48 hours, working to a climax late on 25 July 1916. For all the ferocity of the artillery barrage, the German infantry attack that followed it foundered in the shocking ground conditions. The Germans then fell back. This was just as well as the 1st Division was in no condition to continue.[40] In three days of fighting, it had lost 5285 officers and men. The 2nd Division took its place in the line.[41]

Private Keown, a member of the 5th Battalion of the 1st Division, described the march away from Pozières:

> The weary Battalion marched back two miles or so to the trenches at La Boiselle, and had their well-earned rest interrupted by an intermittent 'tear shell' bombardment. From here to Albert they marched again, now so far recovered from the fearful experiences of Pozières as to be able to raise their voices in singing as they went.[42]

Lieutenant Rule, waiting in reserve with the 4th Division, saw the 1st Division marching through Warloy:

> They came by one morning, having spent the night around Albert … Although we knew it was stiff fighting, we had our eyes opened when we saw these men march by. Those who watched them will never forget it as long as they live. They looked like men who had been in hell. Almost without exception each man looked drawn and haggard, and so dazed that they appeared to be walking in a dream,

and their eyes looked glassy and starey. Quite a few were silly, and these were the only noisy ones in the crowd. Their appearance before they had a night's sleep and clean-up must have been twice as ill as when we saw them ... In all my experience I've never seen men so shaken up as these.[43]

General Gough pressed the 2nd Division on just as relentlessly as he had pressed the 1st.[44] Sweeping aside General White's objections, Gough fixed 12.15 am on 29 July 1916 as the time for the 2nd Division's first attack, from Pozières towards the windmill just north of Pozières. However, heavy artillery fire and a distracting bomb fight hampered preparations for the attack and as a result, the attack failed.

The next day, General Haig received reports of the battle. He was not impressed. He wrote in his diary:

The attack by the 2nd Australian Division upon the enemy's position between Pozières and the Windmill was not successful last night. From several reports, I think the cause was due to lack of preparation.

After lunch I visited H.Q. Reserve Army and impressed on Gough and his G.S.O ... that they must supervise more closely the plans of the Anzac Corps. Some of their Divisional Generals are so ignorant and (like many Colonials) so conceited, that they cannot be trusted to work out unaided the plan of attack.

I then went to H.Q. Anzac Corps at Contay and saw General Birdwood and his B.G.G.S. (White).[45]

It was then that General Haig told Generals Birdwood and White that 'You're not fighting the Bashi-Bazouks now' and that, 'This is serious, scientific war, and you are up against the most scientific and most military nation in Europe,'[46] later confiding to his diary that, 'Luckily, their losses had been fairly small, considering the operation and the numbers engaged — about 1000 for the whole 24 hours.'[47]

Captain Albert Jacka, VC MC and Bar, 'the bravest man in the Aussie Army', is congratulated by General Birdwood on the Bar he won at Bullecourt. General Holmes looks on. AWM E00438

The contrast between Haig and White could not have been more marked, wrote Charles Bean:

> Cyril Brudenell Bingham White was never a typical Australian, unless he was typical of the very best. He was descended straight from the highest pioneer stock, and through careful moulding, and the tests and opportunities that bush and city life provided, became an example of one of the highest types that humanity produces.[48]

A fine general and a brilliant organiser, White had fought with distinction at Gallipoli. He had carried through the reorganisation of the Australian Imperial Force in Egypt, as the Australians made their way from Gallipoli to France. After Pozières, he bristled at Haig's rebuke. When Haig accused the Australians of rough and ready methods, White answered back. Bean again:

... although important errors had been made, they were not of the crude nature indicated by Haig, whose information was almost wholly inaccurate; and, at the end of the interview, White, despite a warning head-shake from the chief of Haig's staff, faced the Commander-in-Chief and pointed this out in detail, item by item. After hearing him thoroughly, Haig laid a hand on White's shoulder. 'I dare say you're right, young man,' he said kindly.[49]

The relationship of brash Colonial with condescending Englishman is confirmed by Haig's diary account of the incident:

I then went to HQ Anzac Corps at Contay and saw Generals Birdwood and (his BGGS[50]) White. The latter seems a very sound capable fellow, and assured me they had learned a lesson, and would be more thorough in future. Luckily, their losses had been fairly small considering the operation and the numbers engaged — about 1000 for the whole 24 hours.[51]

And what of Birdwood? Born in India, Birdwood was also an English cavalry officer. He was the youngest corps commander in the field. From his contact with the Australians, he had developed an affection for the diggers, as well as an understanding of their ways. The diggers, in turn, liked him. Birdwood had also formed a close bond with White. He delegated to White the tasks of organisation and planning, spending as much time as he could with the troops under his command, for whom he maintained a close paternal regard. His experience of the Battle of the Somme, however, was quite different to that of the men under his command:

Back in France, I never had an idle day. I would be on the move soon after 6 a.m., and if the sector to be visited was some way off, I took sandwiches with me for breakfast. If I started later I would have a small breakfast at headquarters, and then, to the dismay of the Staff

Officer accompanying me, would refuse to stop anywhere for lunch ... My Staff, knowing my ways, could always bring chocolate with them. Whenever possible, I arranged to finish my tour at a point about ten miles from headquarters. There our horses would meet us, and we could end the day with a good gallop home over the fields or through the woods ...

Throughout the great part of that summer of 1916 we were fighting along the great road running north-east from Amiens past Albert, Pozières, Martinpuich and Courcelette to Bapaume. The men fought hard and with unflinching courage, taking their punishment without complaint and constantly pushing the Germans back.[52]

If the men had been able to compare the punishment they were taking with the punishment their general was taking, they might well have complained.

Whilst General Haig was applying pressure to his subordinates, he was also under pressure himself. On the very day he visited Generals Birdwood and White, General Robertson, wrote to Haig: 'The powers that be [meaning the War Cabinet] are beginning to get a little uneasy in regard to the situation. The casualties are mounting up and they are wondering whether we are likely to get a good return for them.'[53] This was a good question. Haig reformulated it in his diary as 'Whether a loss of say 300 000 men will lead to really great results, because if not, we ought to be content with something less than we are now doing.'[54]

General Haig gave his response to the Cabinet on 1 August 1916 in point form. He argued that five reasons justified the huge loss of life:

(a) Pressure on Verdun relieved. Not less than six Enemy divisions besides heavy guns have been withdrawn.

(b) Success achieved by Russia last month would certainly have been stopped if Enemy had been free to transfer troops from here to the Eastern theatre.

(c)   Proof given to world that Allies are capable of making and maintaining a vigorous offensive and of driving Enemy's best troops from the strongest positions has shaken faith of Germans, of their friends, of doubting neutrals in the invincibility of Germany. Also impressed on the world, England's strength and determination, and the fighting power of the British race.

(d)   We have inflicted very heavy losses on the Enemy. In one month, 30 of his divisions have been used up, as against 35 at Verdun in 5 months! In another 6 weeks, the Enemy should be hard put to find men!

(e)   The maintenance of a steady offensive pressure will result eventually in his complete overthrow.[55]

Haig was not prepared to change a thing. He continued: 'Principle on which we should act: *Maintain our offensive*. Our losses in July's fighting totalled about 120 000 more than they would have been, had we not attacked. They cannot be regarded as sufficient to justify any anxiety as to our ability to continue the offensive.'[56]

When General Haig spoke to Generals Birdwood and White, he spoke to General Gough as well, warning him of the need to be thorough in his preparations. With luck, this might mean that Gough would henceforth be more accommodating when the need for haste clashed with the need for time to prepare.

The 2nd Division's next attack was postponed from 2 August to 3 August and ultimately to 4 August 1916, although General White had to intervene personally to win the second delay.[57]

Attacking at night, the Australians had found that they often lost sight of their physical objectives. To avoid that confusion, this new attack was fixed for 9.15 pm, when it was still light enough for the troops to see their objectives. These were the crest of the Pozières ridge and the old German line that ran along it.[58] The attack, made on the second anniversary of the declaration of war, succeeded. The four-day artillery bombardment had been effective. For the first time, the Australians were looking from the crest of the Pozières ridge down onto the Bapaume plateau.[59]

General Gough congratulated the 2nd Division for having 'inflicted a severe defeat on the enemy and secured us most valuable ground'.[60] The Germans agreed that the ground was valuable. German command gave the following order:

> At any price Hill [160, the Pozières ridge] must be recovered, for if it were to remain in the hands of the British it would give them an important advantage. Attacks will be made by successive waves 80 yards apart. Troops which first reach the [ridge] must hold on until reinforced, whatever the losses. Any officer or man who fails to resist to the death on the ground won will be immediately court-martialled.[61]

Again, the Australians were repaid for a successful advance with a stiff bombardment. The bombardment began on 5 August 1916 and continued over the next two days. Bean called it 'the crowning bombardment of the whole series',[62] but the Australians repulsed the attacks that followed it.[63] In its turn, the 2nd Division was exhausted. As the bombardment continued, the 4th Division relieved the 2nd Division. Most of the 2nd Division was brought out of the line on 6 August 1916. The relief was completed on 7 August 1916.

In twelve days of continuous bombardment, the 2nd Division lost 6846 killed wounded and missing. In addition to their physical wounds, many of the wounded were suffering from shock. The *Official History* noted: 'An eyewitness has recorded that, of the patients [from the 2nd Division] sitting in front of Vadencourt Château waiting for attention to their flesh wounds, nearly every one was shaking like an aspen leaf — a sure sign of overstrain by shell-fire.'[64] The 2nd Mobile Veterinary Section, which came under shellfire for the first time on the Somme, reported, unsurprisingly, that its horses had also suffered badly from the shelling.[65]

Lieutenant Maxwell recalled the period of rest following the withdrawal of the 2nd Division:

Relief and reorganisation were followed by an inspection by General Birdwood. Lean, short, active, and alert, with grey-blue eyes that twinkled with good humour, Birdwood was our idol. He gave the impression that he knew each man personally and one of his first salutations was:

'Have you written home?'

We were dismissed and the General chatted affably with several of the men.

'How is your father?' he asked of the droll Mick Clarke.

'My father is dead, sir,' he replied.

Birdwood moved about and again encountered Clarke.

'Well, my good man, and how is your father?' he began again.

'He's still dead, sir,' blandly answered the irrepressible Mick.[66]

At the front, the 4th Division took up the cudgels. During a German counterattack on 7 August 1916, a platoon that had taken shelter in a deep German dugout did not realise that the Germans had passed over the dugout, and were advancing towards the Allied positions. Bean wrote:

At that moment the Australians on the flank saw a party of eight Australians, an officer leading, leap from a fold in the ground behind the Germans and charge them in the rear. It was Albert Jacka (of Anzac fame), now Lieutenant, whose platoon, waiting in a deep dugout, had been surprised by the attack. The enemy had bombed the dugout and left a sentry over the stairway. Jacka, firing his revolver from below, had rushed up the stairway followed by his surviving men, lined them out, and then sprung on the Germans from behind, fighting like a wild cat. Not far away, men of the 48th Battalion were resisting; and now they, and other Australians scattered across the slope and on the flanks, joined in. There was a wild mêlée; Jacka was very badly wounded, but supports were coming up. The tables were turned. Most of the captured Australians were freed, many Germans were captured, and the lost ground, and more, was taken.[67]

Lieutenant Rule watched as the stretcher-bearers did their work:

Before the fight had died down, the stretcher-bearers began their usual cleaning up of the field. At intervals, stretcher after stretcher went by, interspersed with the walking wounded.

I called out to one set of bearers: 'Who've you got there?'

'I don't know who I've got, but the bravest man in the Aussie Army is on that stretcher just ahead. It's Bert Jacka, and I wouldn't give a Gyppo piastre for him; he is knocked about dreadfully.'[68]

Jacka had been wounded seven times. He recovered, to be awarded the Military Cross for his exploit. Many (including Bean) thought he had done enough to win a bar to the Victoria Cross he had won at Gallipoli.

General Gough ordered the 4th Division to continue the advance by following the line of the ridge towards Mouquet Farm and Thiepval. General Gough's plan was to take Thiepval by driving a narrow salient past Mouquet Farm and behind Thiepval. Attacking in this unusual way meant that the troops carrying supplies into the salient at the front, as well as those fighting at the front, would be exposed to enemy fire from every angle.[69]

After attacks on six consecutive nights, the 4th Division seized part of the Fabeck trench, north-east of Mouquet Farm on 13 August 1916. Captain 'Mad Harry' Murray led the men of the 13th Battalion in the attack that took the trench, but, finding that they were without support, he ordered them to retire the way they had come, using machine guns and the last of their bombs to cover the retreat. Murray later recalled that close shave:

It looked as if we were to be reduced to our last resort — the bayonet — but then I heard dear old Bob Henderson's voice calling for me. He was our bombing officer and I called out promptly. 'Here I am Bob — have you any bombs?' and back came his reply, like a returning wave, and couched in strong Australianese, 'ANY BLOODY AMOUNT! THROWERS TO THE FRONT!'[70]

The 4th Division was relieved, in its turn. It had suffered the loss of 4649 men.[71]

Meanwhile, they were doing it tough at headquarters. On 12 August 1916, General Haig entertained the King, Raymond Poincaré (the French President), General Foch, General Joffre and several others for luncheon. Haig recorded the event in his diary:

We had 15 at lunch and by the King's desire, only water of various kinds was served. Many of us will long remember General Joffre's look of abhorrence, or annoyance, when Shaddock (my butler) handed him a jug of lemonade and a bottle of ginger beer, and asked him which he preferred.[72]

At much the same time, at Thiepval, John Masefield, later the Poet Laureate, saw something rarer even than French generals going without wine at luncheon:

Once in a lull in the firing a woman appeared upon the enemy parapet and started to walk along it. Our men held their fire and watched her. She walked steadily along the whole front of the Schwaben [redoubt] and then jumped down into the trench. Many thought at the time that she was a man masquerading for a bet. But long afterwards, when our men took the Schwaben, they found her lying in the ruins dead. They buried her there, up on top of the hill. God alone knows who she was and what she was doing there.[73]

Readers, more worldly than the future Poet Laureate, may wish to hazard a guess at who the young lady was and what she was doing there.

The crazy rotation at the front continued, with the 1st Division taking the place of the 4th. The 1st Division had received some reinforcements, but was still at only two-thirds of its full strength. It pressed on with the same pointless series of attacks until 22 August 1916, by which time it had suffered a further 2650 casualties.[74] The 2nd Division then returned to the fray. On 26 August 1916, it reached Mouquet Farm, but could not hold it — there were a further 1268 casualties.[75]

On 26 August 1916, the 4th Division took its second dose of medicine. By 15 September 1916, it had driven the salient as far as it ever went, at a cost of 2409 more casualties.[76]

When the men of the 4th Division made their way back through Pozières, an eyewitness wrote: 'The way was absolutely open (to shellfire), and others were bending low and running hurriedly. Our men were walking as if they were in Pitt Street, erect, not hurrying, each man carrying himself as proudly and carelessly as a British officer does.'[77] Thankfully, this was the last contribution the Australians were asked to make to the Battle of the Somme. Between 19 July 1916 and 5 September 1916, the Australians had suffered 24 139 casualties: 5533 men were killed in action; 1198 died of wounds; 10 died of gas; 133 were gassed in action; 389 became prisoners of war; and 16 876 were wounded in action.[78] They had taken Pozières and the ridge behind it — a small territorial gain for the price paid.

Bean laid the blame for the Australian losses squarely at the feet of the British generals:

In those forty-five days Australians had launched nineteen attacks — all except two being on a narrow front. They knew their constant advance during a time of deadlock would compare with any other achievement on the Somme ... But they felt little confidence in the high tactics and strategy of it all. Indeed not a few British and overseas divisions that served under Gough dreaded ever again to experience the results of his optimistic tactical aims and his urgency when caution was needed.

For the frequent shallow thrusts on narrow fronts Haig's policy was largely responsible. He looked on this as a 'wearing down' phase of the struggle ... Haig was certainly wearing down the enemy; but he did not realise that he was even more quickly wearing down the numbers — though not the morale — of his own army. Apparently no effort was being made to devise special methods of attack which would bring greater loss to the enemy than to the British.[79]

In Haig's conception, what was required on the Somme was 'a steady, methodical, step by step advance'. In Gough's conception, what was required was the same type of advance, but done in haste. Neither conception was adequate to the task.

Colonel Charles à Court Repington, the war correspondent for the *Times* newspaper, supported the tactics of Haig and Gough. Curiously, but accurately, he described them as 'day after day the butchery of the unknown by the unseen, and events decided by the greatest mass of projectiles hurled simultaneously in the general direction of the enemy'.[80]

However, General Haig was well satisfied with his work:

Our advance on Thiepval and on the defences above it had been carried out ... in accordance with my instructions given on the 3rd July, by a slow and methodical progression, in which great skill and much patience and endurance had been displayed with entirely satisfactory results.[81]

Entirely satisfactory? What is truly frightening, in retrospect, is that General Haig may actually have believed that the results of these ill-fated attacks were entirely satisfactory. Whilst ever he clung to that belief, there was no prospect of him even attempting to 'devise special methods of attack which would bring greater loss to the enemy than to the British' — and the men would continue to pay the price for his intransigence.

The price paid by the Australians was only a fraction of the full price. According to Bean, Allied losses in the Battle of the Somme totalled 415000. The British official history put the Allied loss at over 600000.[82]

Lieutenant-Colonel Boraston, who was a member of General Haig's staff and a keen supporter of Haig, was the author of *Sir Douglas Haig's Command 1915-1918*[83] in which he loyally refuted criticisms of General Haig.[84] Boraston ultimately conceded that the Allies suffered 410000 casualties in the Battle of the Somme, whilst the Germans suffered only 180000. Churchill accepted his figures, as did Bean.[85]

In this context, Haig's assertion that the loss of 1000 Australian men in one 24 period at Pozières was 'fairly small, considering the operation and the numbers engaged'[86] is understandable, if chillingly callous. But if Colonel Boraston's figures were correct, what did they say for General Haig's strategy of 'wearing down'? If the Germans had been worn down to the extent of 180000 casualties, the Allies had been worn down more than twice as much.

The diggers knew what was going on. Captain Joynt, who was awarded the Victoria Cross in 1918, wrote of the battles at Pozières and Mouquet Farm: 'Haig's policy of piecemeal attacks created ill-feeling towards General Gough and the British High Command ... The men knew that we had been mishandled.'[87] General Haig, on the other hand, judged his own performance by reference to his stated objectives for the battle:

The three main objectives with which we had commenced our offensive in July had already been achieved ... Verdun had been relieved; the main German forces had been held on the Western front; and the enemy's strength has been very considerably worn down. Any of these three results is in itself sufficient to justify the Somme battle. The attainment of all three of them affords ample compensation for the splendid efforts of our troops and for the sacrifices made by ourselves and our Allies. They have brought us a long step forward towards the final victory of the Allied cause.[88]

Haig made two arguments. First, that the objectives of the battle were valuable; and, second, that the price of achieving them, paid in the lives of other men, was reasonable.

As to the first argument, it was neither an objective nor a result of the battle to advance the front any appreciable distance. By the unbelievable device of claiming that advancing the front was not one of his objectives, General Haig side-stepped the need to explain why so many lives were lost and the line barely moved. If advancing the front was not a goal, why attack at all?

As to the second argument, the notion that the end justifies the means must be tested with rigour when the means involve sacrificing the life of other men. At what point would the price in human lives become too great to justify the attack? 500 000 casualties? 600 000? Was 410 000 casualties a sensible price to pay for the Allies to pay for 180 000 casualties on the German side?

Duff Cooper, Haig's 'official' biographer, contended that questions posed in this way were beside the point. He claimed that 'there exists no yardstick for the measurement of such events, there are no returns to prove whether life has been sold at its market value'.[89] Besides being every bit as callous as General Haig's outlook, this view would never allow an attack to be halted on the basis that the anticipated loss of life did not justify the potential gain.

The Battle of the Somme is the living proof of what can happen if battle commanders exclude from their tactical thinking an obligation to conserve, to the extent possible, the lives of the men entrusted to their command. It is easy enough to characterise General Haig as heartless or callous for pursuing his 'wearing down' strategy regardless of the cost. His supporters might, however, characterise his resolve as a sign of the moral courage that allowed him to withstand in his command levels of adversity that no man should ever have to confront.

CHAPTER SEVEN

WOUNDED

The Australians suffered more than 29 000 casualties in the fighting at Fromelles, Pozières and Mouquet Farm. This represented an average of more than 7000 casualties for each of the four divisions involved.[1] More than 21 000 of the casualties were wounded or gassed.[2]

The wounded had to endure a perilous journey from the front to places in the rear where they could find treatment. Chaplain Tighe, who, like most chaplains, had the task of helping the wounded, reassured a public meeting in North Sydney that the wounded men were being well treated:

> With regard to the treatment of the wounded — nothing can surpass the care and attention shown to them. From the time they are taken by the stretcher-bearers from No-man's land until they are placed in hospital it is nothing but self-denial and mortification and endangering one's life on their behalf. The stretcher-bearers, they who are at the front, are marvellously and wondrously courageous, they risk their lives time after time. I have seen them go forth and within five minutes one is killed; his companion comes back for

another stretcher-bearer to go out and get a wounded man. I have known them leave our dugout after the wounded man is dressed get ten yards away when one man is killed and the other tries to drag back the wounded man to safety. They have really and truly touched my very heart at times when with a sob in their voice and a tear in their eye they would ask me to read the last prayers over the companion who has given his life for them. When you speak of the brave deeds of the men at the front, do not forget a meed of praise and of high praise for the stretcher-bearers.

The wounded man is brought to the Regimental Aid Post and gets his first rough dressing there; he then passes on to the Advance Dressing Station and from there is taken in horse ambulance or motor to the Casualty Clearing Station; from the Casualty Clearing Station on to Blighty. Blighty is an Indian word meaning 'Home'. It is the ambition of every man at the front to get to Blighty. That brings them to England. You are taken in hospital train or hospital ship, and from personal experience I can tell you that the treatment is excellent, the kindness of the Australian nurses and Doctors unsurpassed.[3]

If this gruesome tale was intended to give encouragement to the anxious mothers of North Sydney, it is just as well that the good Jesuit father held back the truth.

The courage of the stretcher-bearers and the skill and kindness of the nurses and doctors could not change the fact that the lot of the wounded men was often desperate. The infantry was trained to press on with the attack if their mates were wounded. It was their duty to leave the wounded men to fend for themselves. The fortunate ones among the wounded walked or crawled to safety. Those who were not so lucky had no option but to wait for the stretcher-bearers.

Private Morrow got a Blighty in March 1917:

A few seconds later I was knocked from the top of the bank to the bottom. Something had hit my right shoulder like a kick from a

Stretchers bearers, everyone's heroes, 'marvellously and wondrously courageous', carry a wounded man through Pozières, 28 August 1916.
AWM E04946

horse, and I found my right arm useless. Blood was running down my sleeve onto my hand. Captain Cherry, of the 26th Battalion, was standing close by, revolver in hand.

'What's the matter, son?'

'Knocked in the arm, sir.'

'Then get out while you can.'

I started off along the road at my best pace. The road was being enfiladed by enemy riflemen, who tried to make a target of me. I zigzagged hurriedly from side to side, and finally got over the brow of the hill, safe from their sight.

Here were more of our men lining the banks, apparently watching for the enemy to come round the rise. They saw me hurrying past and called to know my destination. 'Blighty,' I answered exultantly. I could see the envy in their eyes, and felt a spasm of sympathy for them in their misery.[4]

Sergeant Evans had a harrowing time when he was wounded. When he was well enough, he described what happened in his diary:

Rations had just been dished out and I was holding a dixie of stew in my hand. All of a sudden one of the ration party made a dive into our dugout, where Sergeant Keep was eating. I didn't hear the shell coming — as a rule one can divine the shell will fall somewhere near — but there was blinding flash, the dugout collapsed and out through the door was thrown the poor ration carrier's leg and all his entrails, clean into my face! Dirt and duckboard and splinters of shell, blood and muck hit me all over my legs and arms. I was stunned, my left hand completely numb.

I yelled 'Stretcher-bearers!' but I didn't dare look for Sergeant Keep, when suddenly he burst out of the wreckage covered in mud and blood, right arm half torn off and legs badly hit. Oh my God! I shall never forget it. One man lying in pieces at my feet, Sergeant

Diggers take a dixie of stew to their billets. On the right the farm house manure pit is filled with water. AWM E00092

Keep more dead than alive, and me hardly able to stand with the shock.

Someone dressed my left hand but I wasn't in too much pain. There were a few specks of shell in my arm and I felt generally bruised all over. My head sang and I felt utterly silly. I had the presence of mind to ask for my coat, so thank goodness I have my pay book and a few odds and ends. I have lost my whistle, shaving gear and, worst of all, my watch. But I am alive. Poor Sergeant Keep had a rough spin. He was less fortunate and was badly hit all over the body. Corporal Sturt conducted me to our medical where the doctor gave me a brandy while I waited to be dressed properly.

Well, from the medical, I walked and Keep was stretchered about half a mile … Fritz was shelling pretty continuously, until we struck an old road full of shell holes and ruts. Here an old horse ambulance was on hand to give us a lift.

These stretcher cases on the Menin Road had only minutes to live; a bomb fell and killed most of them. AWM E00711

Keep was in need of urgent attention but never once called out. In fact, he made no noise at all. Just stared upwards. At one point he mustered the energy to look at me and, with an attempted smile, whispered, 'Well, Evans, I guess I'll get Blighty'.

I tried to respond but could think of nothing to say except: 'You'll be right. Think of home, mate'. The truth was that he looked terrible and, at one point, I nearly lost my temper at the length of time it took the ambulance men to mend a wheel.

To make matters worse, Steenwerk's wards were full up and we were directed to Bailleul. Oh God! I shall never forget the nightmare of the ride. The driver got lost and we had to endure four-and-a-half hours in the joint, moving like a snail and jolting like the devil. Went about 10 miles instead of three.[5]

A strange calm came over some wounded men. A medical officer, Captain Huxtable, was following the attack on Passchendaele when he found a friend of his, Elkington, 'lying on the ground. He was a tall, thin fellow with a particularly grim face which now looked grimmer than ever. To my question if he were hurt, he replied, "Only my arm. Lost it". And, true enough, his arm had been blown off. We managed to patch him up, however, and home he went to England, and survived.'[6]

At other times, the scene on the battlefield was so chaotic that there was no time to stop and care for the wounded or the dead. During the Battle of Passchendaele, Sergeant John Linton, a member of the 3rd Divisional Ammunition Column, remembered escaping from heavy shelling, with his cart and donkeys moving at full speed to the rear, when:

'Souvenir', one of my donks, nearly put us into a shell hole, through shying at what, at first glance appeared to me to be a bag lying on the road, but on having another look as we went past, turned out to be two poor 'Aussies', that Fritz had just caught with an H.E.[7] Both were bleeding terribly and were probably dead. I just managed to miss running over them with my near wheel for which you can bet I was terribly glad. Poor lads, the only particulars their people will get will be 'Killed in Action' on the 6th October.[8]

The medical staff was not to blame for the primitive conditions. In most cases, the doctors, nurses and stretcher-bearers had to endure conditions every bit as bad as the men in their care. Captain Harold Lethbridge spent 23 days in November 1916 manning a dressing station on the Somme, called Flat Iron Copse. The conditions were desperate. Medical officers needed a rare mixture of courage, cool-headedness, skill and endurance to withstand them:

> **5.11.16:** Doing the amputation of the thigh — standing in mud with a pair of waders on — a flapping tent — and guns banging all around us was quite a new experience for me. The big Howitzer quite close nearly breaks your eardrums and yet I will sleep through it tonight.

A tressle operating table in the 3rd Australian Field Ambulance near the Menin Road in September 1917. Dressing station conditions were desperate. (Note the wound ticket.) AWM E00714

6.11.16: In bed, in my dugout, after 14 hours strenuous, nervy work. The dugout is small, leaky, muddy floored and musty smelling and not even splinter proof. I trust Fritz doesn't put one on, or else this diary won't be much use. A few came over today ...

This afternoon, one shell killed two and wounded 5 of our [stretcher] bearers, and killed two officers who were riding down. Poor old Ray Walters, what a nice boy he was. So this is war.

Case after case, two at a time in my tent, several died, several dying. One man with about a yard of bowel hanging out, another with brain protruding from his forehead. Fenwick relieved me for a rest. I was just lying down when Moseley and Lewers call me back for one of our poor lads — Atkinson, knee shattered, bleeding profusely, arm shattered and bleeding from a wound in the back. I cut down quickly, Frazelle giving the anaesthetic and tied his femoral. Am giving him a fighting chance.

Two cases lying outside on stretchers. One a Fritz, dying poor devil. I knelt down beside him and asked him what I could do for him. I can't hate a live German, let alone a dying one.

Cars broken down, bearers exhausted, horses knocked up. Sgt Rogers came along and asks for a revolver to shoot a wounded horse.

7.11.16: How splendid the [stretcher-bearers] are — they are having a terrible time, carrying wounded through this mud until they are absolutely exhausted — but never a complaint. What magnificent lads the Australian boys are. Never a complaint from them when they are in this grim hell called the Somme Battle Field.

8.11.16: I feel alright when I am dressing the wounded and can concentrate on the work and pretend only to hear [the shells dropping] out of the corner of my eye. But it is all nerve wracking and horrible and how we will love to get out. We are never safe.

10.11.16: I am syringing out all deep wounds with Eusol, to counteract the sepsis sent in by clothing etc. I think it should have a good effect. It may stop gas gangrene.

12.11.16: We have had a busy day to-day. A battery just on our right had a premature[9] and wounded five. One was bleeding profusely from a fractured humerus and mangled brachial. Fenwick got me to cut down and tie his brachial — they always call on me for any operation work.

The poor 3rd Australian Field Ambulance had rotten luck. An aeroplane came over and dropped a bomb. It killed 11 and wounded 38 ... The plane came down and the pilot gave himself up.

15.11.16: In the morning of the 14th, the wounded started coming in. They were attacking Bapaume Ridge. We put through 375 cases in the day. Fritz started shelling us — shell after shell came all around us, dropping quite close to the horses, spitting our tents with mud and some fragments through our tent. We thought — at least I did — all the time that the next would be among us. About 40 stretcher cases lying out in front and dressing those horribly wounded and dying men, with shells coming all round, was more than we could stand.

16.11.16: Fenwick had a narrow escape. He was dressing a man at McCormicks and a shell came. He crouched and a fragment went through the heart of the man he was dressing.

20.11.16: A man at Pozières lay in No-man's-land for 9 days and lived. Another, with two cobbers — one was killed and one wounded — stayed for four days with his wounded cobber bringing him food. In the infantry, a man's cobber is his very existence ...[10]

For a medical officer manning a dressing station, like Captain Lethbridge, speed of evacuation was the key: 'At the R.A.P.[11] in battle, the great thing is to get the wounded away — not what you can do for them; fix them up and get them away with a hot drink and ¼ grain of morphia — see to the haemorrhage, splints, morphia, hot drinks, and evacuate.[12]

On a stationary trench line, and with casualties at the massive levels they had reached in the trench battles of 1915 and 1916, the army turned its attention to introducing economies of scale to the evacuation of the wounded. Trains could carry many more wounded than ambulances. Trains were already carrying fresh troops up to the front. It was a waste to let them return empty. They could be rigged up as huge ambulances. A M Henniker wrote:

> [The ambulance trains] were to be composed each of 33 of the ordinary continental-type covered goods wagons with the addition of brake vans for baggage and stores, and one carriage for the personnel. In the corners of each of the box trucks was fitted an iron framework known as the 'Brechot' apparatus on which could be placed three stretchers, one above the other. Each wagon thus could take 12 lying-down cases, and the whole train 396 cases.
>
> This type of train could carry more lying-down patients than any of the later types, but it had serious disadvantages. There was no inter-communication between vehicles to permit of attention to patients by the medical personnel while the train was running; there were no means of heating the vehicles, and experiments with stoves showed considerable danger of fire; loose couplings between vehicles and the application of hand brakes gave rise to most injurious jolting of the patients.[13]

The scheduling of hospital trains was part of the planning for all big operations. In the first fourteen days of the Battle of the Somme, 110 ambulance trains were scheduled. By the time of the battle of Messines, eleven months later, a new layer of sophistication had been added. The ambulance trains ran for a few days before the battle, so as to empty the casualty clearing stations to make room for the extra casualties that would come in when the battle began.[14] Over a fourteen-day period before and after the commencement of that battle, 66 ambulance trains were scheduled.[15]

Ambulance trains were not the only innovation. In parts of the front accessible to the canal system, casualties were evacuated by hospital barge.[16] Even with this level of innovation, the progress from the front to a major hospital could be agonisingly slow. Captain Knyvett spent five days on the journey, travelling first on a horse-drawn sledge borrowed from the local farmhouse, then by horse ambulance, to a field ambulance, before being taken on by motor ambulance — 'the most painful trip of my life' — to a casualty clearing station, whence he was loaded onto a hospital train that took him, overnight, to Rouen. He was driven from the station at Rouen to an Infirmary for Aged Women that had been converted to a military hospital, where he was admitted and carried to a ward. From Rouen, he finally went by hospital ship to England.[17]

Men with lesser wounds were treated in hospitals in France. The 13th Stationary Hospital was situated on a hill, just outside the French coastal town of Boulogne. Captain Huxtable, an Australian medical officer, served there. He recalled:

At the hospital there was a Dr Nutall of Birmingham, an excellent surgeon. It was not unusual to learn of a train full of wounded arriving, usually at night, and the ambulances would be at the hospital within half an hour. The admissions on each occasion could be at least 100 to 200 men, and I remember Dr Nutall saying to me that many a man's chances of survival depended mainly upon the amount of time that you could give him. There was so much rush during those times that you could literally save a man or lose him.[18]

There were three Australian General Hospitals in France. AGH 1 was located in tents on the racecourse at Rouen. Conditions were primitive.

There was no water and no drainage. There were no paths or roads.[19] An Australian nurse, Sister Douglas, wrote home that, on 2 July 1916, the day after the Battle of the Somme began, 'freshly wounded poured in to No. 1 AGH as indeed into every one of the many hospitals in the Rouen area ... The base hospital was practically a Casualty Clearing Station at this time.'[20]

Sister Looker was on night duty at AGH 1 in September and October 1917. She recalled that, 'Large convoys of wounded arrived every night ... The wounds were mostly amputations & very severe — Carrell-Dakin treatment was used on these cases with great success.'[21] Carrel-Dakin treatment involved irrigating the wound every two hours with an antiseptic solution made from chloride of lime, sodium carbonate dry and sodium bicarbonate dry.[22] Sister Lucas particularly remembered the conditions in winter: '... we received casualties straight from the field, some very severely wounded, and feeling the cold very greatly. A great number of them had trench feet[23] and frost bite. Several

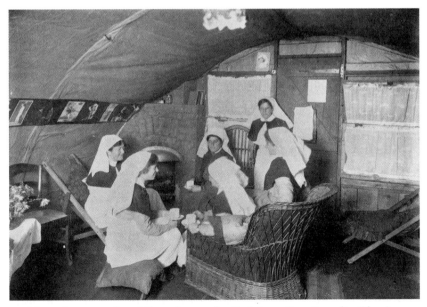

Nurses' quarters in a Nissen hut at the 2nd Australian Casualty Clearing Station Steenwerck, November 1917, appear almost genteel. The reality was that they often had to 'trade their bonnets for tin helmets'. AWM E01280

patients were frozen to death in the ambulances coming down to us.'[24] AGH 1 cared for some 90 000 patients between 1916 and 1918. Most of its patients were evacuated to England within a few days of being admitted.[25]

AGH 2 dealt with a similar number of patients. Like the 13th Stationary Hospital, it was located at Boulogne, on 'a very desolate spot on the sea cliffs, quite close to Wimereux, and about ten minutes tram ride to Boulogne'.[26] According to Sister Hubbard, 'it was a very large tented hospital and most of our patients were battle casualties which kept us very busy. Afterwards this Hospital was converted into huts and they were very up-to-date.'[27]

AGH 2 came to specialise in the treatment of fractures — mainly of the femur. In many cases, amputation was the only treatment possible. So many legs had to be sawn off that the fractured femur ward became known as the 'carpenter's shop'. The ward was fitted out with special beds. One of the nurses recalled:

> As we looked in the door it was difficult to see the patients on account of the wooden frames which surrounded the bed. Sinclairs swing bed. These beds were wonderful. They allowed us to attend the patients without actually disturbing them and we were able to wash and preserve the backs in a wonderful way ... In some cases both their legs were in Thomas's splints and extension applied ... Many of the cases were Gas Gangrenous wounds, some of whom lost their limbs.[28]

The nurses worked in dangerous conditions. AGH 2 was within range of the German artillery. Shrapnel fell on the hut roofs, causing the nurses to trade their bonnets for tin helmets.[29]

The risk of injury to the nurses increased when they were later permitted to work in casualty clearing stations closer to the front. Sister Pratt was wounded in the right shoulder during a bombing raid on No. 1 Australian Casualty Clearing Station in September 1917.[30]

AGH 3 opened in France in May 1917. It was situated in tents and huts at Abbeville, on the Somme. It did general work, and was also a reception centre for patients who had been gassed, although there was little treatment available which the nurses could offer the afflicted men.[31]

There was no extra staff during attacks. As Sister Tilton remembered, the nurses simply had to work harder:

> My duties at night included five wards with two hundred and twenty patients in my care, both medical and surgical. Two orderlies and two VADs assisted me. Almost every night convoys arrived from the line, while evacuations were carried out at the same time. Troop trains tore through express all night. Ambulances rushed backwards and forwards. How they succeeded in avoiding accidents those dark and stormy nights, only those plucky girl drivers knew. Women and girls did all the driving in this sector, and they worked tirelessly, day and night.
>
> The nights were one continual rush and run, with scarcely any time to give to individual patients. We would sponge them if we could, and leave dressings for the day staff. But so often a secondary haemorrhage would occur, necessitating our best efforts to save a life.[32]

Private Morrow, who was wounded in the arm, might have been treated in France, instead of being sent to Blighty. He started out smartly on his journey from the front to the rear, but his condition soon deteriorated. His wound was dressed at a dressing station. He was then told to walk to Bapaume — a distance of a few miles:

> Tired and weary and wet I stumbled along with head down; and other walking cases stumbled and groaned along with me ... At Rouen my wound became badly septic, and an operation was performed which made me a cot case, and marked me for transport

to England. Lying on a stretcher among numerous others waiting to embark, I contentedly watched a colonel doctor moving from patient to patient examining tickets secured to coat lapels.[33]

The 'colonel doctor' was performing a morbid triage, separating those who would be sent back to England from those who would have to stay in France. Morrow lay back, apprehensively waiting his turn:

My heart leapt into my mouth as he stopped at my stretcher and looked down at me. My eyes searched his for some sign of sympathy, some flicker of a cheery smile. But the eyes looked hard and calculating. I wished and hoped that he would move on to some other stretcher. Suddenly he stooped and lifted my card to read. I knew only too well what was written on it, 'G.S.W. right arm. Severe'. He would think an 'arm' case had no right to be a stretcher case and order me to get up and walk away. I was almost ready to weep with disappointment. Finally he stood again, looked at me intently, then moved quickly on. A wonderful weight seemed lifted from my heart. Nothing could stop me now.[34]

Some weapons killed more effectively than others. From April 1916 until March 1919, the Australians suffered most casualties from shell fragments and shrapnel (50.93 per cent). Next came machine gun and rifle bullets (33.93 per cent), followed by gas (11.82 per cent), hand bombs and grenades (1.9 per cent), shell shock (1.14 per cent) and bayonets (0.28 per cent).[35]

Infection could make slight wounds serious. Infection killed just as surely as the machine gun or the artillery. In the days before penicillin, infections were often untreatable. Topical treatments like the Carrel-Dakin treatment could help some infections, but many infections could not be treated in that way.[36] Shock, cold, exposure and delayed treatment were also efficient killers.[37]

At the beginning of the war, the surgeons lacked experience to deal effectively with the type of wounds they had to treat. A G Butler wrote: 'In serious wounds, treated as they were for the most part by immediate suture, with or without some superficial antisepsis, sepsis [bacterial infection] was practically universal; "gas gangrene" was very common, tetanus an ever-present Sword of Damocles.'[38] The surgeons gradually adapted their methods to cope with the trauma they confronted.

In July 1915, the British Army issued a 'Memorandum on the Treatment of Injuries in War', which stipulated:

If it be an open wound, portions of clothing, obvious fragments of shell, and torn or hopelessly damaged portions of tissue should be removed by forceps and scissors. If the wound be not sufficiently open to drain of itself, large drainage tubes should be inserted; and in cases where more must be done an anaesthetic should be given, and the wounds enlarged and held open by retractors so that all recesses may be washed out and drained. A good method of mechanically cleaning the track of a perforating wound consists in drawing backwards and forwards through it a piece of gauze twisted to form a rope. Very large drainage tubes should be used, with numerous large lateral openings. For large deep wounds counter-openings are necessary.[39]

Nature could sometimes treat infection better than the surgeons. A G Butler again:

Colonel David Cade, A.A.M.C., recalls a case at Pozières of a German who was wounded in No-Man's Land and brought in after four days to the R.A.P. with a leg smashed above the knee, and the wound such that gas gangrene would have been expected. It had however been flyblown, was full of maggots and all necrotic tissue had been consumed. There was no gas gangrene, and a clear 'line of demarcation' had formed. At the M.D.S. a 'butcher's' amputation removed the limb and next day the man was asking for a sausage; and was evacuated very well.[40]

Another Australian, Sergeant Campbell, found it easier to get a Blighty after he was wounded at Pozières:

Well Mother, it is quite a treat to get to England for a while. You know I wasn't bad enough to come to England but the old Scotch-Canadian Doctor, Dr Captain Gordon, came & had a look at me on Friday after the scrap & when the nurse told him that I was one of the lads what took part in the scrap for Pozières, he turned to me and said, 'Well, I guess you deserve a holiday, old chap', so he marked me 'Blighty'. Very good of him, wasn't it?[41]

Sir James Elliott, a New Zealand medical officer who served on the hospital ships, described the embarkation process:

At the French port hospital-trains were bringing down the wounded, and the British casualties were dreadfully heavy. At the quayside, the upper part of the large railway station was a military hospital; the lower platforms and all around, were packed with wounded ... As the tide rises and falls about twenty four feet twice in twenty four hours at Havre, the gangways required frequent adjustment. The wounded were carried on stretchers up the steep slope of the gangways by bearers from the shore who had not been asleep, except cat-napping, for thirty hours ... The wounded were passed into the ship at the rate of about two or three a minute, and finally she was packed from stem to stern with 1141 patients on board. The walking cases came first on board. The mud from the trenches is scarce dry upon them. The blood from their wounds soaks their clothes. They come to us still dazed with the crash and roar of rival artillery. They carry their pathetically small bundles of personal belongings, and, if they are lucky, perhaps a German helmet or cap as a trophy.

The singing army has become the silent army.

This man limps painfully, his trouser leg slit to the knee, where the surgeon has adopted the readiest method of getting at the wound. The next man has no sleeve in his coat; it has been similarly sacrificed. There are heads bound up, and arms in slings, and legs dragging painfully. There are others without wounds, which might have saved their nerves from cracking, unfortunates with drawn faces, deeply lined and puckered, and vacant eyes. Many are pre-occupied or dazed, with heavy-lidded eyes. They sink down on the deck, or anywhere, and doze, away from the incessant din. Others, bewildered when spoken to, start suddenly as if a light had been struck in their brains, and follow directions like men in a fog. They are given hot tea or soup and soon fall into a troubled sleep. As in life generally, sadness is mixed with joy and many hearts are gladdened with the prospect of seeing home …

Every patient has two tickets tied to his tunic, each inscribed on the front with his name, number, rank, and unit, and on the back with a concise statement of his wound or disease. In cases that have been in hospital a brief medical history is added. By far the majority of these tickets were labelled G.S.W., gun shot wound; or S.W., shrapnel wound, and there are other labels aplenty, such as trench fever[42], shell-shock, gassed, and so on. Bayonet wounds are rare.[43]

Sir James Elliott saw individual cases of overwhelming sadness: 'A big man had a large flesh wound in his back, both his thighs were smashed and he was trussed in a wooden case. He said it was a relief to get out of the misery of the trench and go over the top, and he saw lines of attackers mown down in swathes.'[44] He also heard stories of extreme pathos:

A few patients had lain out wounded in No-man's-land for a day and night. One of these wounded called out 'Are we downhearted?' There was no reply, so he sang a verse to enliven the proceedings:

I got married to the widow next door;
She'd been married seven times before;
Everyone was an Enery —
She wouldn't ave a Willie or a Sam
Hi ham the heighth called Enery,
Enery the Heighth hi ham![45]

When Gunner William Duffell was gassed, his main emotion was one of relief to be free of the trenches:

The wounded & sick were carried ashore on stretchers and laid in rows in a great iron shed. English women moved about the stretchers offering cigarettes etc to those inclined to smoke. Although I was longing for a smoke it was more than my throat would stand & as my eyes were still shaded I contented myself listening to the voices of those English women & thanking my lucky stars that I was away from the mud & shells.[46]

Diggers gassed defending Villers-Bretonneux on 27 May 1918. Gunner Howell recalled the experience: 'for two days I was completely blind ... this morning I can't talk above a whisper and my head aches fearfully'. AWM E04851

The hospitals in England were a haven for the wounded men. Chaplain Henderson told how 'The first few days pass blissfully in sleep. Even the gramophone is almost soothing after the sound of the guns. Later, when you are well enough to read, there are bookshelves at the end of the ward to explore.'[47]

Private Edgar Morrow was sent to a hospital in Dartford:

My records show it was during the month of May and the joy of life was in me. The long warm twilights were lazily spent lolling in the long lush grass of the pleasant grounds staring at the sky in a vain endeavour to locate the singing skylark; or philosophizing on the behaviour of people in general and girls in particular … [48]

But Morrow was to find that life in clean sheets and a warm bed under the care of a pretty young nurse was not all beer and skittles:

Shortly after my arrival, a screen was put round my bed. I thought some mistake had been made; if not, what was the idea? A pretty Welsh VAD came in behind the screen and turned the clothes down from me. She began to unbutton my pyjama coat. I was astonished and fear I blushed furiously. I was more astonished when I saw that she was blushing just as furiously.

'Hold on a minute, nurse,' I stammered, 'what are you going to do?'

She could speak only broken English and that seemed to make her attractiveness all the more potent. I think she was as uncomfortable over the business as I was.

'Matron says I have to bath you'. She spoke slowly and with a slight lisp.[49]

Captain Lethbridge, relieved from his duties on the front, was posted to No. 2 Australian Auxiliary Hospital, in Southall: 'This place was originally a school, about 9 miles west of London. We have about 500 patients and do all the trimming up of limbs, reamputations, and fit them with legs and arms. It is wonderful to see boys who have lost both legs walking without a stick with artificial legs.[50] The Australian amputees put on a brave face. They called themselves 'stumpies'.[51] When a Salvation Army chaplain on a hospital visit made the mistake of asking one young digger whether he'd soon be on his feet again the soldier replied: 'I don't think so, sir,' and with a merry twinkle in his bright, brown eyes, he drew back the bedclothes and displayed the two stumps of his legs, from which the feet had been severed. 'You talk about one leg in the grave and the other out,' he laughingly continued. 'I've got two in the grave — somewhere in France.'[52]

Arms or legs? Which were more precious? Captain Knyvett recalled that, 'In our ward there were mostly leg injuries, and in the one next door arm cases, and hot and fast flew the arguments as to which it was worse to lose.'[53]

Rehabilitation was not all hard work, according to Bill Oliver:

Padre ran the social element, Aspinall the commissariat and Ivan the sports … A double amputee threw a cricket ball about 70 yards, sitting down. There was a wheel chair race for double amputees as well as a 'hands and knees' race over the ground. There was also a three hops jump for single amputees as well as a race on crutches.[54]

When Gunner Howell was gassed, he wrote in his diary:

For two days I was completely blind and my head and chest are very bad. Got up this morning and am feeling much better. My eyes are still troubling me though … Since coming here I have had no treatment whatsoever and my chest and throat is worse now than the day I was admitted. This morning I can't talk above a whisper and my head aches fearfully'.[55]

Sergeant Evans also experienced a range of symptoms from being gassed:

I was woken by the horrible and familiar stench of gas. I put my respirator on, but began vomiting and was forced to take it off at various intervals. When the all clear was signalled, I continued to be sick and became besieged by bouts of severe coughing fits. It was terrifying. I couldn't get any breath. I really thought I was dying. The lads rushed for the doctor, who said I should be evacuated next morning. My hair was shaved and I was washed down as the gas lingers anywhere it can. All I can remember is the doc telling me I'd be evacuated in the morning, with the words, 'Evans, the war's probably over for you, my boy. Back to Blighty'. Yet I remember feeling no emotion. My God, I felt so sick. My condition was such that a feather could have knocked me down.

Since the gassing I have at times thought I wouldn't make it. Breathing difficulties, a racing heart, violent coughing and sneezing, nausea and diarrhoea. The doc says I've had a kind of chemically induced pneumonia.[56]

When the doctors had nothing more to offer, it was the padre's turn. Kenneth Henderson, an Australian chaplain, described a typical incident:

The bearers enter bringing a wounded man, who is lying relaxed on the stretcher. His eyes are closed, but he opens them as he is lifted to be laid on the table.

The doctor, clad in thigh-boots and leather waist-coat, washes his hands quickly, and switches an electric torch on to the blanketed figure. He pulls aside the blanket. The man's body is bare from the waist, crossed by wide bandages. A red-edged card is tied to the top button of his trousers. A padre stooping over a stretcher in the corner straightens himself, and comes across from a row of stretchers to stand on the other side. The examination is soon concluded, and the doctor and padre stroll to the door, while the new arrival is lifted down and placed in the row of wounded who are all waiting for the ambulance. The padre's experienced eye has seen the damage, and the first question to the medical officer is no more than a formality. 'No chance?' 'No, only a matter of an hour or so, perhaps'. 'Is he conscious?' asks the padre. 'Quite. He will be, too. He's your case now, padre'.[57]

The padre had a depressing task, working with men who were dying so long before their time. Kenneth Henderson recorded what might be said in that awful situation, in a front line dressing station, with shells falling around:

Padre: Chaplain here. Let's get your details. Much pain?

Soldier: No, padre, not much.

Padre: Now, can you give me your people's address? I'll send them a line to say I saw you.

Soldier: I'd be glad — tell them not to worry — I'll soon be right.

Padre: Old man, you soon will be all right.

Soldier: Eh? Oh! Is it come to that, padre?

Padre: Yes, lad, it has.

Soldier: I'm sorry. I don't want to go. You never think, somehow. I want to live.

Padre: Boy, we've each one of us got to go through it alone. Yet we're not alone. Remember, old chap, that our Lord went through it Himself alone. He knows what it's like, and suffers with us. Lean back, lad, and just let yourself lie back in God's arms.

Soldier: I've never been religious, Padre. Never seemed to think somehow.

Padre: Yes, but you're a child in your Father's house all the same. We none of us realise God's love. Only sometimes, when there seems to be no escape from it. And we look back, and think of the things we might have done to help. There's no end in God's patience, no limit to His love.

Soldier: I've never been much good, I'm afraid.

Padre: We can't judge ourselves. Anyway, you came out here, and you knew what it was like. God only wants us to be sincere in our loyalty and love, old man. It's never too late to offer Him that. I think there is a whole eternity of service ahead of you, boy. Are you sorry for all the chances you missed, and the mistakes?

Soldier: Yes, I am. I never thought about Christ. I believed it all, I suppose, but I never thought. You get with fellows, and you don't think. I've been saying my prayers again lately.

Padre: Can you feel, old man, that Christ loves you and really cares?

Soldier: Yes, padre, I believe that … There's just one thing.

[The soldier whispers his confession. The padre grants absolution.]

Soldier: Thanks padre, there's a lot to forgive.

[The padre checks other men before returning to the dying soldier.]

Padre: What messages, old man?

Soldier: Not to worry — I'll see them all again. Tell my mother and sisters it was for them I fought through the battle. Tell my younger brother he's to stop home and look after the place …

Soldier: Padre?

Padre: Yes.

Soldier: Pain's pretty bad. Glad when it's over.

[A new case comes in. The padre sees that the newcomer is able to sit up, and goes back to the stretcher.]

Padre: I'll stay here. Hold on.

Soldier (faintly): Thanks.

[The medical officer comes up, and stooping quickly, injects morphia. The padre tightens his grip, and laying his hand on the man's forehead, makes the sign of the Cross.]

Padre: Unto God's gracious mercy and protection we commit you; the Lord bless you and keep you, the Lord make His face to shine upon you and be gracious unto you, and give you His peace, now and for evermore.[58]

This poor soldier died a young man's death, but he did not die alone. Pity the thousands of men who died alone. Pity those who whose graves are unknown.[59] Pity too their families. Pity also this brave German soldier described by Lieutenant Maxwell:

> ... we happened across a man of the 17th Battalion who was severely wounded in the head. No stretcher-bearers attended him and I stuck a rifle with a fixed bayonet in the ground nearby, so that the bearers who might pass that way later would see him. Two days later, when we passed this spot the poor fellow was still alive, but he was wrapped in the topcoat of a German whose body lay nearby. The German, apparently seeing his end was near had taken off his coat to cover the Australian, whom he thought had a chance.[60]★

In addition to the men wounded in action, the hospital system had to cope with men who were sick. In fact, the number of soldiers who were ill exceeded the number wounded. The total figures for the BEF on the western front for the period 1914 to 1918 were 3 528 486 sick compared with 1 988 969 wounded.[61] Common complaints included respiratory tract infections, skin infestations, fevers, accidental injuries, dental defects[62], venereal disease and complications of exposure to cold conditions. Less common conditions included 'Impaired constitution', 'Results of moral defects' and 'Human idiosyncrasies, undiagnosed, unintelligible'.[63]

The availability of good dental treatment was a novelty for many men at a time when dental hygiene was often lacking. In July 1918,

---

★   Yes, I have considered the possibility that someone else came by and found the German dead and the Australian alive, and covered the Australian with the German's greatcoat, but Lieutenant Maxwell's version is infinitely better.

Sergeant Linton rode one of his donkeys to the dentist's surgery ... to get a tooth stopped. It was a back one and of course he didn't trim me up. I've got to go again on Monday to get it finished ... I paid my [second] visit to the dentist this morning, and put in 10 minutes agony whilst he put on another dressing. I've got to go again on Thursday ... Once more I journeyed to the Dentist at Querrieu ... and would you believe it, this time he pulled the tooth out instead of going on with the filling business. It was a lovely double one with a prong nearly as long as my arm.[64]

Dentistry seems to have changed little since 1918.

Men who were on the mend were sent gradually back into training in convalescent camps in England or in France. Lieutenant Rule was sent to convalesce at the 'Bull Ring' at Étaples. He found himself with members of almost every battalion in the army, having the finishing touches put on their training, or being hardened up after coming from hospital. The Bull Ring was a

... famous French watering-place and a source of great joy and fuddled heads to those who managed to visit it. Adventures with beautiful women who lived in the mansions seemed quite common experiences, and, to the young bloods, this was the spice of life. Could the keenest Puritan blame them?[65]

One person who was certainly no Puritan was the commander of the Australian lines at Étaples, the rotund, humorous and wonderfully patrician Major Clayton. Wounded at Gallipoli, he now commanded this convalescent and training camp, keeping a fatherly eye on the men in his charge. Lieutenant Rule recalled:

Major Hector Clayton addressed us. In an emphatic manner he told us what he would allow and what he would not. Clayton was the most efficient camp commandant I ever knew; to those who kicked over the traces he dealt out punishment just as hard as military law would allow. On the other hand, those who played the game were treated to the best conditions he could give them, and the method worked admirably.[66]

Major Clayton was a solicitor by profession. He knew Lieutenant-Colonel Melville MacNaghten, CMG, from their days in the law together in Sydney, as well as from their shared experiences in Gallipoli and Egypt, where MacNaghten's promising military career had come to an end, thanks to shell shock suffered on Gallipoli.

Clayton was suspicious when he learned that a 'Sergeant MacMelville' had arrived at Étaples wearing the ribbon of the Commander of the Order of St Michael and St George. His suspicions were confirmed when he recognised his old friend. 'Charles, don't be such a goat,' he told him.[67] After MacNaghhten was sent back to Australia with shell shock in 1916, he had gone to Queensland and re-enlisted as a private soldier. He was now a sergeant, and on his way back to the front. Clayton saw his old friend recommissioned as a lieutenant, before 'MacMelville's' nerves got the better of him again, and he was sent home for good in October 1917.

Casualties were not limited to the troops. Many animals suffered terribly. Shelling in the wagon lines killed so many horses that it became standard practice to build anti-bomb walls of earth and sod around the horse lines.[68] Horses and mules were even fitted with their own gas helmets,[69] but this did not stop 250 horses being killed by gas before the battle for Villers-Bretonneux.[70]

There were three systems of evacuating wounded horses: a road service in which grooms led the horses to hospital — the equestrian equivalent of the walking wounded; a barge service from Bac St Maur to St Omer by way of the Lys canal; and a sick horse train that ran from Bailleul.[71]

In April 1917, an Australian veterinary hospital was established near Calais, which was designed to accommodate 1250 animals. The staff was

Horses of the 5th Australian Divisional train tethered in trenches with anti-bomb walls, Amiens May 1918. Many horses suffered terribly; some were even fitted with gas masks. AWM E02432

seven officers and 459 men. It treated 25 000 animals during the eighteen months of its existence.[72]

Lieutenant-Colonel Henry, the Assistant Director of Veterinary Services, described the sorry plight of the horses in the bleak winter between 1916 and 1917:

The country was a howling desolation; it had been torn to pieces by shell-fire and the rain had completed the work of the artillery. The horses were standing in mud to the knees and they were working hard over roads which were cut to pieces by traffic and under conditions which entailed their spending many unnecessary hours in harness and under saddle. As a consequence their feeding was irregular and their time for rest seriously curtailed. Water points were few and far between at first, and in consequence further travelling had to be undertaken by the wearied animals. The weather was atrocious, cold, wet, and miserable. There was at first no shelter, and as a further advance was expected, the authorities were loath to spend time, men and money on building standings. To crown all the food supply could not be maintained at the prescribed ration, and the hospitals became so crowded that orders were received that units were to retain horses which normally would have been sent to the base.[73]

In that dreadful winter, the coldest and wettest of the war, men and horses shared many hardships in common.

Horses were clipped as a precaution against disease. For this, as is so common in army life, there was a procedure designed to stamp out individuality. It was called the 'system of Divisional clipping'. I M Parsonson commented:

> The advantages of this system were that a uniform method of clipping was carried out in accordance with instructions; no CO pet fads were allowed to intrude. (It is curious to note that the greatest difficulty with regard to pet fads arose from the English regular officers attached to the Division. It would appear that in the British Army too much licence was allowed the individual officers).[74]

For once, it was the British, not the Australians, who were playing fast and loose with the King's Regulations.

CHAPTER EIGHT

BREAKING THE DEADLOCK

The prospect of a deadlocked trench war on the western front threw up 'two conflicting schools of military strategy'.[1] Duff Cooper, Haig's 'official' biographer, described the opposing schools of strategy as follows:

> On the one side there were those who, with whatever forebodings, gravely accepted the grim prospect of a long struggle in the main arena [i.e., the western front], entailing slaughter and sacrifice beyond anything previously contemplated, and only terminating when one of the protagonists was reduced to accepting whatever terms were dictated.
>
> There were, on the other hand, some who refused to admit to their minds so fearful a conclusion. Wars had not been so mercilessly fought out in the past, why should the present one prove an exception? Genius could find out a way, closed to the purblind vision of military experts, which would take the professional strategists by surprise and prove a sure and easy way to victory. For the next four years these rival schools of thought strove with one another for

predominance in the councils of war. The majority of the trained soldiers leaned towards the former theory, but a large number of the more active-minded politicians adopted the latter. They knew enough of the subject to be aware that the main principle in strategy is to turn the opponent's flank. Assuming that this was no longer possible on that line that was held from the North Sea to the Swiss frontier, they argued that it was necessary to go beyond these limits, and by winning a decisive victory in the east render the position of the Central Powers in the west no longer tenable.[2]

General Haig was firmly of the first school. He was steadfast in the view that the war would be won or lost on the western front. In May 1917, he wrote:

> The guiding principles are those which have proved successful in war from time immemorial, viz., that the first step must always be to wear down the enemy's power of resistance and to continue to do so until he is so weakened that he will be unable to withstand a decisive blow; then with all one's forces to deliver the decisive blow and finally to reap the fruits of victory.
>
> The enemy has already been weakened appreciably, but time is required to wear down his great number of troops. The situation is not yet ripe for the decisive blow. We must therefore continue to wear down the enemy until his power of resistance has been further reduced.[3]

This represented a marked departure from the approach that Haig had sought to implement in his plans for the Battle of the Somme. There was no mention here of a single, decisive battle. Haig was now advocating a war of attrition, in which the enemy's forces would be worn down gradually.

If the Australians coming under Haig's command in May 1916 had known that 12 months later the Commander-in-Chief would conclude that the process of wearing down the enemy still had a long way to go, they would have been alarmed, but they should not have been surprised. In 1916, the Germans held the western front with a force of some 120 divisions.[4] It would inevitably take time to 'wear down' so large an army.

The objection to the strategy of attrition was obvious to many. A strategy of attrition suits an army with superior manpower. Haig did not have superior manpower, nor did he have the luxury of waiting whilst German manpower was gradually ground down.

Churchill was a bitter critic of the strategy of attrition. He believed that Haig and Robertson together forced the strategy of attrition on the War Cabinet, against its better judgment. In *The World Crisis 1911-1918*, written in the 1920s, he said of General Robertson:

This officer was Chief of the Imperial General Staff with unprecedented powers during the whole of 1916 and 1917. Robertson's doctrines were clear and consistent. He believed in concentrating all the efforts of the British and French armies upon offensive action in France and Flanders, and that we should stand on the defensive everywhere else. He advocated and pressed every offensive in which the British armies were engaged, and did his utmost to procure the compliance of the Cabinet in every operation. In an illuminating sentence [in Robertson's memoirs], he complained that 'certain Ministers still held fast to the belief that victory could never be won — or only at prohibitive cost — by *straightforward action on the Western Front*, and that it must be sought through lines of indirect attack elsewhere'. 'Straightforward action on the Western Front,' in 1915 (when Robertson was Chief of the Staff in France) and in 1916 and 1917 (when he was C.I.G.S.), meant, and could only mean, frontal assaults upon fortified positions defended by wire and machine guns without the necessary superiority of numbers, or an adequate artillery, or any novel offensive method. He succeeded in enforcing this policy against the better judgment of successive Cabinets or War Councils, with the result that when he left the War Office in February, 1918, the British and French armies were at their weakest point in strength and fighting power, and the Germans for the first time since the original invasion had gathered so great a superiority of reserves as to be able to launch a gigantic attack.[5]

David Lloyd George believed that opening up other fronts of the war would relieve pressure on the western front. On 13 October 1916 (before he became prime minister), Lloyd George met with Lord Hankey. At that point, the Somme offensive was grinding to a halt. Hankey made the following note of the meeting:

> Lloyd George … was very depressed about the offensive, which he does not consider to have produced results commensurate with the effort. He is evidently longing to carry out a big offensive at Salonica — his old love, is very apprehensive about Roumania, but cannot get his generals to agree with him. I told him I had great sympathy with his point of view, and that I had always had the same misgivings about the Somme offensive. Nevertheless I had deliberately muzzled myself because I wanted Robertson to have a perfectly free hand.[6]

The option of an offensive in Salonica was possible because there was already a large Franco-British force in the region, which could be used to attack Bulgaria, one of Germany's allies, along her southern frontier.[7] The politicians who advocated opening a second front faced two huge hurdles. First, the strategy of opening a second front had failed dismally in the Dardanelles. Second, the professional soldiers would not buy into the strategy. As Hankey told Lloyd George,

> I said that the Dardanelles expedition had failed because the soldiers did not believe in it, and consequently had insisted on the best of

everything being sent to France. Salonica would fail in exactly the same way unless he could induce the soldiers to see that it was the best course and to go for it hard. In military affairs you are dealing with flesh and blood and men's minds, and not mere machines. It was better to have a second best plan and to conform your whole policy to further it, than to have a plan that your soldiers didn't believe in.[8]

Hankey was only too well aware of how little career politicians and career bureaucrats could influence the views of career soldiers. When he and Herbert Asquith[9] had gone to the Somme to attempt to influence the military to use that surprise new weapon, the tank, in mass formations, Hankey despaired that he and Asquith were unable to influence the soldiers. Hankey wrote:

It was on this account that I left my work at the War Committee to accompany Asquith on his visit to the Somme. It was, however, very difficult for anyone from home to influence those on whom fell the day-to-day responsibility of fighting this great battle. One could not pretend to knowledge of local conditions and one's status was necessarily that of an amateur, or at best of a professor, an academic student without practical experience. Yet in this instance (as the attack at Cambrai proved) the amateurs and 'professors' were right and the 'professionals' were wrong ... For the remainder of the fighting season the tanks were used for the most part in small groups. To those who promoted and designed them this misuse of tanks came as a cruel disappointment. The refusal of the Staff to listen to their views aroused indignation.[10]

By 1917, the battle lines between the politicians and bureaucrats on the one hand, and the staff on the other, were clearly drawn. Generals Haig, Robertson and the staff held firmly to the western front school of strategy. General Henry Wilson was the only senior general who was prepared to countenance some alternative strategy, but his views were not then in vogue.

To the extent that British lives would be sacrificed by the strategy of continuous attack, General Haig made no apology:[11]

[The] object of all war is victory, and a purely defensive attitude can never bring about a successful decision, either in a battle or in a campaign. The idea that a war can be won by standing on the defensive and waiting for the enemy to attack is a dangerous fallacy, which owes its inception to the desire to evade the price of victory.[12]

In this context, of course, 'the price of victory' was a euphemism for the casualties sustained.

Among the politicians, Lloyd George advocated opening a second front, while Churchill argued that Haig had been too hasty in seeking to commit under-prepared troops to relentless, but hopeless, attacks that only drove up the casualty figures. For him also, the tank might have been the harbinger of a new strategic approach:

The flower of the nation, its manhood, its enterprise, its brains were all freely given ... The front had to be defended, the war had to be waged, but there was surely no policy in eagerly *seeking* offensives with immature formations, or during periods when no answer to the machine gun existed. Suppose that the British Army sacrificed upon the Somme, the finest we ever had, had been preserved, trained and developed to its full strength till the summer of 1917, till perhaps 3,000 tanks were ready, till an overwhelming artillery was prepared, till a scientific method of continuous advance had been devised, till the apparatus was complete, might not a decisive result have been achieved at one supreme stroke?[13]

Churchill contended for one supreme stroke. Unlike Haig, however, Churchill saw that the stroke should not be delivered until it could be delivered at an acceptable price in lives forsaken.

General Haig was aware that frontal assaults carried a high cost in the lives of the men in his command, but he believed that the cost was part and parcel of modern warfare. After the war, Haig wrote that:

> certain general factors peculiar to modern war made for the inflation of losses. The great strength of modern field defences and the power and precision of modern weapons, the multiplication of machine guns, trench mortars, and artillery of all natures, the employment of gas and the rapid development of the aeroplane as a formidable agent of destruction against both men and material, all combined to increase the price to be paid for victory.[14]

The 'general factors' he identified were all the results of the recent development of new military technologies. Whilst Haig recognised the problems that the new technologies created, he was slow to take advantage of the opportunities they offered. What was missing from General Haig's conception of the strategy of the war on the western front was any appreciation that it may have been his role to reduce the 'price to be paid for victory', and that he might reduce the price by taking a different tactical approach.

As the spring turned into summer, and the fighting season of 1917 drew closer, the British generals and politicians were at odds over the challenge of how to break the deadlock on the western front. This was not so much a dilemma for the generals and politicians as for the front-line troops. It was they, and not the generals and politicians, who would pay the price for the leadership's failure to break the deadlock.

CHAPTER NINE

BULLECOURT

The diggers fought their first major battle of 1917 at Bullecourt. The winter of 1916–17 was the wettest and coldest for 40 years. The constant bombardment during the Battle of the Somme had thoroughly churned up the rich soil. The rain now turned it to mud. Major Mackay described the conditions: 'Trenches very wet, narrow boggy. In some places, mud up to a man's fork. The mud is so sticky that it is almost impossible to lift one's foot out of it. The effect on a weak man would be disastrous.'[1]

In the wet, care of the men's feet became a priority. Loss of circulation could lead to the debilitating condition known as trench foot. Trench foot was officially regarded as a crime, although it was no respecter of rank. General Birdwood confessed that he had 'succumbed to it': 'Even though I wore good, thick boots laced lightly to encourage the circulation, I found the many hours I had to spend tramping through icy mud turned my feet into blocks of ice, and gradually a couple of toes gave out and troubled me for years to come.'[2] The men lived in the icy mud for days on end, and were 'crimed' if they succumbed.

Ambulance men carry diggers stricken with trench foot, December 1916. The condition was officially regarded as a crime, though it was no respecter of rank — General Birdwood 'succumbed to it'. AWM E00081

Mackay's routine was to remove his socks twice daily, rub his feet hard, and then turn his socks inside out.[3] Private Keown reported that, in the 5th Battalion, 'whale-oil was used extensively as a liniment, and was undoubtedly effective if applied in time. The only other practical safeguard was a change into dry footwear as often as possible, which, while the sufferer's duty was in the front line, was practically never.'[4]

Lieutenant Semple suffered from the condition:

I am on my way to hospital, suffering from trench feet due to being in water up to my knees for 72 hours without a break. There was not a place anywhere in the trench where we could stand clear of the water ... as soon as I took my boots off my feet swelled rapidly so that I could not put on my boots again & I had to make my way to the ambulance station, barefooted. The distance was something like two miles and I had some difficulty in negotiating it.[5]

It took great resilience to cope with the cold, the wet and the mud, as Sergeant Simon's matter of fact description demonstrates:

Our rations came to Bull's Trench in bags of ten, per mules, and were carried thence by human mules. No water was brought, but the ice in the shell-holes was melted to obtain water ... An axe would soon be the means of filling dixies with lumps of ice. We used it for tea for several days until one chap noticed a pair of boots sticking out ... and discovered they were attached to a body ... We generally managed to sleep warm by sleeping close together and sharing blankets — each man carried two. The cold, however, was preferable to the mud.[6]

By January 1917, Sergeant Downing had become demoralised by the mud, the cold and by the demands of returning, time and again, to the front line:

Back to the line tomorrow. We just go into the line again and again until we get knocked. We'll never get out of this. Just in and out, in and out, and somebody stonkered every time. Australia has forgotten us, and so has God. I wouldn't wish my worst enemy to have to put up with this life. But we've got to, and why shouldn't they too. All bound to get our 'issue' sooner or later.[7]

Out of the line, the Australians were polishing their French. Sergeant Denning and his mates, Nugget, Fatty and Phil, found that the lock-keeper's cottage was a private *estaminet*:

Not only were beer and fried eggs an attraction, the daughter Marie was a very buxom Mademoiselle. Nugget was already on very good terms with her. We weren't as raw as on our first encounter with the French girls and had picked up a bit of French.

Marie was all smiles and attention — Nugget all amorous and complimentary. He was getting bolder and bolder. As a rule he was a moderate drinker but that night he seemed as if he were trying to work up some 'Dutch courage'.

Madam and Papa were dozing in their chairs, when Nugget, a little blurry in his speech by now, blurted out as Marie leaned over the table, 'What about sleepin' with yer tonight Marie?' Marie, who understood English quite well when she wanted to, said very demurely 'No compré, Nugget.'[8]

'No compré be damned. You compré all right. Couchez avec moi.[9]'

'Après la guerre,[10] Nugg-et,' she smiled.

'No, not after the war, tonight.'

'No Nugg-et. Piccanin — no bon.'[11]

Nugget's French may have improved, but his style was still very ordinary.

Other diggers struggled with the French and Belgian languages. The French word Étaples is pronounced Aytarple. The diggers had no time for such linguistics. They called it Eat-apples. The diggers invented many of their own words. Ypres became Wipers; Ploegsteert became Plug Street; Doingt became Doing It; and Poperinghe simply Pop. *Estaminet*, the French word for pub, became just-a-minute. The white wine served in the just-a-minute, *vin blanc* (pronounced van blonk), became plonk. *Beaucoup*, the French word for a large quantity, became boko. *Ça ne fait rien*, the French for it does not matter, became san fairy ann.

German 77 artillery shells were called whizz-bangs. Another large artillery shell was called a Jack Johnson, after a prize fighter.

The Australians often called English soldiers chum, but pronounced, Lancashire style, as choom.

The radio codes also fell into common usage: emma gee was used for machine gun; toc emma for trench mortar; ack ack for anti-aircraft, and Toc H for Talbot House, the famous refuge for resting troops run by the Reverend Tubby Clayton★ in Poperinghe.

False rumours were furphies. The derivation of the word is uncertain. On one version, it comes from John Furphy, the Victorian manufacturer of water and sanitation carts, whose eponymous carts were reputedly places where men congregated to gossip. Another story is that the first tanks to arrive in France were disguised from the Germans by being delivered in crates marked with the Furphy brand. A third story is that the word derives from the Irish word 'murphies', meaning potatoes, in honour of the Irish talent for telling tall tales. At least two of these derivations are furphies.

The diggers adopted a morbid phrase at roll calls. When a man did not answer his name, his mates answered: Hanging on the barbed wire.

Il n'y a plus, the French for there is nothing left, became napoo. If the estaminet ran out of wine, it was napoo; if a man was blown away by a shell, he, too, was napoo. And the cemetery was the rest camp.

Lieutenant Maxwell had a bombastic commanding officer, who had his own way of coming to grips with the French language:

The crowd of us of No.8 platoon were swallowing beer in an estaminet controlled by a voluble French dame, when the 'skipper' entered and grasped the opportunity of demonstrating before us his linguistic abilities. For five minutes he harangued Madame with the rapidity of a machine-gun burst. The mystified Madame merely puckered her eyebrows and with a shrug of her shoulders murmured:

'No comprends vous, Monsieur'.[12]

Disgustedly turning to us, the captain snorted: 'Confound the damned woman, she can't understand her own language.'[13]

★   No relation.

While the diggers endured the miserable winter conditions, changes of leadership and political and military upheavals were afoot. In Britain, David Lloyd George replaced Herbert Asquith as prime minister. In Russia, the Tsar was deposed in March 1917. His replacement by a provisional government cast doubt on the continuation of Russian resistance. In France, a series of sixteen mutinies in May 1917 rocked the army. In the state of uncertainty that followed, the burden of the offensive on the western front fell on the British more heavily than before.[14]

In Germany, General Falkenhayn, the original commander on the western front, was replaced by General Hindenburg, who had made such a success of fighting the Russians on the eastern front. Hindenburg brought with him his chief of staff, General Ludendorff, who became the most influential figure in the prosecution of the remainder of the war for Germany.

Hindenburg and Ludendorff took a different view of strategy than Falkenhayn. Their concept was to reactivate unrestricted submarine warfare. By this means they hoped to reduce Britain by starvation. The German naval staff believed this would be achieved in six months. In the meantime, Germany would stand on the defensive on the western front.[15]

To facilitate the defensive policy, the Germans resolved to shorten the line of the western front. On a broad section of the front, from Arras to Soissons, they fell back from the line they held in January 1917 to the newly prepared fortifications of the Hindenburg line — a retreat of some 10 to 30 miles. The effect was to reduce the number of divisions the Germans (and the Allies) would need to man the line. The retreat took place in February and March 1917.

Whatever savings of manpower or energy the Germans were able to make by shortening the line, the decision to reactivate unlimited submarine warfare backfired disastrously. Unrestricted submarine warfare meant torpedoing United States shipping. Until that happened, the United States had adopted a position of neutrality in a war they regarded as European, but they would not take the torpedoing of their shipping lying down. On 6 April 1917, after the sinking of the *Lusitania*, the United States declared war on Germany.

The retreat to the Hindenburg line gave the diggers momentary release from the mud, as they pursued the retreating Germans into the open fields. Charles Bean wrote: 'Rarely did Australian soldiers experience such exhilaration as on that morning when, with the Somme morass finally behind them, they skirmished across green fields ...'[16] Despite the exhilaration of the pursuit, and despite General Haig's boast that the advance of Thiepval had been 'a slow and methodical progression, in which great skill and much patience and endurance had been displayed with entirely satisfactory results',[17] the truth was that the Allies were still a long way from developing 'a scientific method of continuous advance'[18] that was capable of dislodging the Germans from their fortified positions, especially now that the Germans were ensconced in the newly built Hindenburg line.

Many problems had been identified with the use of an artillery bombardment in combination with an infantry attack. The bombardment was guaranteed to sacrifice the element of surprise, but it was not guaranteed to clear the wire protecting the enemy positions, or to kill the enemy, or to dislodge them from their positions.

Lack of accuracy of artillery fire had contributed to the debacle on the Somme. Worn artillery pieces and imperfectly made ammunition compounded the inaccuracy of artillery fire. Maps were primitive, as were methods of aiming and ranging artillery. If the artillery did not have the opportunity to range on critical targets, its fire would inevitably be inaccurate.

To counter the problem that the enemy had time to set up its machine guns after the bombardment ended and before the advancing troops reached the enemy lines, the technique of the creeping barrage was developed. Under this technique, the barrage continued across no-man's-land after the advancing troops had left their trenches, but was 'lifted' by 50 or 100 yards at timed intervals — generally 100 yards in three minutes, but varying according to the circumstances. Advancing troops followed as close as they dared behind the creeping barrage, enabling them to enter the enemy's trenches before the enemy could recover from the bombardment and set up their guns.

This technique demanded excellent communication between the infantry and the artillery. Poor coordination between artillery and infantry could have disastrous results. If the creeping barrage lifted too quickly, the infantrymen would be left exposed as they crossed no-man's-land. If it lifted too slowly, shells might drop short on the advancing infantrymen. Newton Wanliss describes a British howitzer dropping shells into advancing British infantry in an advance in 1918. The shells were falling more than a mile short of their target.[19]

It was also vital to maintain communications after the infantry managed to attain its goals. If, having taken a trench, the infantry apprehended a counterattack and called for support fire by sending up flares, the artillery was understandably reluctant to fire if it did not know precisely where either the advancing infantry, or the counterattacking Germans were. In fact, communications in the heat of battle — whether by runner, telephone or carrier pigeon — were so difficult that coordination between the infantry and the artillery often failed.

Gunner Howell described the task of the signallers attached to the artillery, as he experienced it at the Battle of the Somme:

All communication having become impossible by means of telephones, I was told to make an attempt to get into communication with one of the balloons by means of a lamp. I didn't go much on the job, but there was nothing else to be done so I set the lamp up on a small hill and endeavoured to call up the nearest captive balloon. It was a waste of time and after running the gauntlet of the barrage for about half an hour I was called in. I hope to heaven I never have to do that again. Goodness knows how I escaped the machine gun fire and I never want to try that experiment again. Although the attempt was after all a failure the Captain seemed pleased. The only thing we could do then was to carry messages to the nearest station that was in telephone communication and this proved to be an awful job. The night was as black as a dungeon and the flares only made the darkness more intense. While they were in the air the light showed everything up as clear as day and during that short space I had to dodge into a shell hole to escape being riddled by a machine gun and look around for my bearings.[20]

The diggers at Bullecourt once again came under the command of General Gough, the notorious 'thrusting' cavalry officer,★ and, partly for that reason, one of Haig's favourite generals. Gough's impetuosity had cost the Australians dearly at Pozières. He was now to repeat the dose at Bullecourt.

The aim of the attack on Bullecourt was to support a larger British attack which had opened on 9 April 1917 at Arras, a few miles north of the position at Bullecourt. If a breakthrough could be achieved at Bullecourt, the attack would swing north in support of the attack on Arras.

Bullecourt was part of the new Hindenburg line. It was a position of enormous strength, heavily fortified with barbed wire. The diggers, who had only recently arrived in the area, were under pressure from General Gough to move quickly to support the attack at Arras, which had already begun.

The attack at Bullecourt represented a new departure in tactics. Instead of an artillery barrage, the attack was to be led by twelve tanks. The hope was that the use of tanks would introduce the element of surprise, whilst the tanks would be able to destroy the barbed-wire

---

★   Some would argue that 'thrusting' and 'cavalry officer' were synonymous.

entanglements. The attack would be on a narrow front, with the infantry following the tanks. This was the brainchild of a tank officer, who sold the idea to General Gough. According to Bean: 'Gough leapt at the project, asked how soon it could be carried out … He hurried with the tank officers to Birdwood's headquarters. Birdwood and White were full of doubts, but, as Gough pointed out (and the tank officers undertook) the wire should be broken before the infantry was asked to attack, they agreed to the attempt.'[21]

The attack was fixed for 4.45 am on 10 April 1917. The weather was bitterly cold. In fact, it was snowing. At midnight, the Australians took up positions in front of the railway embankment behind which they had set up their headquarters in anticipation of the attack. As zero hour approached, there was no sign of the tanks. Every ear strained to hear their engines, but no tank arrived.

As dawn approached, 'an exhausted tank officer stumbled into a telephone office in Noreuil valley, a mile behind the railway embankment, and told the 4th Division's headquarters that his machines had met blizzard weather and could not be [there] in time'.[22] A more amateur situation could not be imagined.

As dawn broke, the troops were hurriedly withdrawn from their exposed positions in no-man's-land, 'cursing the tanks and everybody connected with them'.[23] The attack was a non-event. Fortunately, the retreat was achieved with few casualties. The enemy, however, was now aware that an attack was in the offing. The element of surprise was lost. The enemy had time to reinforce the position with machine guns and storm troopers.[24]

Undeterred by the loss of surprise and by the men's exhaustion from spending the night lying out in the snow, General Gough ordered them to make the attack the next day. The plans were not changed. 'Upon strong protests from Birdwood and White, General Gough telephoned to GHQ, and presently returned to say that Haig considered the attack to be urgently required. This settled the matter.'[25] Once again, an order from Haig in the comfort of his headquarters overruled the divisional

A digger grabs a sleep during the Bullecourt battle May 1917. He was fortunate: the first and second Bullecourt conflicts cost 10,000 Australian casualties. AWM E00455

commanders on the spot, and tipped the scales in favour of impetuosity over caution.

The next night, the troops once again took up positions in no-man's-land. By 4.30 am only three tanks had reached position. Captain White wrote that, of the remaining tanks:

> One had had an 'accident', one complained of 'engine trouble', and the other had lolloped into a sunken road whither it had gone contrary to the directions by a 14th officer.[26] These tanks were out of action before the battle commenced, and, not only the three that had arrived, but the others had made squeals, screeches and sparks that must have warned the enemy. Our men cursed them and the 'silent artillery'.[27]

The attack went ahead with only three tanks.

At zero hour, the order to advance was given.

Newton Wanliss wrote:

There were about 1000 yards to reach the first objective [the first German trench]; there was not any cover — the ground was as flat as a billiard table. Unprotected by a barrage, the attacking force was absolutely at the enemy's mercy until it reached the wire; there could not be any retaliation until it got to grips with its opponent; the first problem was how many would survive to do so.[28]

The troops advanced across the snow in four long lines, almost in parade order, until the German artillery burst forth. The men in dark uniforms made stark targets against the white background of the snow. The tanks attracted the German fire, so much so that their 'shapes were outlined by the sparkling of bullets'.[29] This took some of the pressure off the advancing troops, who were able to reach the barbed-wire entanglements.

The wire was '60 or 70 feet wide, breast high, with enormous protruding one inch barbs, and so thick that anyone lying down could not see through it, and was admirably sited so as to enable the German machine gunners to fire along its fringe'.[30] The wire had been broken in some places, but the machine guns concentrated on the gaps, and many men were killed trying to get through.[31] Only one of the tanks reached the German trenches, but some of the men did, and the first trench was taken in a rush, with Mills bombs thrown and hand-to-hand fighting carrying the charge.[32]

The next objective was the second German trench. It was also protected by heavy belts of barbed wire, this time unbroken. By 6.45 am the second trench had been taken.[33] Captain Murray organised the men in the second trench. He sent a hand-written message calling for artillery support. His message read: 'With artillery support we can keep the position until the cows come home.'[34] The men in the trenches sent up the SOS flares eighteen times calling for artillery support, but there was no response.[35] Aerial reports had convinced the high command that the attack was continuing beyond the German trenches, so they refused to order the artillery to bomb that area, leaving the way clear for the German counterattackers to advance with impunity. The Australians in the trenches were stranded. By 11.30 am, with ammunition running low, the only course was to attempt to return to the Australian lines. Looking over the vicious fire that was sweeping the way back, Murray told his men, 'It is either capture, or go into that.'[36]

The achievement of occupying part of the Hindenburg line without a barrage was one of the great feats of arms of the war, but there was nothing else to recommend the day. Seventy-nine Australian officers and 2260 other ranks were listed as casualties and 1300 Australians were taken into captivity, making Bullecourt the only occasion in the war when the Germans took a considerable number of Australian prisoners.[37]

Officially, the loss of the battle was attributed to the failure of the tanks. The diggers heartily endorsed this verdict. The tanks of 1917 were 'mechanically deficient, the crews were half-trained and new to battle, had never co-operated with infantry, and there were far too few of them'.[38] Their movement was difficult. Not only were they unreliable under their own power, but, when they had to move long distances, they had to go by train. Loading and unloading from the trains caused headaches and not a few engineering problems.[39] Newton Wanliss, the historian of the 14th Battalion, saw a deeper cause of failure: the impetuosity of General Gough and the Fifth Army command.

The whole plan seems to have been based on numerous misconceptions, and was evidently the handiwork of someone dominated, not by reason, but by impulse. The decision to persist with the attack on April 11, under the same original conditions after the fiasco of the previous day, was a lamentable and unfortunate error of judgment, entailing the most disastrous consequences. It seems inexplicable, and can only be explained as another example of that intense spirit of optimism which permeated British leadership throughout the whole war, and which seemed almost immune to the many and bitter fruits of experience. Though the battle was splendidly fought, it was crudely planned.[40]

Nor did General Birdwood conceal the failures of General Gough's command from his men. Lieutenant Rule, a member of the 14th Battalion, recorded a visit from General Birdwood a few days after the battle, when Birdwood told the troops:

> 'Boys, I can assure you that no one regrets this disaster that has befallen your brigade more than I do; and again, 'I can assure you that none of your own officers had anything to do with the arrangements for the stunt'; and lastly, 'We did our utmost to have the stunt put off until more suitable arrangements could be made'.[41]

From this criticism, Rule realised that Gough and his ilk 'were fallible flesh and blood, the same as we'.[42]

It was not difficult for Rule to pinpoint the faults in General Gough's plan to attack the Hindenburg line. The available Australian artillery was so lacking in firepower that it could not be relied on to give support. Gough's plan was to make up for the absence of artillery with only twelve tanks. The men had never attacked with tanks before, nor had the tanks ever been used in the manner Gough proposed.[43] The men were given no opportunity to train with the tanks, or to learn their capabilities.

The Germans, meanwhile, were equally anxious to divert Allied reserves from the offensive at Arras. Using similar logic to Gough's, on 15 April 1917, they attacked the Australian 1st and 2nd Divisions at Lagnicourt, near Noreuil and just south of Bullecourt. Fighting on the defensive this time, the Australians had the better of the battle, sustaining some 1000 casualties compared to the Germans' 2313.[44]

The Australians made a further attempt on Bullecourt at 3.45 am on 3 May 1917, but this attack was made behind a creeping barrage, and without the false security of the tanks. The attack was partly successful, with the 6th Brigade seizing part of the Hindenburg trenches and extending its hold with bombing raids down the trench lines. Fighting raged backwards and forwards between the trench line and a sunken road half across no-man's-land. By nightfall, the Australian still held the trench line. The Australians held on to this narrow foothold in the Hindenburg line, gradually extending it to a front of 600 yards by 6 May 1917.[45]

By 7 May 1917, most of the 1st and 2nd Australian Divisions were engaged in the second Bullecourt battle. Captain Joynt, VC, described the next period of the battle:

> The Germans kept counterattacking from front and flanks without success; altogether twelve Hun counterattacks were defeated. None of them reached our front line, each attack disintegrating fully two hundred yards short of our trenches. German officers could be seen bravely attempting to lead their men on to come to grips with us, but the Huns wouldn't follow.[46]

On 12 May 1917, it was the turn of the 5th Division to take over the burden, repulsing a strong German counterattack on the morning of 15 May 1917. This was the Germans' last roll of the dice. When their attack failed, they decided to withdraw from Bullecourt.[47]

Although Haig described it as 'among the great deeds of the war', second Bullecourt, fought between 5 and 17 May 1917, cost the Australians 7000 casualties, compared to some 3000 in a single night at first Bullecourt. For this price, the Australians had secured a foothold in the supposedly impregnable Hindenburg line, and held it through seven general counterattacks and a dozen minor ones, but had achieved little of lasting value.[48] For Joynt, the diggers paid this price to indulge General Gough's penchant for 'clutching at valuable strategic ends by impossible tactics'.[49]

Once again, the diggers bore the brunt of the impetuosity of General Gough, and of the inability of the Australian commanders to counteract it.

CHAPTER TEN

MESSINES

After Fromelles, Pozières and Bullecourt, the diggers were wary of their British commanders, and with good reason. Captain Behrend, an Englishman who served as an adjutant in France and Flanders in 1917 and 1918, gave an English perspective of the British high command:

> … whatever may be thought or written today [1963] about the tactical and strategic skill, or the lack of it, possessed by our high command, we [English soldiers] in France and Flanders in 1917 and 1918 had no complaints about the way in which we were administered. Our medical, transport, and supply services had advanced a long way since the days of the Boer and Crimean Wars. We were well fed and clothed; when we were wounded or sick we were admirably looked after; leave was given fairly, regularly, and generously; during my time with the B.E.F. there was no shortage of guns or ammunition, motors, maps, or indeed of anything. To us it seemed that the vast if at times cumbersome machine worked smoothly, and to us it was the last word in modernity.[1]

Behrend's accepting frame of mind stood in marked contrast to the more questioning attitude of the Australians. Indeed, Behrend's account illustrates to a number of contrasts between the Australians and the British: 'It was not our habit to criticize our top Generals … For we did not know our Generals, nor did they seem to want us to know them.'[2] There was a stark contrast between the aloofness of the British generals, and the more friendly approach of Birdwood and the Australian generals under him.

Behrend 'saw Haig but once, and then only from a distance. Whatever the capacity of his brain, he was a fine and upright figure on a horse; he looked the part and thus left one in no doubt that he was the sort of man well able to shoulder his responsibilities'. The connection between a man's seat on a horse and his capacity to command a large army is obscure. Behrend evidently did not know that Lloyd George described Haig as 'brilliant to the top of his boots'.

The rose-coloured glasses Behrend reserved for his superiors at least saw clearly in relation to one of the British high command — the avuncular, even grandfatherly, General Plumer:

> It was noticeable and therefore common knowledge that Second Army under Plumer cared for and looked after its troops better than any of our other Armies. Hence Plumer, a small white-haired man with pink cheeks, was rated as a good general, and his battle of Messines — for he, or maybe Harington his Chief of Staff, planned and executed it — was so much a model of what a battle for limited objectives should be that it was a pleasure to take part in it.[3]

The Australians were now to get their chance to work with this different type of British general.

After the rigours of first Bullecourt, the 4th Division was not happy at the prospect of continuing in the line. According to Lieutenant Rule:

> Somewhere about the end of April we had a big divisional parade and march past. General Birdwood said good-bye to us, as we were

being sent away from the I Anzac Corps to operate with the II Anzac Corps up at Messines. This [being sent to Messines without a rest after Bullecourt] is where the 4th Division received such a rough spin. The rest of the Aussie divisions were allowed to rest until the Passchendaele battle came on in September, but we were kept hard at it, going into the line three times.[4]

Whilst the battles on the Somme and at Bullecourt had bogged down in relentless trench fighting, Haig's plan for both battles had been that the initial advance would open up gaps in the enemy's trenches, through which the cavalry would pass. Once the cavalry was through, it could range widely behind the German lines, breaking free of the trenches and restoring the war of movement.

With solid roots in the cavalry, this form of aggressive, mounted warfare was the bread and butter of many of the British high command. There were some, however, who questioned whether the cavalry had any role to play in trench warfare, and who advocated the adoption of different methods. General Rawlinson was one such. As early as March 1915, he had written to Clive Wigram, the King's secretary, describing the new approach he favoured:

> What we want to do now is what I call 'bite-and-hold'. Bite off a piece of the enemy's line … and hold it against counterattack. The bite can be made without much loss, and, if we choose the right place and make every preparation to put it quickly into a state of defence, there ought to be no difficulty in holding it against the enemy's counterattacks, and inflicting on him at least twice the loss that we suffered in making the bite.[5]

The merit of the bite-and-hold tactic was that it allowed the Allies to advance their infantry without their ever leaving the protection of their own guns. When they seized limited parts of the German front, they could hold them against counterattack with the help of their static artillery. When the positions were secure, they could move up their artillery, and repeat the process.[6] Progress in this way would never be dramatic, but it might be reliable.

The Battle of Messines was to be a bite-and-hold operation. The battle had been in planning since June 1915. General Plumer had taken command of the Messines sector in January 1916. He planned the battle with intricate thoroughness.[7] Plumer's methods of command were in marked contrast to other British generals. His watchword was that the army command served the needs of the divisions and the men.[8] From a regimental background, Plumer believed in making himself and the other members of the army staff highly visible to the men in their command. His chief of staff, General Harington, described how Plumer's daily routine began with a meeting of the headquarters staff:

Directly after the daily conference, the Chief with an aide-de-camp went off on his rounds. He must have averaged 100 miles a day. I think most of us did. We used to leave with the Signals our general direction, including some Headquarters at which we were certain to call. My tours were generally in the opposite direction to those of the Chief in order to visit as many formations as possible, though we would often arrange to meet during the day at some Corps Headquarters to discuss any problem.

By this means it is fair to say that every Corps and Divisional Headquarters and most Brigade Headquarters were visited almost daily by either the Chief himself or one of his team and always with the object of ascertaining if there was anything we could do to help. It was by this means that he won … trust and confidence …

In his daily tours none were forgotten. One moment he was in the forward area visiting various Headquarters the next he was in the back areas saying a kind and encouraging word to men in rest billets or horse lines, visiting gun positions, workshops, railheads, hospitals and Army schools. He made all realize that they were part of his big machine.[9]

The contrast between Plumer's style of leadership and the hectoring approach of General Gough could not be greater. According to Harington, Plumer 'had been a regimental soldier and he never forgot it'.[10]

Not only was Harington a huge admirer of Plumer, the two of them formed a formidable team. Haig's intelligence officer, Brigadier Charteris, described them as

> the most even-tempered pair of warriors in the whole war or any war. The troops love them … The two men are so utterly different in appearance, Plumer, placid and peaceful-looking, rather like an elderly grey-moustached Cupid, Harington always looking rather fine-drawn and almost haggard. Neither has ever been known to lose his temper … nobody knows where Plumer ends and Harington begins.[11]

The Battle of Messines formed part of a larger operation by which Haig hoped to clear the German Army from the Belgian coast north of Ypres. This was to be achieved by an attack on Passchendaele. Before he could do that, Haig needed to secure his right flank by straightening the salient that pushed into the Allied line at Messines, south of Ypres.

The town of Messines sits on top of a high hill. The Douve River flows to the west and south of the hill. Since 1914, the Germans had held the top of the hill, overlooking (and bombing) the British trenches in the valley of the Douve River, at Ploegsteert to the south and at Kemmel to the north. The object of the attack was to bite off the top of the Messines ridge down to the Oosttaverne trench line in the flat country on the eastern side of the ridge, and to hold it against counterattack.

Plumer had the luxury of time to prepare for the attack, and he did not waste it. During 1915 and 1916, companies of tunnellers (coal miners before the war) had driven mine shafts for miles under the German lines. There were nineteen of these shafts. The ends of the shafts had been packed with a total of 957 000 pounds of explosive, ready to be set off at zero hour of zero day — 3.10 am on 7 June 1917. In fact, the majority of the mines had been ready since June 1916.[12]

During 1916, the railway system that connected the Channel ports to the front had been extensively overhauled. Haig had appointed a civilian, Sir Eric Geddes, to overhaul the transport system by which supplies of food, ammunition and all the essentials of life were transported from Britain across the Channel and on to the front. Geddes worked on the philosophy that warfare consisted of men, munitions and movement. In 1916, the British had the men and the munitions, but they had forgotten about the movement.[13]

Three main rail lines serviced the front from the ports of Calais, Boulogne and Dunkirk. These now operated more efficiently, bringing an end to the problems of ammunition shortage that had bedevilled some stages of the Battle of the Somme.[14] In the twelve-day bombardment before the Battle of Messines, the artillery was sufficiently well-supplied to be able to fire 3.5 million shells.[15] A shortage of water had also been solved by laying pipes that supplied between 450000 and 600000 gallons daily.[16]

The men who were to fight the battle rehearsed their roles repeatedly. They were briefed on the task with the aid of a huge three dimensional model of the battlefield that covered 'about an acre of ground' — a novelty for the Australian troops, and one that engendered confidence in the planning of the battle.[17] Artillery and machine gun plans were made and rehearsed on the enemy himself.[18] The original plans were checked, settled and reinforced in consultation during Plumer's visits to divisional and brigade commanders.[19] Here again, the contrast with Gough's dictatorial style was evident. Harington described Plumer's consultative style as the reverse of the normal picture:

> When lower formations were not consulted but merely ordered into action with the result that they thought that neither the stages nor the time of attack nor the place of the barrage was correct, [they]

did not start in good heart. Simply the difference between the art of commanding by trust as against distrust.[20]

Technical innovation was to the fore in the planning of the battle. A new communications system had been developed in which a hot-air balloon anchored to the ground by wires was sent aloft behind each corps. The balloon had a basket attached in which an artillery observer sat precariously perched, watching the battle through binoculars or a telescope. The brave soul in the basket was connected to a forward report centre by telephone lines which ran through the anchor cables of the balloon. The forward report centre was, in turn, connected to Harington's office at headquarters. This allowed Harington to maintain instant communication with the progress of the battle on each corps front.[21]

Of course, hot-air balloons were easy targets. When a balloon was shot down — which was frequently — the long-suffering observer had to jump out of the basket and hope for the best, relying on his 1917-

Hot-air balloons were an easy target and so the observer in the basket always had a parachute at hand, ready to leap, hoping for the best. AWM E01125

model parachute. If, miraculously, the parachute saved the observer's life, he could look forward to being sent aloft again as soon as another balloon could be inflated and launched.

At the beginning of the war, artillery aiming was notoriously inaccurate. The inaccuracy came from a multitude of causes: the weather; the wind; worn barrels; inconsistent manufacture of shells; differing muzzle velocities; and the movement of the guns as they fired and recoiled. This inaccuracy of the guns was compounded by haphazard methods of target location. Traditionally, enemy artillery was located by artillery observers in forward lookout positions, who did their best to mark the enemy positions on maps. The best observers found it difficult accurately to estimate the direction and range of the enemy gun emplacements, most of which were heavily camouflaged.

One option was trial and error. The artillery would fire a few shots and the observer would watch where they fell, calling adjustments until the gun was on target.[22] This, of course, put the enemy on notice that he had been spotted.

Gradually, instruments were developed that took observations more scientifically. The instruments took timed rangings on the sounds and muzzle flashes of the guns. From these, it was possible to pinpoint enemy guns by triangulation without letting the enemy know that his positions had been found out.

Aeroplanes also helped with target spotting. The pilot of an RE8 had a morse code transmitter by which he could transmit a message to an artillery battery. In the battery, a signaller had a crystal set receiver through with which he could hear the morse signal, but only if he could hold the wire continually in contact with the right part of the crystal.* This was not two-way radio — the pilot could only transmit and the signaller could only receive.

---

*   Australians of a certain (but great) age will remember using the same technique to listen, late at night, to cricket Tests in England.

The message was a single morse letter, corresponding to the numbers on an imaginary clockface, centred on the target, with twelve o'clock to the north of the target. The artillery fired a test round; the pilot observed where it dropped; the pilot tapped out the appropriate letter in morse indicating where the shell had landed; if the signaller received the message, he laid on the ground a piece of canvas in the shape of the letter; the pilot meantime flew back over the battery to check that the correct message had been received; if it had, the artillery adjusted their aim; fired another test round; and the process was repeated. The benefit of this process was that it accurately ranged the target. The detriment was that it also gave away the position of the battery.[23] In theory, at least, the sausage balloons could help collect and disseminate this information. Often, the observer's view was obscured by the dust and smoke of the battle.

At Messines, the Australians were stationed on the right (or southern) side of the line of attack. The 4th Division — reputed to be the toughest of all Australian divisions — was under the command of General Holmes.★[24] It would take part in the second stage of the attack, following the New Zealanders and sweeping across the ridge to the final objective. The 3rd Division — the newest Australian division — was under the command of General Monash. Its task was to sweep up the far right flank, in conjunction with the 4th Division. Monash, who was to take and develop Plumer's approach to battle planning, described the preparations for the battle in a letter home on 19 May 1917:

I am now in the thick of preparation for our forthcoming offensive operations. My job is to capture the southern spur of a famous ridge, and to form a defensive flank for our army. For weeks past, we have been making roads, building railways and tramways, forming ammunition-dumps, making gun emplacements and camouflaging them, preparing brigade and battalion headquarters and laying a

---

★   My great-grandfather — the father of my father's mother.

complex system of underground cables, fixing the position of machine guns, heavy guns and howitzers … There is a mass of field engineering work to be done, in large dugouts, approach avenues, assembly and jumping off trenches; most voluminous orders to be got out, controlling the action of the whole of my 20 000 men and animals — feeding organisation, transport organisation, ammunition supply, cutting the enemy's wire (an operation now in full blast), the preliminary destructive bombardment of his field works, the completion and blowing up of mines, and finally the preparation of the 12 000 infantry, for the actual work of 'going over the top'.

The Army commander spent all yesterday afternoon with me, going patiently and minutely through the whole of my plans, and said he felt sure that I had done all that was possible to ensure success.[25]

At 3.10 am, nineteen mines blew under the enemy lines. The explosion 'seemed to cause the ground to rise up and go down'.[26] The blast was like an earthquake. It was felt in Lille, ten miles away, causing the inhabitants to rush out of their houses. 'The earthquake came first and then there were 19 immense pillars of fire, first red, then white, then all the colours of the rainbow, accompanied by great masses of clay and sand and debris, dug-outs, machine-gun emplacements and so on.'[27]

The creeping barrage began at the same time. The infantry advanced on the assault as the debris from the mines subsided. Following closely on the creeping barrage, the infantry carried the enemy front line in a few minutes, pressing up the western slope to the crest of the ridge.[28] The surviving Germans were 'too dazed to offer serious opposition'.[29] The infantry took the first line of trenches without effective opposition.

Whilst the long barrage had warned the enemy of the impending attack, the explosion of the mines had injected a true, and devastating, element of surprise. At headquarters, Plumer 'was kneeling by his bedside praying for those gallant officers and men who at that moment were attacking'.[30] Shortly, he joined Harington to listen to the news of the attack from the sausage balloon communications, which Hartington described in 1935 as, 'an eye-witness account such as we are now accustomed to on the wireless'.[31] With luck, this technological advance would soon spell the end of the carrier pigeon as an instrument of war.[32]

Tanks followed the infantry. Only fifteen of them reached the first objective line, but there was little for them to do, so complete had been the success of the infantry. When the first wave of attacking troops reached their objective at the top of the ridge, they halted to allow fresh troops to 'leap frog' over them and press on with the attack on the Oosttarverne line. This could only be done at the time coordinated with the artillery. The fresh troops resumed the attack at 3.10 pm, pushing down the eastern slope of the ridge. Within an hour, the Oosttarverne line had been taken.[33]

The value of the sausage balloon communication system was demonstrated when a tank became stranded on top of the ridge, and was coming under heavy artillery fire. The observer in the sausage balloon saw which enemy battery was firing on the tank, and reported its location to Harington, who, in turn called in artillery fire with the result that, 'in thirteen minutes that Battery was bombed and silenced and our tank escaped'.[34] This story also illustrates how far artillery aiming techniques had improved.

By the end of the day, the objectives of the attack had been achieved and the work of holding had begun. The wireless reported a possible counterattack that day from the direction of Warneton. Plumer had three mines in reserve, in case the counterattack developed, but, as events turned out, there was no counterattack that day.[35] The enemy did launch a heavy bombardment and a strong counterattack on the evening of 8 June 1917, but without success.

The Battle of Messines was an immense success. Confidence in leadership (or, at least, leadership by trust) was restored. The salient was eliminated. The Germans suffered a huge setback. The way lay clear for the assault on Passchendaele. Losses, however, were not curtailed. Casualties were roughly even on both sides, with the British sustaining 26 000 casualties, including 13 900 in II Anzac Corps (which, in that battle, included the 25th British division).[36] These figures are high, but Harington later wrote that they were 'one-fifth of the casualties we had anticipated'.★[37]

One casualty, in particular, struck the Australians. On 2 July 1917, the commander of the 4th division, Major-General Holmes — a loyal, brave and most able man[38] — was killed. He had been doing one of the less spectacular of a general's duties: entertaining visiting dignitaries. This time it was W A Holman, the Premier of New South Wales. The General was taking the Premier to see the Messines battlefield. For this purpose, Holmes had his chauffeur drive the party up the west side of Hill 63, a hill directly south of the Messines battlefield, which commands a magnificent view of the town of Messines, and the ridge that was overrun in the battle. As the car approached a small shrine, an enemy plane was under fire from an anti-aircraft battery. Holmes said, 'Come on, we must not run a risk with this precious Premier. We'll run on past the shrine where it will be safe.' According to Holman, Holmes laughed and said, 'They have spotted you, Holman. This is unhealthy. Let's move.'

They drove past the shrine (which still stands) and up the western face of Hill 63 to the White Gates (which no longer stand) where they stopped. The party walked up towards the crest of the hill. Holmes returned to the car to get his cap. At 10.20 am, a high explosive shell fell among the group. The others were shaken and bruised, but unhurt. Holmes had a wound that extended from under the left ribs in his back as far as his neck. He died before reaching the dressing station.

It was one of Holmes' quirks that he never hesitated to wear his full uniform, complete with red staff tabs and cap band when visiting the front line. This did not necessarily endear him to his men, as the sight of the red trimmings often prompted the enemy to fire on the trenches long after the general had left them. Perhaps, in this instance, the trait had led to the General's death.

★ Could Harington and Plumer really have anticipated 130 000 casualties?

Haig was grudging about Plumer's success. He had previously thought of dismissing Plumer from the command of the Second Army. According to Lieutenant Charles Edmonds, an Englisman, this was the product of an old grudge on Haig's part: '[Haig's] attitude … dated from the time when Haig was a student at the Staff College and Plumer, as an outside examiner, gave Haig a low place, which was the sort of thing Haig never forgot.'[39] What goes around comes around, even for a person as kind and likeable as General Plumer.

Far from being embarrassed about having once attempted to remove Plumer from his command, when Haig came to confide in his diary on the night of the Messines battle, he wrote:

> Soon after 4 pm I visited General Plumer at his HQ at Cassel, and congratulated him on his success. The old man deserves the highest praise for he has patiently defended the Ypres salient for 2½ years, and he well [knows] that pressure has been brought to bear on me in order to remove him from Command of the Second Army.
>
> The operations today are probably the most successful I have yet undertaken … [40]

At 60 years of age, Plumer was only four years older than Haig. The difference in ages does not explain why Haig, at 56, was still immature enough to take for himself the credit for Plumer's victory.

CHAPTER ELEVEN

PASSCHENDAELE

With the clearance of the salient at Messines, Haig had secured his right flank in readiness to drive the Germans away from the Belgian coast. His plan involved advancing north-west from the ruined city of Ypres, across the Passchendaele ridge, and on to the coast.

Passchendaele, or Third Ypres, as it is sometimes called, are names given to a series of eleven limited battles fought in succession between 31 July and 30 November 1917. I or II Anzac was the spearhead in five of the attacks: the third to the seventh inclusive. In only three of the attacks — the first three that the Australians led — were conditions suitable for the type of operations that had been planned. The other attacks were all made in oppressively wet conditions, that turned the ground into mud, and the battlefield into a slaughterhouse.[1] Ultimately, the mud of Flanders did as much to blunt the Allied attacks as the stout resistance of the Germans.

Haig gave the command of the Passchendaele operations to General Gough. This may not have been surprising in light of Haig's condescending attitude towards Plumer, but it meant that this 'thrusting' general was once again calling the shots.

Haig's own role in the planning of individual battles was declining as the size of the force under his control increased. With the number of men under his command now around 1.8 million,[2] the challenges of commanding an organisation of that size and complexity, as well as of dealing with his political masters, increasingly diverted Haig from the day-to-day planning of operations.

This meant that the responsibility for operational planning devolved on the commanders of armies, corps and divisions. Interference in matters of detail best decided by the officers on the ground, of which Haig's telegram instruction to General Monro at Fromelles, and his telephone instruction to General Gough at Bullecourt were examples, became less frequent. The scope of Haig's own task meant that he had no option but to rely on his army, corps and divisional commanders to take the initiative.

The conflict between Haig and his political masters came to a head in mid-July 1917.[3] The question was whether the Cabinet would trust Haig with the lives of the men, if all he intended to do was to repeat the discredited tactics of the Battle of the Somme. As Bean put it, the War Cabinet feared that 'Haig would involve the British Army not in a mere step-by-step offensive but in a single-handed, unlimited attempt to break through the strongest defences of the strongest enemies'.[4] The Cabinet's apprehensions touched on four controversial issues: the reckless waste of lives; the inadvisability of attacking the enemy at its strong points; the fear that Britain was shouldering France's burden; and the western front/second front controversy.

On 8 June 1917, Lloyd George established a War Policy Committee, separate from the War Cabinet, to consider these issues. The committee consisted of Lloyd George, Curzon, Milner, Smuts, with Lord Hankey as its secretary.[5] Between 8 and 29 June 1917, the committee held sixteen meetings, before reporting to the War Cabinet.

The committee's recommendation was to give artillery support to the Italians, who were fighting the Austrians in the north of Italy, by transferring 300 heavy guns from the western front to the Italian front.

If Austria was tired of the war, a stronger blow might cause her to sue for peace, in which case, there would be the added advantage that Bulgaria and Turkey would both be isolated from Germany. This policy was known as 'knocking away the props' that supported Germany.[6]

Not only did the War Policy Committee believe there was merit in opening a second front, it had doubts about the policy of concentrating on the western front. Was there sufficient manpower for the attack? Was it possible to advance far enough to achieve Haig's and Robertson's goals? Would failure further reduce morale at home? 'To all these criticisms Haig and Robertson were able to give a plausible reply' wrote Lord Hankey.[7] Their objections were both powerful and well-rehearsed.[8] Haig and Robertson insisted on the attack in Flanders. They argued that the attack had been in planning since January 1916. The French had agreed to it in May 1917.[9] The British and French Governments had already committed to the war of attrition. That was true. At a meeting on 4 and 5 May 1917, Haig and Robertson had agreed with the French Generals Pétain and Nivelle that: 'It is no longer a question of aiming at breaking through the enemy's front and aiming at distant objectives. It is now a question of wearing down and exhausting the enemy's resistance and if and when this is achieved, to exploit it to the fullest possible extent.'[10]

Haig argued that Messines, and Vimy before it, had been successes. Indeed, he offered 'his' success at Messines as 'a happy earnest of his proposed plans'.[11] With the zest of a convert (an insincere convert, at that), he promised that the next offensive would be a Plumer-style, bite-and-hold operation, limited in scope, with the infantry never moving beyond the protection of the artillery. Casualties would be limited as much as possible. If the British did not attack, the Germans would, and greater casualties would be suffered. There could be no guarantee, of course, but Haig and Robertson were adamant that the Flanders option was better than the Italian.

Moreover, the navy supported Haig's plan.[12] A breakthrough in Flanders would make the way clear to Ostend, Ghent, Bruges, Brussels and the Ardennes, clearing the ports and compromising German railway communications, by disrupting the railhead at Roulers.[13] As soon as the plans were articulated in this form, it became obvious that they represented a huge departure from the notion of a series of bite-and-hold attacks. It was some fifty miles from Ypres to the Belgian coast, and even further from Ypres to the Ardennes. Objectives of that distance and scale could only be achieved if there was a truly spectacular breakthrough, allowing the cavalry to wreak havoc behind the German lines. But Haig could never resist the carrot of the spectacular breakthrough.

Lloyd George summoned Haig to London for a week of meetings with the War Policy Committee starting on 19 June 1917. According to Hankey, there was a 'regular battle royal (conducted in the best possible spirit) between Lloyd George on the one hand and Robertson and Haig on the other'.[14] The question was whether Haig's and Robertson's plans offered reasonable prospects of success.[15]

Haig recorded his disappointment with the politicians. 'The members of the War Cabinet asked me numerous questions all tending to show that each of them was more pessimistic than the other!'[16] Haig recorded his arguments in his diary:

> *now* was the favourable moment, and … everything possible should be done to take advantage of it by concentrating on the Western Front *all* available resources. I stated that Germany was within 6 months of the total exhaustion of her available manpower, *if the fighting continues at its present intensity.*[17]

Notoriously taciturn, and a poor debater, Haig stuck to his guns. Robertson was equally resolute. Absorbing the relentless pressure that could be applied in a week of Cabinet committee meetings, Haig wrote that, 'Robertson would not budge! All he would say was that my plan was the only thing to do.'[18] From the navy perspective, Admiral Jellicoe strongly supported the goal of clearing the Belgian coast.[19]

The committee gave the generals one last chance to change their minds. Lord Hankey wrote:

All the week the controversy went on, but on Monday (June 25), after the Committee had adjourned to give Robertson and Haig time to think it over, they adhered to their opinion and Lloyd George felt he could not press his amateur opinions, so he gave in, and Haig was authorized to continue his preparations. The final decision, however, was postponed until after a conference with the French, as Lloyd George declines to agree finally until assured that the French will do their bit by attacking simultaneously. A fortnight was left for this ... [20]

On 28 June 1917, Haig recorded in his diary that he had spoken to General Wilson, who thought that 'our continuing offensive is the only way to save France',[21] but Wilson's version of the same conversation contained a critical reservation: 'we should attack all we could right up to the time of the mud'.[22]

In the event, the decision was taken over dinner on 16 July 1917, without meeting with the French. Lord Hankey wrote:

In the evening Lloyd George gave a dinner at 10 Downing Street to the War Policy Committee ... Balfour and Carson being also guests. We went over much the same ground as at the last dinner at Curzon's, and the final decision was to allow Haig to begin his offensive, but not to allow it to degenerate into a drawn out, indecisive battle of the 'Somme' type. If this happened, it was to be stopped and the plan for an attack on the Italian Front would be tried.[23]

According to Hankey

The decision to allow Haig to undertake the Flanders offensive was taken by Lloyd George and by most of his colleagues with reluctance and misgiving. No one believed that a strategical result could be achieved, and all shrank from the terrible losses which they knew it must involve. But the consensus of naval and military opinion was so overwhelming that the War Cabinet could not take the responsibility of rejecting the advice thrust upon it with so much cogency.[24]

The professional soldiers had carried the day. It is an interesting reflection on the nature of courage to compare the courage it took for the politicians to take that fateful decision with the courage the troops would need to carry it out.

Certainly, in the next war, there would be no question of the British prime minister deferring to his advisers on account of his 'amateur' military status, yet Churchill and his Cabinet had to take ultimate responsibility for invidious decisions in that war as well. What sets the Flanders decision apart is that, although the best brains available were working to solve the stalemate on the western front, 'no one believed that a strategical result could be achieved'. A sense of hopelessness — of damned if you do and damned if you don't — surrounded the decision.

Third Ypres began with an aerial offensive combined with what Haig characteristically called 'a methodical and comprehensive artillery program'.[25] The barrage lasted two weeks, again robbing the offensive of the element of surprise.[26]

The first attack, by British troops, took place on 31 July 1917. The men set out from Ypres to attack along the Menin Road. Their ultimate objective was the ridge of high ground five to eight miles east of Ypres. The fact that the objective of the attack was so far away was also inconsistent with the bite-and-hold principle.

Major Davidson, the Director of Military Operations at GHQ, had written a monograph questioning whether the objective should not be 1500 or 3000 yards. General Gough responded that the 'attacking force would waste a valuable opportunity if it did not reap from the first attack all the advantages possible; the first organized stroke should be quickly followed by others',[27] but he did not favour limiting these too strictly in depth.

The objectives for the first attack were the three German trench lines and the Passchendaele-Staden heights, which were to be reached by exploitation if opportunity permitted. The hope of a spectacular breakthrough had not been dropped. The date of the first attack was chosen with a view to launching the 'offensive beyond [the Passchendaele-Staden heights] in time to enable the coastal attack to catch the high tides of August 7 or 8'.[28] This allowed only a week for the infantry to advance more than 50 miles — something that had not been achieved since the trenches were dug.

Gough was adamant that Haig intended a major breakthrough. In 1944, he wrote to General Edmonds, the British official historian:

I have a very clear and distinct recollection of Haig's personal explanations to me, and his instructions, when I was appointed to undertake this operation. He quite clearly told me that the plan was to capture Passchendaele Ridge, and to advance as rapidly as possible on Roulers. I was then to advance on Ostend. This was very definitely viewing the battle as an attempt to break through, and moreover, Haig never altered this opinion till the attack was launched, so far as I know.

The G.H.Q. plan failed to amass anything like sufficient forces to carry out so ambitious a task — 20 to 30 divisions were necessary — and the front of attack was too narrow and directed at the wrong place …

It was also a mistake not to entrust the operation to the General [Plumer] who had been on that front for more than two years, instead of bringing me over on to a bit of ground with which I had practically no acquaintance.[29]

Far from being a bite-and-hold operation, this attack was planned as a hybrid, with the mixed aims of wearing out and penetrating.[30] This not only evidenced tactical confusion, it also had the practical effect of diluting the artillery barrage. If the objective was limited to 1500 or even 3000 yards, artillery fire could be concentrated on the German positions in that limited area. If the objective was extended to five or eight miles, the effect of the artillery was dispersed over that much greater area, reducing its effectiveness exponentially.[31] Moreover, Gough was correct in saying that the preparations, and the available resources, were insufficient for an attack of that magnitude.

Haig, for his part, blamed Gough for the lack of resources. In his diary, he recorded:

> As regards future operations, I told Gough to continue to carry out the original plan: to consolidate ground gained, and to improve his position as he may deem necessary for facilitating the next advance: the next advance will be made as soon as possible, *but only after adequate bombardment and after dominating the hostile artillery*.[32]

It was a failure of command that each general accused the other of attacking with inadequate resources. They both recognised the problem — one should have assumed the responsibility for solving it.

No Australian infantry took part in this battle. The Australian divisions were still resting on the Somme. Australian artillery and some Australian airmen took part, the latter flying with the Royal Flying Corps. They were the first Australian pilots to take part in the war.[33]

It rained solidly for four days. The attack foundered in the rain and mud. The coastal attack remained a pipedream. The line bogged down within sight of the city walls of Ypres. Conditions were deplorable. General Haig wrote in a despatch:

> The low-lying, clayey soil, torn by shells and sodden with rain, turned to a succession of vast muddy pools. The valleys of the

choked and overflowing streams were speedily transformed into long stretches of bog, impassable except by a few well-defined tracks, which became marks for the enemy's artillery. To leave these tracks was to risk death by drowning, and in the course of the subsequent fighting on several occasions both men and pack animals were lost in this way. In these conditions operations of any magnitude became impossible, and the resumption of our offensive was necessarily postponed until a period of fine weather should allow the ground to recover.[34]

It was not solely the rain that caused the deplorable conditions. The low-lying country around Ypres had been carefully drained over centuries of intensive farming. The bombardments destroyed the drainage systems, leaving the water with no way to escape.[35]

Even Gough was now attempting to persuade Haig to break off the offensive. Surprisingly, it was Plumer who advocated continuation of the attack.[36] Haig eventually sided with Gough. On 4 August 1917, he conceded, 'As the rain still continues I cannot say when it will be possible to continue the offensive.'[37]

Gough and Haig were correct. Bite-and-hold tactics could only work in fine weather. Charles Bean wrote:

The step-by-step method, as practised at … Messines [and in the later battles at Ypres] was effective only in fine weather. Then, with an immense artillery functioning at its best; with airmen spotting the targets; with guns, men and supplies moving across the country on dry tracks; with nearly all shells bursting on the surface as intended, scattering fragments up to half a mile, and raising a dust cloud (which was more helpful than a smoke screen, and rolled ahead of the infantry, who worked in the haze on its rear fringe) — in such conditions the infantry was almost certain to capture its objectives, no matter what the enemy attempted. But with the ground a slough; with guns and ammunition constantly bogged; with air observation difficult and uncertain; with the shells failing to explode in the soft mud or their bursts muffled and barely visible; with no dust or smoke, and the unscreened infantrymen often unable even to detect the barrage they were ordered to follow, and in any case unable to keep up with it across the sea of brimming shell-craters — in these conditions, though part of the infantry often struggles through to sections of the objective, they could not link up or receive supplies. With disastrous regularity their efforts failed and their losses rose — as did the spirits of the Germans beholding these failures.[38]

Lloyd George was devastated by the failure of the attacks. Hankey described it as a time of unrelieved gloom for the prime minister. 'On this muddy and bloody battlefield he saw realized all that he had predicted only a few weeks before. The moment seemed at hand to fall back on the alternative plan for an operation in Italy ... First, however, he had to persuade military opinion ...'[39]

Lloyd George remonstrated with Robertson, reminding him of the condition that, if the attack proved unsuccessful, the offensive should move to the Italian front. Robertson remained adamant. He blamed the weather, and said that, as soon as the weather improved, the advance would resume. The offensive had worn down the Germans. It would be wrong to give in when a real triumph might be at hand.[40]

In his frustration, Lloyd George became, 'despondent at the failure of the year's campaigning, and disgusted at the narrowness of the General Staff, and the inability of his colleagues to see eye to eye with him and their fear of overruling the General Staff. He was also very annoyed at the way the General Staff twist their facts and estimates to suit their arguments'.[41] But Lloyd George could not carry the War Cabinet with him to overrule the General Staff. It weighed heavily with him that he had ordered an attack which he believed 'had not the remotest prospect of success.'[42] The question of why he did not order the end of the campaign, as he certainly had power to do, remains controversial,[43] although Hankey suggests that Lloyd George was 'obviously puzzled, as his predecessor was, how far the Government is justified in interfering with a military operation'.[44]

When the weather improved, and the offensive was resumed, I Anzac Corps was ordered to take part. They would come under the command of General Plumer who, thankfully, had replaced General Gough in command of the offensive on 28 August 1917. I Anzac Corps moved from the Somme, north to Flanders. On 16 September 1917, the diggers marched east, through what remained of Ypres, along the Menin Road.

At dawn on 20 September 1917, after a bombardment of five days, the 1st and 2nd Divisions advanced side by side (for the first time) in the Battle of the Menin Road. In the fine weather, the bite-and-hold attack succeeded. The plan worked perfectly. The Australians were elated. They took Glencorse Wood, Nonne Bosschen swamp, Black

Diggers march by what remains of Ypres, the ruins of the Cloth Hall, 'past its walls of hard and hoary bricks', on their way to Passchendaele, 25 October 1917. AWM E04612

Duckboard tracks provide a precarious route for diggers near the Menin Road, 29 October 1917. AWM E01220

Watch Corner and part of Polygon Wood. Casualties, however, were heavy. The Australians suffered some 5000 casualties. The British suffered four or five times that loss.[45]

The contrast between the British and the Australians was as marked then as now. An English subaltern, Lieutenant Edmonds, described attacking alongside the Australians, and gave a description that only an Englishman could give:

> On our right were Colonial troops attacking in much greater numbers than ours, so that my own front looked empty but theirs crowded with men, and before long one of the platoons came straying across my front. It suddenly struck me that I knew the platoon commander; I seized him by the hand and introduced myself. As we exchanged civilities I became aware that we were under machine gun fire.[46]

The 4th and 5th Divisions followed the 1st and 2nd Divisions into the attack. Sergeant Walter Downing wrote that they also marched through Ypres: 'past its walls of hard and hoary bricks and the deep moats where bullfrogs croak among the reeds that grow in the black water … Splintered corduroys [roads made of logs] wind across the foul mud along the road. On either side is a long mound of wagons, rifles, ambulances equipment'.[47] The corduroy road was the Menin Road, and the rubbish beside it was debris of the battle that had just taken place there. It was not an inspiring sight. Leonard Mann described the scene:

> Further along the road, where a light railway broke off, there was a scattered dump and a number of low humpies. Not far off, on the other side, were some horse lines, and a sprinkling of tents and scattered shelters almost hidden in the old trench line. Around these a few men were also moving. All over the place the eye, now keener, could pick up signs of low-lying life and activity. A good way further

A shell crater amongst the debris of battle near Ypres, 3 October 1917.
AWM E00707

down, a sausage balloon was up. Approaching out of the mist, along the road, came a line of donks, from which, as they passed, the weary drivers of an ammunition column looked down at the straggling line of infantry. It was slowly dawning on the troops that they were on the Menin Road.[48]

The 1st and 2nd Divisions were now withdrawn for a period of rest. Captain Joynt wrote of that time: 'We have been here a week, resting and playing games and not doing any drill. At Steenvoorde, the divisional concert party has been giving a fine show, which I attended twice — quite as good a show as any of the shows at St Kilda beach. General Birdwood visited us yesterday and presented a few medals.'[49]

In his autobiographical novel, *Flesh in Armour*, Leonard Mann described a rare sunny period of respite during the Passchendaele battle:

During the afternoon, whoever came up the duck board track could see men taking advantage of the sun's warmth to sit at the doors of huts and chat themselves.* In the soft field in front, a number were throwing blank Mills bombs, testing their length and accuracy in a game improvised from the old iron quoit game, which was commonly played up till ten years previously in the old midland towns and settlements. You pitched the bomb to a piece of white paper stuck on a ring of mud. In a firmed paddock on the other side of the huts a football was being kicked about. Charl, anxious for a part in which he knew he could shine, had gone off there as soon as he could, dragging Bill rather unwillingly, for Bill was no footballer. Down the road, near where the duck board track turned in, was a brick cottage where an old Froggie and his Madame still hung on obstinately under a roof which some time or other had been blown half off by a shell, and which had been patched with odd bits of iron and sand bags sewn together. They lived by selling hot baths at a franc per tub.[50]

---

* Chats were lice. Chatting was the process of removing lice from the body and the clothes.

A period of respite in the sun allows diggers to 'chat' — try and remove lice from their shirts — after a spell in the line, June 1916. AWM EZ0009

Meanwhile, the artillerymen, engineers, pioneers, transport drivers and other support troops worked to advance the support services in time for the next attack, in which the 4th and 5th Divisions were to advance through Polygon Wood to the rifle range on its eastern perimeter, arriving at the foot of Broodseinde ridge.

Demands on support services peaked during the battles of 1917. Whereas it took 128 trains a day to supply the Battle of the Somme, the average number of trains used each day in the period of a week before and after zero day of the 1917 battles was: Messines — 242; the battle outside Ypres on 31 July — 261; and the battle at Passchendaele on 12 October — 271.[51]

At Polygon Wood, tactics were again well executed. Charles Bean recorded: 'At 5.50 am on September 26 there descended the most perfect barrage that ever protected Australian troops. Rolling ahead of them "like a Gippsland bushfire" it raised a fog of dust in the edge of which the troops were by now sufficiently skilled to advance, fighting down enemy groups.'[52]

An edge of experience was beginning to play a part in the Australians' success.

In the fine weather, air support played a role in the attack. Harrington wrote: 'All day on the 26th our aeroplanes were very active; contact patrols flew low over the enemy's positions from early morning onwards, searching for reserve troops, and harassing hostile troops and transport from an average height of about 300 feet.'[53] German planes came over as well. Sergeant Lawrence looked on from the ground: 'Continually the Hun planes are over us — low down so that we can see the observer leaning out — can see his goggles. But at last one of our slow old observer machines comes over — very low — the observer leans out as the machine banks — waves his hand — gee, it is the finest tonic ever handed out to fighting troops'.[54]

After Polygon Wood, I Anzac moved north in the line, allowing II Anzac to enter the line on its right for a third attack, this time on Broodseinde ridge. The 1st, 2nd and 3rd Australian Divisions and the New Zealand Division would form the centre of the line. This was the only time four Anzac divisions attacked side by side.[55] The attack was fixed for 6.00 am on 4 October 1917. As the Anzac troops waited for zero hour, a German bombardment began. F C Trotter recalled:

We got up and went forward over our own front line, over towards the Germans. It was dawn, and fast growing towards full light of day, and it was surprising to discover that so many of our men were left after such a heavy bombardment. Like ants swarming about when their ant-bed has been disturbed, did our men keep coming out from everywhere — out of their shell holes. It was a happy diversion this, for out in what was formerly 'No Man's Land' we had advanced beyond the German barrage, and whilst we waited for our own first line of barrage to lift from the German front line, we busied ourselves going from hole to hole, binding the wounded and making them more comfortable. Our front-line barrage then lifted, and forward we went. And what did we find? Germans massed for attack — laying out in 'No Man's Land' in front of their trenches awaiting their signal to advance on us. We had beaten them by only three minutes — that is the great joke of that morning's attack. Imagine their surprise, in waiting for the correct minute to advance on us, to find themselves attacked instead. Then there was a commotion — but our lads had the upper hand. A few Germans resisted our attack, others came running excitedly towards us, their hands upraised in surrender; some of them holding out their watches and rings as barter for their lives, completely demoralised.[56]

The two attacks had commenced virtually simultaneously. 'The Lewis gunners in the advancing Australian line opened fire; the Germans broke; the Australian lines rolled on over the remnant and up the slope.'[57]

The attack was the high point of the Passchendaele battle. Coming on top of Menin Road and Polygon Wood, the taking of Broodseinde ridge demonstrated the effectiveness of the bite-and-hold tactics, at least in fine weather. Again, however, the victory came at a high price. Australian casualties numbered 6500; the New Zealanders' 1700. It was some consolation that 5000 German prisoners were taken.[58]

As the Allied generals debated whether German morale was so low that it was now time for a decisive blow on the ridge at Passchendaele, it began to rain again. The night of 6 October 1917 was 'wild and wet and not fit for a dog to be out in'.[59]

As usual, Haig was more bullish about the prospects than most, believing that the victory at Broodseinde ridge had so demoralised the Germans that it was worth taking risks attacking the Passchendaele ridge, even though the artillery preparation would be shorter, and the proposed advance longer, than in the previous attacks.[60]

Three old problems had crept back into Allied planning: undue haste; disregard for the adverse weather conditions; and the dilution of the artillery barrage. When the attack on Passchendaele began, the barrage was so weak as to be 'imperceptible'.[61] The rain was heavy and the barrage was light — exactly the opposite of the correct formula.

The attack was launched at dawn on 12 October 1917. The 3rd and 4th Australian Divisions and the New Zealand Division attacked with five British divisions. The mud, and determined German machine gun fire from concrete gun emplacements, defeated the attack. Conditions were, once again, appalling. As the German commander, Crown Prince Rupprecht, observed: 'Rain; our most effective ally.'[62]

The mud got into everything, disabling both rifles and machine guns. The soft, semi-liquid ground also affected the detonation of percussion shells. They either failed to detonate, or burst harmlessly in the mud.[63] Although the conditions must have affected the British and Germans equally,[64] they were not reflected in a reduction of Allied casualties. In the 3rd Division there were 3000 casualties; among the New Zealanders 3000; and in the 4th Division 1000.[65]

General Monash wrote home, 'Just in the degree that the battle of 4 October was brilliantly successful, so were the operations of 12 October deeply disappointing, although the 3rd Australian division did magnificently under the most adverse circumstances.'[66] He blamed hasty preparation.

At Broodseinde ridge, the 3rd Division had barely succeeded in making all the preparations for the battle in three days. This had involved making 'roads, tracks, pushing forward its guns, supplying its ammunition dumps, burying its telegraph cables, establishing its numerous headquarters, aid-posts and report centres, and a thousand and one other details'.[67] At Passchendaele, 'the Chief' allowed only 24 hours for the same preparations. It was not enough. Moreover, he overruled Monash's request for a postponement of the battle.[68] No wonder the bombardment was imperceptible.

Like Monash, Gough also asked to postpone the attack, but, in a reversal of their accustomed roles, Plumer overruled him.[69] After one day, Plumer changed his mind and decided against continuing the attack.[70]

The Australians continued fighting until the Canadians relieved them on 18 October 1917. The Battle of Passchendaele continued into November 1917, when winter caused another pause in the offensive before the capture of the Passchendaele-Staden ridge could be completed.

Third Ypres was better executed than the Somme, and the casualties, totalling 400 000, were fewer. The victories in which the Australians took part — Menin Road, Polygon Wood and Broodseinde ridge — were fine victories. Indeed, Bean rated them higher than Messines.[71] But there was no escaping the fact that the battle had gone nowhere near clearing the Belgian coast.

If the objective of the battle was wearing down, it had worn down the Allies as well as the Germans. If the objective of the attack was penetration and the resumption of a war of movement, or to take the coast, it had failed utterly. The confusion surrounding the planning of the battle was reflected in its outcome.

An 18 pounder gun requires the combined strength of diggers and horses to haul it through mud on Broodseinde ridge in preparation for the attack on Passchendaele, 10 October 1917. AWM E01208

General Sir Launcelot Kiggell, General Haig's chief of staff, was reduced to tears when he saw the Passchendaele battlefield: 'Good God, did we really send men to fight in that?' AWM E00952

General Haig blamed the failure on the rain: 'Despite the magnitude of [the enemy's] efforts, it was the immense natural difficulties, accentuated manifold by the abnormally wet weather, rather than the enemy's resistance, which limited our progress and prevented the complete capture of the ridge.'[72] Harington also blamed the rain, but he understood better than Haig the reaction of others to the losses:

> Thus ended what may be called the Passchendaele operations with Passchendaele in our hands and a substantial footing on the Passchendaele-Staden ridge. Critics will say and have said 'Yes, and at what price?'
>
> I cannot dispute that. Those stages up to Passchendaele have always been a nightmare to me as they were to my Chief. They were all right up to and including Broodseinde, 4th October. After that Fate was very cruel to us. It is easy to say now that that everyone knew it was going to rain like that except those at G.H.Q. ...[73]

More dramatically, when General Sir Launcelot Kiggell, Haig's chief of staff, was taken to see the Passchendaele battlefield, he broke down in tears, saying: 'Good God, did we really send men to fight in that?'[74] As disturbing as it may have been that a general was weeping, it was a little late for the staff to start learning the ground conditions. Controversy surrounds this story, which may not be true. Another version of the story has it that it was General Davidson and not General Kiggell, and that the general was not weeping, but merely 'holding his hands to his face to show that he was dumb to enquiries and not to hide tears'.[75]

Duff Cooper, whom the Haig family invited to write his biography, had a bet each way, denying the truth of the story in one breath, and belittling the officer who wept in the next:

[The officers at GHQ] were not ignorant of the conditions in which the men were fighting. Six young officers of brigade-major rank were deputed to visit regularly the front line and to report to the general staff on the state of the ground as well as on other matters. In addition, the general officer commanding royal artillery, the engineer in chief and the quarter master general had each a liaison officer whose duty it was to keep his chief informed of the effect of the weather upon the operations of their various branches. They in turn informed the Commander-in-Chief. The legend of the staff officer who wept when he saw the mud at Passchendaele is either apocryphal or does little credit to the nerves of the man who could not bear to see the conditions concerning which he had already received full information.[76]

From the soldiers' viewpoint, neither story reflected well on the staff. Which was worse: ignoring the weather conditions, or ignoring reports about the weather conditions? Either way, the ignorance of the staff sent many good men to the grave.

Captain Behrend can have the last word. If Haig did not know the conditions in which the men were fighting, 'It was a pity he was not standing beside me at the Menin Gate [in Ypres]. For had he witnessed with his own eyes the decimation of so many of his Divisions, he would surely have called a halt to this senseless and bloody struggle for the prize of a few more thousand feet of mud.'[77]

Haig acknowledged the limitations of the bite-and-hold technique, particularly in the mud. As long as his men could reach the enemy, they could prevail, but physical exhaustion placed narrow limits on how far they could advance, and necessitated long pauses between advances.[78]

It is difficult to argue with Haig's conclusion that, in the circumstances of 1917, with little support from the Russians or the French, the British armies had 'taken their full share in the fighting on the Western front',[79] although it was a stretch for him to claim that, 'No other example of offensive action on so large a scale, so long and successfully sustained, has yet been furnished by the war,'[80] unless he had forgotten the German thrust into France and Belgium in 1914.

For the Australians, there was some consolation in Haig's improving opinion of their fighting qualities. When Haig told the Duke of Connaught that he thought I Anzac Corps was among the best disciplined troops in the BEF, the Duke said, 'You surprise me. I had heard that discipline among the Australians was bad.' Haig replied:

That depends on what you mean by discipline. I can only say this: that I have never yet called on the Australian Corps to undertake a difficult and hazardous operation — and I have often done so — without the operation in question being carried through with success, and always with good spirit and keen determination. From the top down to the most junior commanders, details have been most carefully worked out, and the plan is executed with coolness and courage. And that is what *I* call discipline.[81]

This, not saluting, was the real test of mettle.

CHAPTER TWELVE

PRISONERS OF WAR

During the First World War 4084 Australians became prisoners of war — 173 officers and 3911 other ranks.[1] Being a prisoner of war was no soft option. The moment of capture was especially dangerous. With emotions from the battle still running high, it was often unclear if the enemy wanted to surrender, or if the fight was still on.

After capture, the prisoner of war confronted the disappointment of defeat, and maudlin uncertainty as to his future. This uncertainty lasted throughout his captivity, with the prisoner not knowing from day to day how his fortunes would fluctuate. The extreme danger of the moment of capture may have abated over time, but the threat hanging over the head of the prisoner persisted until the prisoner was finally reunited with his own people.

In the aftermath of the fierce battles at Pozières, the *Official History* recorded:

... throughout the village could be seen isolated Australians 'ratting' occasional fugitives from the rubble heaps, chasing terrified and shrieking Germans and killing them with the bayonet, or shooting from the shoulder at those who got away, and then sitting down on the door-steps to smoke and wait for others to bolt from the cellars.[2]

After the battle at Dernancourt in 1918, Australian prisoners encountered similar treatment at the hands of the Germans. Private Curtis and seven men of his platoon surrendered after a hard fight. As they climbed out of the trench, a German officer asked who they were. On being told they were Australians, the officer drew his pistol and shot poor Curtis through the stomach. Curtis was fatally injured.[3]

Private Savage was wounded through the elbows when he was captured. He asked some Germans for a drink. They asked who he was. When he told them he was Australian, they punched him in the mouth and told him if he made a noise again, they would bayonet him.[4] Similarly, when a German officer spoke to Captain Frazer in French, thinking he was a Frenchman, and Frazer replied that he was Australian, the officer struck him across the face with his riding whip.[5]

Upon being captured, one Australian officer drew his pistol and fired six wild shots at the German officer who had captured him. All missed. 'The German officer, white with anger, wrenched the revolver from him and said, "Do you know I could shoot you for this?"'[6] — a very restrained, magnanimous and courageous response in the circumstances.

An Australian officer showed similar restraint and courage when he was shot whilst taking the surrender of a German headquarters during the Messines battle:

As [the Germans] began to come out [the Australian officer] was shot through the shoulder. The Australians behind him, thinking that the shot had come from the building, would have killed every man in it, but the officer, though in much pain, stood in their way and they had to allow 30 unwounded Germans to troop out and move off unhurt as prisoners.[7]

Many diggers would not have spared the Germans in the same circumstances. During the Menin Road battle, the 5th Battalion was attacking a two-storey pill-box:[8]

> Captain Moore, a beloved officer, now ran towards the pillbox, but was immediately shot by a German who, according to the reports afterwards made, had already surrendered. The Victorians at once killed this man and others, and only interposition by their officers stopped them from exterminating the whole garrison.[9]

Captain Joynt described an Australian attack on a series of five blockhouses during the same battle:

> Around each blockhouse was a party of Australians, firing at the loopholes in the blockhouses from which the Huns were firing out. Disdaining to take cover, some men were standing up full length and firing at the standing position. Soon the marksmen got direct hits through the loopholes and the Hun rifles and machine guns, one by one, ceased firing. The concrete blockhouses were then rushed. The Huns, seeing the rush coming, in some cases rushed out first with their hands up to surrender. This would not do for some of our fellows — this bad sporting spirit of shooting as long as they were safe and then rushing out expecting mercy.[10]

General Monash disavowed any brutality towards prisoners. He also used a sporting metaphor:

> Australian soldiers are nothing if not sportsmen, and no case ever came under my notice of brutality or inhumanity to prisoners. Upon the contrary, when once a man's surrender had been accepted, and he had been fully disarmed, he was treated with marked kindness. The front line troops were always ready to share their water and rations with their prisoners, and cigarettes were distributed with a liberal hand.[11]

Monash, a lawyer by training, was careful to make a distinction that Bean and Joynt did not: a prisoner is not properly a prisoner until his surrender is accepted, and he is fully disarmed. A man who pretends to surrender only to attempt to kill his captors is still a combatant, and not a prisoner.[12]

At other times, the heat and speed of the battle meant there was no time to make nice distinctions about the motives of the enemy. In 1918, Lieutenant Maxwell was mopping up after the battle of 8 August when 'A German leapt from a shell-hole and rushed towards me. I shot him dead. It was only then I found that his only desire was to hand me his Iron Cross to ensure his safety.'[13]

The capture of prisoners could be tiresome for the captor, who had to take the surrender, disarm the prisoners, and take them into custody. In the heat of battle, this was often inconvenient. If the captor had to escort prisoners out of the fighting, he would have to lead them back to the rear trenches, through whatever artillery fire was falling. The prisoners would then be safe, but the escort would have to return to the front through the same artillery fire.

In some circumstances, it was not possible to take prisoners, even if the enemy may have wanted to surrender. In a trench raid, for instance, there was often no question of taking prisoners — it was a case of kill or be killed.[14] It was equally impossible to take prisoners in hand-to-hand fighting.[15] At other times prisoners were taken with ridiculous ease. The historian of the 14th Battalion, Newton Wanliss, recounted this story:

Just before daybreak ... four men were plainly observed walking leisurely along in front of our wire, evidently seeking a passage through. They wore greatcoats, and little notice was taken of them, as our wiring and trench mortar parties were often out near the wire. Having found an opening, the party filed through, and the leader (a corporal) on reaching our parapet, was challenged. Simultaneously he was recognised as a German, and apparently being too bewildered to surrender, was promptly shot dead. A second later, a bomb was thrown at his comrades, wounding one in the foot. The three survivors (one of whom could speak fairly good English) then surrendered and it was ascertained that they had lost their bearings and wandered into our lines by mistake.[16]

Their mistake was minor compared to the mistake that Sergeant Hawken and Sapper Hughes, both members of the Australian Broad Gauge Railway Operating Company, made in the confusion of the retreat on 25 March 1918: '[They] had been sent out from Albert with some Canadians in a train to destroy railway lines, bridges and watering points, [and] drove their train deep into the German line without being aware of it. "By the time we had pulled the train up, German bayonets were sticking through the doors."'[17]

Prisoners were frequently pressed into service as stretcher-bearers, also a risky activity. The rules of war allowed them to be used for one carry only. Strictly, prisoners could not be forced to go back for a second load, although some did so, voluntarily or otherwise.[18] Prisoners could also be used as labourers, but not on defence works, and not in range of their own shells. By the end of 1917, there were 69 720 German prisoners of war at work in Allied labour units.[19]

At Messines 7261 German prisoners were captured in that one battle.[20] There, the prisoners were dazed by the underground mines and, as the oncoming troops stormed their trenches, they 'came out, some of them cringing like beaten animals. They "made many fruitless attempts to embrace us," reported Lieutenant Gerard. "I have never seen men so demoralised."'[21] When the enemy surrendered in such high numbers (not frequently) there was often no real option but to leave those who surrendered to make their own way to the rear.

Prisoners sometimes found themselves used as pawns in mindless games of tit-for-tat. Bean describes how the Germans mistreated a group of Allied prisoners, including some Australians, captured after the Bullecourt battle:

Each party was placed into a room of the fort ... floored with stone or concrete, with little air or light. For all purposes of sanitation, there was placed in the corner a single tub, which quickly overflowed. The men were allowed neither straw nor blankets, but must sleep on the bare damp floor, and were fed with one slice of bread daily, and coffee "substitute".[22]

The Germans announced that this treatment was in revenge for the British having defied convention by employing German prisoners within range of German guns.[23] To this charge, Bean cheerfully pleaded guilty:

> The complaint against the British command was true enough — through a recklessness that later brought grievous trouble and much suffering to others, German prisoners had, like the Egyptian labourers in Gallipoli, been employed in areas subject to fire. The characteristically brutal methods of the German commanders in retaliation had little effect, except to win for their whole people a reputation which, in this generation at least, will continue to do great harm to their country.[24]

Bean seems not to notice the similarity between the mistreatment of the prisoners on both sides. Bean was an eye-witness to many of the events he describes, and knew personally many of the men involved. He often brings to his descriptions a clinical matter-of-factness about terrible events. He is always unashamedly partisan.

The diggers were invariably curious to see their opponents closeup. They compared what they saw with the stereotypes they had in mind. Lieutenant Rule was distinctly unimpressed that Germans captured in the battle at Pozières were happy to be out of the fighting: 'About eighty [Huns] came by us in the trench, and they were certainly the most joyful looking Huns I'd ever seen. They were clean-shaven and had hardly a dirty article on them. They looked as if they were all off to a wedding and not a hop-over.'[25]

In September 1917, the 5th Battalion took 200 prisoners of a different stamp in the Passchendaele battle: 'Generally, they were not the be-spectacled, puny, spiritless Germans who so often gave feeble and short resistance. Hefty, hardbitten, and well fed, these men gave little support by their fighting to the theory that the man-power of the German army was deteriorating in quality.'[26]

Monash was amused to meet captured German officers. They would, of course, give away no information of value. What amused him was their air of wounded pride.

It was a feeling of professional pique which dominated their whole demeanour. They were always volubly full of excuses, the weather, the fog, the poor *morale* of their own men, the unexpectedness of our attack, the Tanks, errors in their maps — anything at all but a frank admission of their own military inferiority.[27]

This last claim was a harsh verdict — if there is one conclusion that stands unchallenged from any account of the First World War, it is that the Germans were equal to, if not better, than the Allies in most aspects of the military arts.

A W Keown noted that the diggers were not always gracious hosts of their prisoners:

The prisoners carried our wounded from the front line, and greatly lightened the burden of the over-worked stretcher-bearers. One of the Fifth [Battalion], unarmed in the excitement of the moment, took charge of a stretcher for his wounded mate, and requisitioned five Huns as bearers. One proved recalcitrant, and the Australian, after searching in vain for a weapon, at length clenched his fists and threatened to punch the German's jaw if he didn't get on with the job ...

Some of the captives freely offered their belongings, and some of the Australians made their choice from the contents of parcels which had evidently just been received from home by the Germans. One man collected eighteen watches and two purses from the prisoners, and strongly resented the implications that any duress had used in obtaining them. 'They must have liked the look of my face,' he explained to his scoffing comrades.[28]

When Private Harney went into the business of watch-stealing, he bit off more than he could chew:

I said: 'Blimey! This is where I'm going to make a few bob'.

So I started. As the prisoners would come back, I'd just go over to them and they were satisfied to give you anything. They were happy to get out of it, the business on the other side of the line ...

So a bloke came along, very important lookin', like a German general. I looked at him and thought, he's mean.

I had a Very pistol[29] and I held it up and I said, 'Hands up' ...

Diggers search a German prisoner for souvenirs. The unfortunate prisoner could be 'fleeced of everything but his name and his clothes'. AWM E03919

Blimey! It was an English colonel ... one of these real pukka English colonels, and he'd got wounded in the arm and he was coming back, and he put on a great big German overcoat ...

He come over to where our officer bloke was and he said: 'One of your men held me up with a revolver'.

And the captain bloke said: 'It couldn't be my men. They don't do that kind of thing'.

'Well', he said. 'He's somewhere 'ere. I'd know him again'.

And I thought to meself, will you know me? I said: 'Well, I'm out of this'.

So I hid away and me mates all chucked some old bags over me, and they come and they said: 'Well, he's not here, sir'.

So, he went on and the captain said, 'How'd ya get on?'

'I got sixteen watches'.

Blimey! Any good 'uns?'

I said, 'Yes', and held one out.

He said, 'That's a good 'un. I'll give you forty francs for that'.[30]

Horses could become prisoners as well as men. Many German horses were captured during the final advance that began in August 1918. An Australian veterinary officer wrote: 'They were of all kinds and sizes and showed very little evidence of care. The shoeing, however, was excellent.'[31] It fell to the veterinary service to take care of these prisoners.

Captain Dent was captured on 14 November 1916, during the Somme battle, near Flers.[32] He ran the full gamut of the prisoner of war experience. Injured by shrapnel, and semi-conscious, he lay out in the battlefield overnight, when, unbeknown to him, the Germans occupied the old British trenches. Captain Dent was captured when he returned to what he thought were the Australian trenches, but were now full of Germans.

He was taken to a dressing post. There, he was treated last, after all the wounded Germans. In hospital, he was well treated by three doctors, who were both conscientious and skilful. The senior doctor operated, successfully, to staunch an internal haemorrhage. His treatment deteriorated when a Prussian unit took over the hospital. It deteriorated further still when he was moved to a second hospital near Cambrai.[33]

The food was bad, but the doctors told Dent that he was being fed the standard issue for all Germans. Things improved when he was moved to a hospital in Hamburg, staffed by Red Cross orderlies. A wound in his heel had become septic. It was only then that Dent began to receive proper treatment for this wound. One doctor, who treated Dent kindly and with skill, told Dent that he 'was a fool for coming all the way from Australia to fight and give [his] health and strength, and perhaps, [his] life, for "Damned England".'[34]

The British also treated German prisoners who were casualties in the same hospitals as the British. This did not necessarily lead to peace and harmony, as Captain Knyvett recorded:

> In the bed opposite me in this hospital there was a German officer and he bellowed like a bull all night. We got pretty sick of his noise and told the medical officer in charge of the ward when he came on his rounds in the morning that if he did not chloroform or do something to silence the hound, we would. I suggested he go and tell him that if he did not shut up he would be sent into the ward with his own privates. He did so and there was not another squeak from him.[35]

In February 1917, Captain Dent had a visitor. It was a Mr Morgan, from the American Embassy.[36] Dent was imprisoned with three other officers. Morgan wrote to all of their families. Morgan also told the prisoners that the rations they were receiving were, indeed, the standard German rations and that 'we could not expect what the Germans had not got and that food shortage was being felt throughout the country'.[37]

In June 1917, Dent was sent to an officers' prison camp at Augustabad. He eventually began to receive food parcels from the Red

Cross and from home.[38] When these became plentiful, one of the camp guards commented on a load of parcels: 'All this is a bluff by the English. Why, look at the papers, look at what our U-boats are doing. England is starving, and she is sending you out all this stuff to make us think she is not.'[39]

The prisoners at Augustabad occupied themselves with running a camp newspaper, amateur dramatics, knitting, reading and studying a range of subjects including foreign languages, navigation and typing. They also played sports — tennis, hockey and football, in particular.[40] There was even a system of parole, under which officers could leave the camp on their word of honour to return. The American Express Company in Berlin honoured the Allied prisoners' cheques, even after America joined the war.[41]

Captain Dent recounted that his fellow prisoners dug a tunnel, but the Germans discovered it before they could escape. The prisoners dug a second tunnel. This time, nine or ten prisoners escaped, with the result that the camp commandant was sacked and replaced by a colonel from the Prussian Guards. The overbearing behaviour of the Prussian redoubled the enthusiasm of the would-be escapers. Seventeen men escaped through a third tunnel. The uproar amongst the Germans was gratifying, but none of the escapers made it out of Germany.[42]

In December 1917, Dent was moved to a camp near Mannheim for assessment for possible repatriation. When he was there:

> ... an Allied raiding party visited Mannheim. We were all sitting at dinner one day when some of the Frenchmen spotted the red, white and blue rings on the wings of the aeroplanes. Then began the little white bursts of smoke in the air and the boom of the guns. The Huns had spotted them, too. About a dozen planes, altogether regardless of the anti-air guns, circled over Mannheim, dropped their bombs, and gradually faded away again. It was a splendid sight to see some of our own forces operating again, more especially as we were in German country. The prisoners could not restrain themselves and

all turned out on the grounds to cheer. The French were particularly enthusiastic.[43]

On Christmas Day, 1917, Dent received word that he, and all the prisoners in the camp, would be repatriated. They were taken by train to Constance, a town that straddles the Swiss/German border, where they were put on another train that took them into Switzerland:

> The Swiss people had heard of our coming and they, too, cheered us all along the route. At the stopping places they were assembled in crowds to welcome us, and showered down upon us all sorts of luxuries that we had almost forgotten were in existence.
>
> The two largest receptions were at Berne and Zurich. We arrived at Berne about 2 am but the people were waiting for us and welcomed us in large numbers. They gave us an excellent meal, after which speeches were made in our honour, and altogether our entertainers spared no pains to express towards us their sympathy and goodwill.[44]

For all the joy of the welcome of the Swiss, and of returning home, being a prisoner of war is a tough and thankless form of service.

CHAPTER THIRTEEN

LEAVE

The trip from the western front to London took a day. It was possible to be in the trenches one day and London the next. Paris was closer still. For most English soldiers, leave meant going home to wife or family. Many of the English soldiers felt uncomfortable, or misunderstood, when suddenly translated from their mates in the trenches to their families.

Leave was often given on short notice. Siegfried Sassoon gave a taste of the dislocating sensation in *Memoirs of a Fox-hunting Man*:

That same day, at about midnight, I was awakened by Dottrell, who told me that I was to go on leave next morning. I drove to the station in the Maltese cart; the train started at 9.30, crawled to Havre, and by ten o'clock next day I was in London. I had been in France less than four months. As regards war experience I felt a bit of an impostor. I had noticed that officers back from their ten days' leave were usually somewhat silent about it. Then, after a few weeks, they began to look forward to their next leave again ... There wasn't much to be said about mine, for it was bitterly cold and a heavy fall of snow knocked my hopes of hunting [with hounds] on the head. So I remained quietly with Aunt Evelyn at Butley, telling myself that it was a great luxury to have a hot bath every day … And kind Aunt Evelyn talked bitterly about the Germans and called them "hell-hounds". I found myself defending them … Perhaps, after all, it was better to be back with the battalion.[1]

The diggers did not share the same burden of visiting home and family. For them, leave meant the chance to see Britain, which many Australians still called 'home'. Many had relatives in Britain. For those who did not, hospitality was generously extended to men on leave from the front.

Leave came annually. The diggers who were given leave took special leave trains that connected with boats to Folkestone. These connected with trains to Victoria Station. There was a threat of U-boats, so destroyers escorted the cross-Channel ferries on their trip, which lasted around two hours. Sergeant Linton was held up on his trip back to France because a gale had swept floating mines away from the Allied minefields, and minesweepers had to clear them.[2]

At other times, the trains could be the hold-up. Sergeant Chapman took a trip from the front to Le Havre — a distance of 60 or 70 miles — that lasted fifteen hours. As he wrote home, 'It is little wonder that the troops were getting out and picking blackberries on the way. The train contained two engines and 55 carriages, so you can imagine its length.'[3] The number of carriages may have explained the slow speed.

By the end of the war, the arrangements for taking leave were well worked out. With an army of 1.8 million, it only took a small proportion to be on leave together for there to be thousands of men taking the leave trains to and from London at any one time, and many more were in London itself.[4] As they passed through the ports, the troops picked up fresh uniforms and underwear, before launching themselves on a London, which, by the end of the war, was inured to the antics, not only of the diggers, but of all the men who found themselves on a short break from the horrors of the front.

The diggers were not cast entirely adrift amid the glories of the big city. The administrative headquarters of the AIF were in Horseferry Road, in London, and the diggers paid a visit there as part of their leave, not least to draw pay. For many diggers, leave was combined with a visit to the Australian training schools that had been established on Salisbury Plain. Others took leave as part of their convalescence from injury or illness.[5]

Sergeant Ray Denning (then a corporal) was sent to London to join the 16th Field Company Engineers, which was being formed in England. In the process, he was sent on a training course, promoted to sergeant and took leave in London. He even paraded for the King.[6]

His first task in London was to report to the Horseferry Road headquarters. After a night in London, he found himself at Park House Camp on Salisbury Plain, where the new unit was assembled, and trained. Denning became the sergeant of No. 1 section. When the men in the new unit paraded before the King, they were confronted not only by the King, but also by an impressive array of generals in uniform, and one man in black civilian clothes and a high top hat. Denning recalled:

> We didn't know who he was, perhaps the King's chamberlain, or the Prime Minister.
>
> When we were dismissed, we were told to line the road and give His Majesty a rousing cheer as he passed. No need to tell the Aussies that. We gave three dinkum Aussie cheers for the King. Then some wag yelled, 'What about three cheers for the bloke in the top hat'. They were given just as lustily, much to the amusement of His Majesty.[7]

The school at Park House ran on regimental lines, which came as a shock to Denning after his time at the front: ' … there seemed to be dozens of Military Police pulling us up for some minor offence — a button off, or the wrong belt on — and our arms got tired swishing up and down from saluting'.[8]

Denning and his mate, Mc, took leave in London, where they met a 'gentleman', Mr Courtier, who took it on himself to entertain the diggers at his own expense. He took them punting on the river, in the hope of finding 'more congenial company':[9]

As we glided along, we saw two attractive young ladies having lunch on the bank a little apart from the rest of the groups. To our surprise Mr Courtier called, 'Coming for a little run, girls?' They turned away from us. He was snubbed. It did not worry him, he paddled on and said, 'Don't worry, let them finish their lunch. They are decent girls. We'll come back'.

'And risk another snub,' Mc said.

'Oh no. It is not considered so improper as it used to be for young ladies to accept such an invitation, especially as I am here as a kind of chaperon'.

We came back and Mr Courtier did the talking. They looked us over and consented to come along with us. Mc and I felt a bit embarrassed at first, and Mr Courtier set to work paddling with his back to us … We had a really happy day, and before parting, we arranged to meet the girls again.[10]

It was not easy for the diggers to adjust from the rough manners of the Australian trenches to the arcane conventions of English society, nor to overcome the shyness that, surprisingly to some, was very much part of the Australian character.

Far from being the shady character that Denning's description might imply, Denning learned that Mr Courtier was the very reputable proprietor of Courtier & Sons, Book Binders and Publishers.[11] His generosity to two diggers he had never before met was typical of that of many English men and women.

Denning did manage to meet his own English girl, whilst on leave from Park Camp. They spent days together, picnicking and walking hand-in-hand as young lovers, and talking about the war:

I think I was jealous of her admiration and loyalty to her English soldier brothers and friends, which in reality was only natural, and greatly to be admired. I had dreamed of and desired to have the true admiration of the Aussie girls for their own Aussie boys.

I was no better and no worse than most men brought up in a sheltered environment. I had the longings, desires and frustrations of all men. There was no doubt early training held a man in good stead.

Previously in Egypt, France, and London, the fear of infection threatened promiscuity. I hadn't availed myself of the opportunity of promiscuous sex.

Shirley was a decent, good girl, full of fun and mischief. She liked to be kissed and cuddled but drew the line there. She was broad-minded yet honest. I was very attracted to her.[12]

Ray Denning met Shirley in London on his final leave, where they whiled away the hours until it was time to take the train back to the front. 'The hours of my last leave soon passed and the time arrived to say goodbye to my dear friend. To dwell in detail about the goodbye would be 'to tell tales out of school'.[13]

The meticulous Sergeant Lawrence did not have as much luck when he and his mate met two girls on leave in Scotland. His mate had persuaded the girls to accompany them on a train trip to Loch Lomond:

We caught our train and off we went. After about 10 minutes I summed up enough courage to have a screw at her (sic). Help! For scrimey! Shades of hades! Her face was just perfect, profile, etc. fine, but her ears, full of dirt, her neck ditto, and her nails supporting enough black for the whole army. How I hate and detest one speck upon a girl … During the whole afternoon I felt that dirt near me. Thank God the trip as regards scenery was glorious.[14]

If Lawrence 'had the longings, desires and frustrations of all men', as Denning had put it, they were not strong enough to overcome his neat streak.

Bert Bishop was more thoughtful, but was not interested in casual sex. His mates asked him to go into the town of Eu for a good time:

> 'There are some wonderful tarts in there. What's the matter with you? Are you mad?'
>
> 'Not mad. Only an idiot'.
>
> I only had to think of the lovely, laughing, clean girls I had grown up with, the fun we'd had at beach picnics, tennis parties, singsongs and dances, and I didn't want to go to Eu.
>
> I had often thought of the attractive girl I had met in Euston Road, London. She seemed quite genuine in what she told me. Since then I had heard quite a few of our chaps tell of their sexual adventures whilst on leave. Several of them praised their ladyloves who had lost their husbands in the war. Quite a few had lost lieutenants, there was an odd captain or two, but when one fellow told me of his two weeks with a major's widow — I began to wonder.[15]

Now this was taking respect for the uniform to ridiculous lengths. It does not seem to have dawned on Bishop that women may have had 'longings, desires and frustrations' just like men, nor that they would feel the longing equally, whatever ranks their gallant husbands may once have held.

Of course, there is a tremendous and understandable bias in what the diggers wrote home, or even in their diaries, about their sexual escapades. It was one thing for Lawrence or Bishop to boast about abstemious behaviour. It was quite another for those who were not so restrained to write home to tell their mothers or girlfriends what really went on. What goes on tour stays on tour, even in those days.

Cities like London and Paris, and towns closer to the front, like Poperinghe and Amiens, more than accommodated the sexual appetites of the soldiers. There is no basis to suggest that the soldiers of the First World War were more or less promiscuous than the soldiers of any other war. It must also be acknowledged that there were some, like Bert Bishop, who did come from sheltered backgrounds, and maintained what they had been taught in their youth: 'I was not alone in the way I saw things, many had the same outlook. Brought up in a small country town, church at least once on Sunday, kept at Sunday school till fifteen, I had little opportunity to develop ideas about that part of life.'[16]

Sergeant Maxwell was sent to a four-month officer training school at Balliol College, Oxford, but he was sidetracked on his way there by a cabaret in Piccadilly, where he found 'a jostling pack of party girls, a gust of assorted talcum and heated flesh, a whirl of wet scarlet lips, a flash of white teeth and lecherous smiles that held in them the promise of devilry before dawn'.[17] As the party reached its climax:

> Australian military police cluttered the stairway. Their sergeant dramatically demanded silence with uplifted hand. I recognised him as a member of my own battalion. To evade the front line he had blown off his left thumb at Gallipoli.
>
> 'I am sorry to break up the party,' he began, with the arrogant voice of a colonel, 'but I want to examine the leave passes of all you Australians. Anyone who is absent without leave I intend to arrest'.[18]

Maxwell did not care. He had a pass. When the sergeant asked for it, Maxwell said: 'With pleasure, old man,' and then I could not forgo the temptation to ask after the condition of the stump of the finger he had destroyed at Gallipoli.'[19]

This was a step too far. When Maxwell fished in his pocket for his pass, it was not there. He had left it in the hotel room. A sharp brawl ensued, and Maxwell was taken into custody, whence he came before the Bow Street magistrate, who looked 'like Methuselah', was 'very hostile to Colonials' and fined Maxwell £20.[20] The police them delivered Maxwell to a 'Brass Hat at Horseferry Road' who told him, 'You're a disgrace to Australia ... The sergeant will accompany you back to France.' Maxwell gave his escort the slip, but took the first train to Folkestone and the ferry to Flanders, where the story of his escapade had already arrived in the English newspapers.[21] His mates chipped in the £20, his colonel, although stern, was forgiving. Maxwell was later awarded the Victoria Cross.[22]

One digger was on a course in England. The ground was frozen hard. The digger was miserable, feeling the cold. To his surprise at that early hour, he saw General Birdwood out for his morning exercise. Birdwood said, 'Better come and have a little rum.' The digger agreed, and off they went. After a few miles the digger was tiring, and had to ask the general how much longer they would be:

Digger: When are we getting to that rum, Sir?

General: Rum! What rum?

Digger: Didn't you say, sir, 'Come and have some rum'?

General: Good Lord, no. I said 'run' — not 'rum'.[23]

With his usual forbearance for Australians, the general recorded only that the digger's response was quite unprintable.[24]

Sergeant Whitelaw's leave from the Ypres front in August 1917 was 'ten days of freedom in a civilized English speaking country'.[25] With £5 in his pocket and £20 in his paybook, he was ready for a high time. From Victoria Station, 'We marched to the A.I.F. headquarters in Horseferry Road, where we received our pays and had orders and regulations of London read to us, and then we were dismissed on our free ways.'[26]

Whitelaw saw all the sights of London — the Strand, Fleet Street, the Houses of Parliament, Trafalgar Square, Buckingham Palace, Marble Arch, St Paul's, Big Ben and Westminster Abbey with its collection of tombs of the great and famous — 'In fact it's a blessed church yard with a roof over it where they stored most of the greatest men England had since Jimmie made the place.'[27]

Whitelaw and his mate, George Muller, visited the Clement Talbot motor works, where Lord Sainsbury, the chairman, who had fought earlier in the war as a colonel, greeted them personally and showed them round the plant. Mr Shorland, one of the executives, took Whitelaw and Muller home to his house in Hertfordshire, where he entertained them for dinner and they stayed the night.

The next morning, the two diggers were taken on a 'walk around part of the grounds which were well laid out and really beautiful. I had to smile when the gardeners and groom etc. touch their hats and say "Good morning sir", just fancy Australian workmen doing that.'[28] Like so many other diggers, they found themselves playing the roles of Connecticut Yankees in King Arthur's Court.

The London shows were popular among the men on leave. Captain Lethbridge, a doctor, managed to squeeze *La Bohème, Aida* (twice), *Madame Butterfly* and the variety shows *Big Boys, High Jinks, The South Polar Pictures* and *Daddy Long Legs* into ten days' leave in 1916.[29] George Muller and Ray Whitelaw saw shows at the Holborn Empire and at the Palladium, but the highlight of their leave was going to Her Majesty's to see *Choo Chin Chow*, starring Arch and Lily Brayton. This was the smash hit of the time. On his leave in July 1917, Sergeant Lawrence saw its 400th performance.[30]

Sergeant Clay went one better with *Choo Chin Chow*. One of his mates knew a girl from the cast — an Australian girl at that. 'This girl (Miss Telfer) was very good to us. Several mornings she took us round and pointed out lots of places of interest that otherwise we would not have seen ... She sang beautifully, too, and often, after breakfast, we would go to where she boarded for an hour and have some music. I gave my lungs a little exercise, too.'[31] With his theatrical guide, Clay saw *High Jinks, Daddy Long Legs, A Royal Divorce* and *Wanted — a Husband*.[32]

Gunner Howell took leave in England in September 1917. After seeing London, he took the train to Edinburgh and on to Aberdeen, where he met some of the local girls:

> The Aberdeen Flappers, or as our chaps call them 'Jeans' all want to do something for us. They are not the regular variety of Flapper who want so much amusement as they can get but are quite anxious to make Australians welcome. And I must say I didn't let <u>all</u> opportunities slip. When my leave is over my stay in the British Isles will ever remain one of the most pleasant times in my life.[33]

Howell noticed that Londoners had come to the stage 'where they expect anything and are not either moved by victories or reverses … The only thing which seems to concern the Londoner is the likelihood of an air raid, but still there are some who regard an air raid as some special form of excitement arranged for their special benefit.'[34]

Sergeant Lawrence had more than his fair share of excitement as he drove in a London cab:

> We had gone no distance before I noticed everyone looking up and when I followed suit I saw about 20-odd aeroplanes. It needed no-one to tell me that they were Hun machines and as we drove along we watched them coming over. They flew in perfect formation and very low, so low in fact that you could just distinguish the crosses upon them. Just before they got immediately overhead our taxi driver made straight for an underground railway (tube) entrance. At first I thought he was going to drive, taxi and all, down, but he sprang out and said, 'No good to me, I'm off' and he bolted down the tube. People were running in all directions and as they give you no medals for standing outside upon a show like this, we sought cover too. Then down came the bombs, about 20, one every second. Directly we could see that they had all passed overhead we ran out. They had dropped all around us (at the bank of England corner) and the air was full of brick dust and fire engines.[35]

Sergeant Linton prepared for his leave in February 1918 with 'a bonzer hot bath tonight and ... a clean rig of clothes. I am now free from chats for a day or so.'[36] Once in London, they were marched to Horseferry Road 'where we got a bit of a lecture as to what we were to do and what not to do by the Doctor',[37] suggesting that some of the men were not as punctilious in matters of romance as Private Bishop had been.

Linton drew £2.10.0 in pay, and, with two mates, Ron Pow and Snowy Wilson:

> ... set off up the Strand for a feed. We were fixed up at Slaters and had a real good tuck in. There are girls by the million so we weren't long in getting hold of 3 decent looking tarts. They took us all over the place and we eventually went to see a picture in Leicester Square. It wasn't a bad programme. I've seen better, but we sat it out after which we took the girls round to supper. Of course they had to go upstairs and ordered ham and eggs, which cost me 13/-.[38] We had no sooner been served than the sirens were sounded and thousands of whistles blown which of course was the tip for us to get under cover ... the two girls we were with almost went mad with fear. I tried to console them in a rough old way but they wouldn't listen to me and declared that they wouldn't eat a mouthful so to quieten them we agreed to take a trip down to Charing Cross Tube and leave them there ... Ron and I went back to the Tea Rooms and had their supper and ours as well.[39] ✦

It was not such a promising start, but at least the boys had full stomachs. Linton and Wilson took the overnight train to Edinburgh, where they stayed with Sergeant Linton's Aunt Jean, and his cousins Sarah, Sandy and their friend, Nan. He met his Aunts Sarah and Annie, and his Uncle Jim. His Scottish family gave him all the comforts of home — Aunt Jean even gave him a 'Hot Toddie' for the tickle in his throat.[40]

Nan was his favourite, and though it was one thing to 'get the usual salute from Aunt (kissed) … Nan came in a little later and I collected another kiss (did real well on the kissing line in Scotland). She was terribly worried because a couple of days previous she had visited the dentist and had her top teeth pulled out. Of course I made her laugh as much as possible and she soon got tired of putting her hand up to hide her gums'.[41]

While in Edinburgh Linton noticed that the tram driver was a girl, the tram conductor was a conductress and the ticket inspector was a lady, so 'the whole joint was run by the fair sex'.[42] For Nan and Alice, 'the Mill hours [were] now 9.30am to 4pm, times being hard'.[43]

At the end of his leave, Nan saw Linton off at the station, and as the train headed back to London, Linton 'started to realize I was a soldier again'.[44]

Sister Donnell fell ill after arduous service in France following the Passchendaele battles. In February 1918, she was sent away to the 'Sick Sisters' at Abbeville, near the border of France and Italy, to regain her health. Here she recovered in the 'scenery … the blue sky, the warmth and sunshine, and the sweet scent of mimosa' — a far cry from the bleak winter of northern France.[45]

Paris was another option for leave. Gunner Howell took his leave there in February 1918. In less than a day, he made his way by train from the front at Steenwerk to the Gare du Nord.[46] Whilst bombs were falling on London, there was little sign of war in Paris. There seemed to be no food restrictions — an excellent meal was available from five francs upwards.[47] But it was the theatre that fascinated Gunner Howell, especially the Casino de Paris and the Folies Bergères:

These two have a grand promenade garden attached. Here a band plays lively airs all the evening. Tables are scattered about, half hidden by palms and gaily-lit stalls. Multi-coloured lights hang from chandeliers and walls. Sitting at the tables are groups of men and women listening to the music. As the music livens, parties can be seen dancing in the spaces set apart for the purpose and the whole show is extremely fascinating and to me rather novel. This keeps on during the whole of the time the show is in progress and as one gets tired of the performance it is an easy matter to make for the promenade and watch the crowd. Both these halls are very well patronized and a dull moment never finds its way into the entire evening.[48]

In May 1917, Lieutenant Rule and his mates went AWOL[49] from a promotion school in Albert, and took the train to Paris, evading British military police checking passes at the Gare du Nord. Their trip was not a success. They found the prices crippling, the French maid in the hotel unwilling, and the Parisian pissoirs a source of endless amusement.[50]

Paris even stirred the sanctimonious Lawrence, who had now been promoted Lieutenant. In June 1917, he wrote home to one of his mates:

All I have to write about is Paris. First of all until you have seen it there are two subjects you know nothing about. Cities and women. In both it surely stands without equal ... Some of these boulevards have upon the footpath as many as two rows of trees and as these are in full foliage now you can imagine what it's like. Right in the centre of the city you come across stretches of footway a quarter of a mile long, just a shady walk, through the top of which one can only catch occasional glimpses of the sun above. It's great. Imagine the Block in Collins Street with the footpath easily twice the width it is at present.[51]

Not much could top that, but Lieutenant Lawrence had more surprises up his sleeve:

Imagine a gloriously hot day, yourself seated in the shade at one of those tables with iced lemon water in front of you and passing you in hundreds superbly gowned and beautiful women ... I never saw a plain girl the whole time I was there, neither did I see a thick pair of ankles ... Only small it's true, but they are just bubbling over with the very joy of life, chock full of spirits and enjoying love and passion to their utmost capacity. Surely they were only made to tempt man, these women, and they well know how to do it.[52]

Lawrence was enjoying leave in Paris far more than Loch Lomond. What would the evening bring?

In Paris the girls are allowed to accost you, and they do it well too … The first one pressed one firm little breast against me and gasped 'You Darling'. Oh hell, I looked at her, she was divine, I felt myself slipping, going, going — Higgins grabbed my arm and we pass on. Another step and I do him a like service … After five months in the mud, it's hard. Anyhow we manage by dint of helping one another to pull through the ordeal and return safely to our hotel.[53]

Lieutenant Lawrence found it an uplifting experience:

The streets of Paris are absolutely thronged with these girls, not the slovenly, washed–out cheeky looking little sluts that get about our streets, but gloriously and correctly dressed women of rare beauty. Women whom one could take anywhere and feel secure in the knowledge that she would look and behave the part of a lady.[54]

With two others, Lawrence met an Englishman who had lived in Paris for twenty years. He sent them to a 'fine place with decent girls'.[55] Here Lawrence met a 'little lady [who] had a superb little figure, round, soft, firm just in the right places, black silk stockings with openwork clocks, dainty little feet in suede Merry Widow shoes, clean cut slim ankles (my one failing) and a right royal regal little head'.

Things were looking promising:

To most fellows it would have been the height of delight to witness her disrobing but somehow I just couldn't, her whole being seemed too sacred to intrude upon at such a time, so I stayed chatting to Higgins and when I went into the room she was in bed. I turned off all but the small lights and hopping into bed beside her would have bolted again had it been possible. We lay and talked for some time and although she knew no English we got on fairly well. As we talked I lay and looked at her. God she was glorious, and as I looked, the more I disliked the task before me. *However,* I switched out the light.[56]

The next day, the girls persuaded Higgins and Lawrence to take them on a tour of the town. Nothing was too good for them — parasols, hats, a ride in a Rolls Royce, a lavish dinner and 'one or two little articles'.[57] But, after his spree, Lawrence was left with a serious case of lover's remorse: 'Afterwards we totted up our expenses, 900 francs, £33 for the three … but when I came to reckon it up I wished I had not spent *so much* and *such time* in *merely looking at her.*'[58]

CHAPTER FOURTEEN

THE BIRTH OF THE AUSTRALIAN CORPS

After Third Ypres, the sense of frustration within the War Cabinet was palpable. Churchill argued for the adoption of new tactics. Lloyd George and Churchill both advocated opening a second front. All Cabinet members were appalled at the failure of the frontal assault. Yet none could find a general who was prepared to put forward an alternative to all-out assault on the strongholds of the western front. Lord Hankey wrote:

> The failure of the Flanders front to achieve any immediate strategical result, the terrible losses and the fact that the plan had worked out exactly as he had anticipated had affected the Prime Minister's usual sense of buoyancy of spirit. His conviction that the war could not be won on the lines hitherto adopted was only too strongly confirmed. Yet his professional advisers could suggest nothing better. Every alternative he had proposed had been rejected. The obvious remedy was to find new advisers. But where? The General Staff trained at [the British Staff College at] Camberley nearly all shared the view of their superiors and they held together,

a veritable band of brothers. Their opinion might be right or wrong, but their unanimity was remarkable.[1]

The sense of frustration stemmed from the fact that the greatest brains in the Empire had worked to solve the problem of the deadlocked front, but all had failed utterly. It seemed that there was nowhere to turn. Lloyd George complained that the only option seemed to be to 'repeat the fatuous old tactics of hammering away with human flesh and sinews at the strongest fortresses of the enemy'.[2]

At this low point, the British took one last swipe at the Germans which shone a ray of light on the question of tactics. In a battle at Cambrai late in November 1917, they attacked with tanks, but with no bombardment. The surprise attack allowed them to penetrate the German lines for six miles.

Although the Germans won back the ground gained at Cambrai before Christmas, the battle showed that using tanks in surprise attacks, in sufficient numbers, and on solid ground that had not been churned up by artillery could lend a decisive edge to infantry operations.

Whilst Haig wrote that, 'throughout these operations the value of the services rendered by the tanks was very great, and the utmost gallantry, enterprise and resolution were displayed by both officers and crews',[3] other responses were less muted. Churchill, now back in the War Cabinet as Munitions Minister, went directly to the point:

Accusing as I do without exception all the great ally offensives of 1915, 1916 and 1917, as needless and wrongly conceived operations of infinite cost, I am bound to reply to the question, What else could be done? And I answer it pointing to the Battle of Cambrai, '*This* could have been done'. This in many variants, this in larger and better forms ought to have been done, and would have been done if only the Generals had not been content to fight the bullets of machine guns with the breasts of gallant men, and think that that was waging war.[4]

The British generals were not alone in their failure to appreciate the true potential of the tank. For their part, since Bullecourt, the diggers had held a low opinion of this new weapon. Moreover, the Germans, normally so innovative, eschewed the development of the tank until it was too late in the war to use them effectively. It is an interesting speculation that the person who best learned and adapted Churchill's lesson was General Rommel. In any event, the Cambrai battle finally drove home the lesson that the tank must be added to the mix of tactics to be adopted for future Allied infantry offensives.[5]

Internationally, three developments were unfolding that influenced events on the western front in 1918. The first was the slowness of the build-up of the American force in France. Although it was now almost a year since the Americans had entered the war, their cautious, stepwise approach to training their men and transporting them to France was causing delays that frustrated the British commanders.[6] In December 1917, General Pershing, the American commander, told Haig that only four divisions would be trained by June 1918,[7] and only eight or nine divisions were expected to be in the line by the end of the summer.[8]

The second was the collapse of Russian resistance. The Bolshevik government sued for peace in November 1917. The Russian armies simply dissolved.[9] This left the Bolsheviks in the position of attempting to negotiate the terms of a peace treaty from a position of abject weakness — and that with an enemy that was in no mood to forgive. Trotsky resorted to the ploy of inviting all the Allies to the peace negotiations.

Trotsky's ploy did not work,[10] but it did lead to the third development: a round of abortive peace offers. On Christmas Day, Count Czernin, the Austrian delegate to the talks with Russia, made an offer of peace on behalf of the Central Powers. The offer was hardly a compromise. It was rejected.[11]

In response, however, President Wilson outlined fourteen points on which the United States would agree to end the war. Lloyd George was also forced to state his position, which he did, reinforcing Britain's resolve to continue the war until the weight of numbers drove the Germans to defeat. Billy Hughes supported Lloyd George.[12] The offers of peace were so far apart that there was no hope of agreement. The peace initiatives broke down 'in a crossfire of generalisations'.[13]

The collapse of Russia allowed Ludendorff to begin moving troops from the Russian front to the western front. By Christmas, he was moving divisions at the rate of two a week.[14] There was an obvious threat that, with the reinforcements from the Russian front, the Germans would be in a position to launch a well-supported attack on the western front when fighting resumed in 1918.[15] While the Germans were reinforcing their forces, the strength of the Allies remained depleted from the battles of 1917. Churchill, then Minister for Munitions, wrote:

> Sir Douglas Haig vehemently and naturally called for all the officers and men required to bring his divisions up to full strength at the earliest possible moment. Robertson supported him, and was evidently seriously alarmed. From my central position between the Army and the War Cabinet, with, I believe, the whole information available in my possession and with constant intimate access to the Prime Minister, I never ceased to press for the immediate reinforcement of Sir Douglas Haig.[16]

As vehement as Haig may have been in his demands for reinforcements, he remained confident of the outcome of the war. Haig, who had been promoted Field Marshal,[17] evidently interpreted the German peace offer as a sign of weakness. He was not convinced that the Germans would go on the offensive in 1918. His diary for 9 January 1918 record:

> I lunched with the PM ... We had a very cheery party. Conversation turned on the length of the war and some betting took place. Derby bet the PM 100 cigars to 100 cigarettes that war would be over by next new year. LG disagreed. I said I thought the war would be over

because of the *internal* state of Germany. She could not continue after the coming autumn, because her population was degenerating so fast that even if she won, there would not be the men to exploit and develop the country after she won the war etc. etc.

I also emphasized the critical nature of the coming 4 months on the Western Front if Germany did not make peace. Germany having only one million men as reserves for this year's fighting, I doubted whether they would risk them in an attempt to 'break through'. If they did, it would be a gambler's throw.[18]

Both Churchill and Lloyd George were resigned to the war continuing into 1919, when they thought the weight of American numbers would tip the scales in favour of the Allies.[19]

The active mind of Lloyd George refused to countenance that there was only one choice. He identified four alternatives. The first was to concentrate all forces on the western front — this was Haig's and Robertson's view. The second was to concentrate mainly on the western front, but to use forces in other theatres when winter prevented fighting on the western front — Wilson expressed some support for this alternative. The third was to stand on the defensive on the western front until Russia recovered and the numbers of American troops became decisive — Pétain favoured this course. The fourth was to weaken Germany by attacking her Allies — this approach was called 'knocking the props'.[20]

Lloyd George and Churchill argued that the British must nurse their troops through 1918, conserving numbers and resources for a final blow in 1919. Haig held to the view that victory would come in 1918, by repeating the tactics of 1916 and 1917. He and Robertson wanted to resume the offensive on the western front.[21]

It was a classic stand-off. On the one hand, articulate and intelligent politicians were using all their powers of persuasion to argue that the war must continue into 1919. On the other hand, inarticulate generals, probably less intelligent than the politicians, were using all their powers of stonewalling to argue that repeating the tactics of 1916 and 1917 would end the war in 1918.

The generals had far the worse side of the argument, yet events proved them correct. In their persistent opposition to Lloyd George and Churchill, the generals were the embodiment of one of Churchill's favourite sayings: never give up.

It is a matter of conjecture whether the alternatives that Lloyd George postulated would have proved equally successful. Certainly, Bulgaria sued for peace in September 1918, Turkey did the same in October and Austria-Hungary at the beginning of November. Who is to say that 'knocking the props' would not have worked as effectively as continuing all-out on the western front?

Haig spoke casually of the prospect of casualties — Germany putting a million reservists at risk was an example. His manner betrayed heartlessness rather than resolve. Lloyd George approached the prospect of casualties with apprehension and revulsion, something that emerges fully in Churchill's melodramatic account:

> Mr Lloyd George viewed with horror the task imposed on him of driving ... the remaining manhood of the nation [to war]. Lads of eighteen or nineteen, elderly men up to forty-five, the last surviving brother, the only son of his mother (and she a widow), the father the sole support of the family, the weak, the consumptive, the thrice wounded — all must now prepare themselves for the scythe.[22]

Churchill was never one to hold back from a dramatic turn of phrase. When he wrote this, he had just turned 43. There was no way he thought of himself as 'elderly': not then, and not when he became Prime Minister for the second time, at the age of 77. But his hyperbole did not detract from Lloyd George's determination to resist Haig's demands in any way that would curtail the slaughter on the western front. Churchill wrote that he:

urged that the Cabinet should send all the men that were needed to reconstitute the Army, and should at the same time forbid absolutely any resumption of the offensive. The Prime Minister however did not feel that, if the troops were once in France, he would be strong enough to resist those military pressures for an offensive which had so often overborne the wiser judgment of Statesmen. He therefore held, with all his potent influence, to a different policy. He sanctioned only a moderate reinforcement of the army, while at the same time gathering in England the largest possible number of reserves. In this way he believed he would be able ... to prevent a British offensive and to feed the armies during the whole course of the fearful year which was approaching.[23]

Lloyd George and the War Cabinet adopted a second device to thwart Haig's and Robertson's offensive ambitions. It was the establishment of a Supreme War Council in Versailles. Robertson objected strongly to the initiative, which he believed would complicate the chain of command. In this, Robertson was correct. Indeed, Lloyd George intended the council to act as a brake on the offensive ambitions of Haig and Robertson. Robertson's objections were overruled and he was eventually dismissed from his position of Chief of the Imperial General staff.

Robertson was the scapegoat for the friction between Lloyd George and Haig. Lloyd George would have sacked Haig himself if there had been a suitable replacement, but, as Lloyd George wrote in his memoirs:

Who could be put in [Haig's] place? It is a sad reflection that not one amongst the visible military leaders would have been any better. There were amongst them plenty of good soldiers who knew their profession and possessed intelligence up to a point. But Haig was all that and probably better within those limits than anyone else in sight.[24]

Lloyd George's manoeuvring had the result he intended. It scotched Haig's plans of resuming the offensive in the spring of 1918.[25]

The Australians were as poorly placed as the British to resist a German attack. I and II Anzac Corps suffered 55 000 casualties in the battles of 1917, 38 000 of them at Third Ypres. In a total force with a nominal strength of around 150 000 men, this was a huge loss. Of the nominal roll, around 50 000 were corps troops used mainly in support roles. The nominal strength of each division was in the order of 18 000, making a total of 90 000.

The actual strength of the divisions in November 1917 was far below that number. Efforts to reinforce the divisions over the winter, mainly with convalescent men, had not brought them remotely near full strength. Bean gives the following numbers for the actual strength of the divisions over the winter of 1917–18:[26]

Division	1 November 1917	31 December 1917	28 February 1918
1st	11 476	12 694	13 531
2nd	11 805	12 583	13 579
3rd	8503	11 626	13 097
4th	9787	11 098	12 021
5th	10 192	13 070	13 577
Total	51 763	61 071	65 805

Each division was, therefore, missing about 6000 men, and doing its best to make do at around two-thirds of normal strength. No easy solution for this predicament was in sight.

Australian manpower was fully stretched. Australia had sent two divisions to Gallipoli: the 1st and the 2nd. After Gallipoli, it doubled (or rather, split) these two divisions to form the 4th and 5th Divisions. These four divisions went to France in the first half of 1916. Meanwhile, the 3rd Division, the youngest of the Australian divisions, was raised in Australia and sent to England, where it completed its training on Salisbury Plain, under the command of General Monash. It arrived in France in December 1916.

Australia set about raising a 6th Division in 1917. The 6th Division was to come mainly from men recovering from wounds in England. The flood of casualties from the great battles of 1917 put an end to this idea. All available reserves were needed to plug the holes in the existing divisions.[27]

Unlike the British, Australian soldiers were all volunteers. Whilst men had enlisted in huge numbers in the first three years of the war, by the end of 1917, the available pool of able-bodied men had shrunk, and the numbers of potential volunteers had diminished to the point that it was unlikely that the casualties of Bullecourt, Messines and Third Ypres could be replaced.

The shortage of manpower led Billy Hughes to propose a referendum for the adoption of conscription. The referendum, held in October 1916, was defeated. According to Bean, some voters were swayed by the fact that Australia itself was not in imminent danger from the war, others by Archbishop Mannix, whose opposition to conscription stemmed from the troubles between Great Britain and Ireland in Easter 1916.[28]

A second referendum, held in December 1917, was also defeated. Mannix again opposed the proposal, and the majority against it actually increased. Feelings ran high. Following Mannix's second campaign against conscription, Bean commented that, 'future students of this episode may wonder whether his concern was really with Australian interests'.[29]

Hughes had touted the second referendum as a vote to separate the sheep from the goats. When the referendum was defeated, Archbishop Mannix told his flock from his pulpit how appropriate it was that the prime minister's name was Billy.

There had been huge patriotic support for the King and the Empire at the outbreak of war, and enlistments had increased after Gallipoli. The miserable results of the Somme battles and the battles of 1917 had evidently dampened the appetite of Australian parents for sending their children to a European war. Moreover, whilst the soldiers voted in favour of conscription on both occasions, they did so by fairly narrow margins.[30] Despite, or, perhaps, because of their experience of fighting with British troops, many diggers were uncomfortable with the notion of fighting alongside men who were not volunteers.[31]

Even with a volunteer army, the Australian divisions had more deserters than equivalent British divisions. When a battle was in the offing, or when things were tough, there was a small percentage of Australians who went missing from their units.[32]

General Glasgow called this group, 'men "whose sense of honour was weak" [who] preferred imprisonment to front line service'.[33] Birdwood called them men who, 'when their battalion was ordered into the trenches "quietly slipped away to the rear"', but distinguished the genuine cases 'whose nerves have suffered' who should 'be quietly withdrawn, and utilized in suitable positions behind the firing line'.[34] Bean, more directly, called them, '"hard cases" and ne'er do wells … in some cases actual criminals who had enlisted without any intention of serving at the front, and ready to go to any means to avoid it'.[35]

A solid rump of generals, including Generals Haig, Birdwood, Monash and Holmes, attributed the greater rate of desertion among the Australians to the fact that Australian law did not impose the death penalty for desertion, whereas British law did. They pressured the Australian government to bring Australian law into line with the British.[36]

This exposed a fundamental difference between the Australian outlook and the British. The Australian public felt it was unfair to impose the death penalty on men who had volunteered to fight in a cause that was not strictly their own.[37] Recognising this difference, the Australian government refused to bow to pressure to introduce the death penalty.

The diggers themselves resented the system of punishment used in the British Army. They were made to stand on parade while the death sentences of British soldiers were read out, in a bizarre spirit of *pour encourager les autres*.[38] This ceremony 'aroused in the Australians, officers and men, only a sullen sympathy and a fierce pride that their own people was strong enough to refuse' the death penalty to the generals who sought its imposition.[39]

Private Bishop described how the Australians felt about British military justice:

One morning a sergeant, for some trifling offence contrary to good order and military discipline, had been sentenced to lose his stripes and revert to the ranks. What a ceremony was made of this! Various NCOs and Tommy officers played their part ... The sergeant was ordered here, he was ordered there. Finally they got him where they wanted him. Particulars of his offence were read out. The verdict and sentence were read out. Most of the troops in the camp were Australians, and to us the whole thing seemed like comic opera. The sergeant stood at attention, all by himself. As each separate order was barked, some master-at-arms or warrant officer stepped this way, stepped that way, till he stood beside the poor Tommy sergeant. Then the fellow doing the stripping, still under orders, placed his right hand on the top of the sewn-on stripes, gave a heave, and the sergeant was a full private.

'What a victory', the man beside me said. 'That should win the war for us' ...

On some mornings there would be as many as half-a-dozen particulars of courts martial, all Tommies. They all went through the same stereotyped phraseology.

First there was the name, the rank, the man's number, his unit, the offence with which he was charged. The date of his court martial. The findings of the court martial.

'Found guilty and sentenced to be shot by firing squad. Sentence duly carried out at dawn on such-and-such a date'.

None of these courts martial were of Australians. No digger was ever shot by his own men because of an offence against King's Rules

& Regulations. The heads knew it would not work with us. The terrible part of it all was that in practically every case the offender was a young English boy. Dragged from their homes at the age of nineteen, given about three months' training, they were dumped into battle as soon as they hit France.[40]

The fact was that many of the 'heads' did think the death penalty would work for the diggers. Thankfully, Hughes and the members of his Cabinet did not. They, not the 'heads', had a better sense of what motivated Australian soldiers: carrot, not stick. The revulsion that the British approach inspired in Bean and Bishop pulsed through their writing, so many years after the event.

Opposition to conscription did not suggest that Australians were not proud of the diggers and their achievements — quite the opposite. Gallipoli, although a failure in outcome, had been an immense source of pride for all Australians. The battles in France, however, had come to be recognised for what they were — some successes, but many failures — and the successes often came with a huge price. Messines, Menin Road, Broodseinde and Polygon Wood made a forlorn list of successes, without counting the many failures.

The failures were often blamed on the British generals. Moreover, the failures complicated the debate over conscription. Those in favour of conscription argued that Australia was not doing enough for the war effort. Those opposed to it argued that the British generals had squandered the troops they had been given, and there was no justification for giving them more.[41] This, of course, was precisely the argument that David Lloyd George made so capably and forcefully.

Monash also thought the Australians had been misused during the battles of 1917. On 18 October 1917, he wrote home:

Our men are being put into the hottest fighting and are being sacrificed in hare-brained ventures, like Bullecourt and Passchendaele, and there is no-one in the War Cabinet to lift a voice in protest. It all arises from the fact that Australia is not represented in the War Cabinet, owing to Hughes, for political reasons, having been unable to come to England. So Australian interests are suffering badly, and Australia is not getting anything like the recognition it deserves ... [42]

For Monash to describe Bullecourt and Passchendaele as 'hare-brained ventures' demonstrated that if the Australians had ever treated their British superiors with deference, that notion had well and truly gone — not that White's answering back to General Haig after the battle of Pozières had been exactly deferential. By the end of 1917, the Australians knew from bitter experience that the British did not have all the answers, and never had.

The answers, such as they were known at the end of 1917, had been developed by trial and error over the last two years. Plumer's copybook attack on Messines, and the bite-and-hold battles on the Menin Road, at Broodseinde and at Polygon Wood had proven an approach to battle that, when used in good weather, could help attacking troops advance to the enemy trenches and drive the enemy back. So far, the Germans had no answer to that approach.

Monash's complaint that British generals had misused Australian troops raised another issue. Why should Australia not have its own army? If the British generals were sacrificing good Australian men on 'hare-brained ventures', there were plenty of Australian generals who could take their place. It was hardly likely that they would do a worse job, and they might do better.

Early in the war, Australia had accepted that the divisions it supplied would be absorbed into the wider British Army. When the divisions were split and reformed after Gallipoli, they were organised along British regimental lines, just for that purpose. Since then, under the umbrella of I and II Anzac Corps, they had been shuffled from army to army, often without due care for their situation, and sometimes with disastrous results.

In May 1916, when Hughes offered to raise the 6th Australian Division, it was a condition of the offer that an Australian army corps be formed. British generals opposed him on the ground that, if five (or six) Australian divisions were combined in one army corps, that corps would be larger than any existing army corps, and too unwieldy for one commander too handle. The decimation of the Australian divisions in 1917 provided a bleak answer to this justification.

The Americans insisted that their army, now building in size, should always fight under American command. The Canadians, with four divisions, had always fought as a single Canadian corps.

According to Monash, it was:

> impossible to overvalue the advantages which accrued to the Canadian troops from this close and constant association of all the four divisions with each other, with the Corps Commander and his Staff, and with all the accessory Corps services. It meant mutual knowledge of each other among all Commanders, all Staffs, all arms and services and the mutual trust and confidence born of that knowledge.[43]

The diggers shared Monash's view.[44] There was, however, one overwhelming reason behind the desire to form a single army corps. Monash asserted: 'It was founded upon a sense of Nationhood, which prompted the wish, vaguely formed early in the war, and steadily crystallizing in the minds both of the Australian people and of the troops themselves, that all Australian Divisions should be brought together under a single leadership.'[45]

British opposition persisted until, late in 1917, when Hughes cabled the War Cabinet:

> I desire to emphasise the point that it is strongly desired by Commonwealth Government that all Australian troops should be grouped together under General Birdwood, and that Australian troops

should be commanded and staffed by Australian officers, of whom most have had several years' war experience in addition to former peace training in Australian permanent and militia forces. This would appeal most strongly to Australian national sentiment, it is most keenly desired by the troops, the Commonwealth Government presses for it.[46]

The cable tipped the scales. Almost to the surprise of the Australian troops, the decision to form a single Australian Army corps was taken on 1 November 1917. The corps would consist of four divisions: the 1st, 2nd, 3rd and 5th. The threat that the 4th Division would be dissolved to supply the manpower shortages in the other divisions was not carried out. Instead, the 4th Division was withdrawn as a depot division, to act, in effect, as a reserve division for the Australian Corps.

The New Zealanders opposed the split with the Australians, but for the Australians, the advantages of a single Australian command outweighed the sense of regret that the troops felt at 'the dissolution of the close comradeship which had existed between the troops from the sister Dominions of Australia and New Zealand'.[47]

Following the collapse of the Russian front, no one doubted that the Germans were preparing to make a massive assault on the western front as soon as fighting began in 1918. No one, that is, except General Haig. His diary is remarkable as much for its failure to treat the enemy build-up as an occasion for alarm, as for its complacency at the prospect. On 2 March 1918, he did warn his army commanders to be 'ready as soon as possible to meet a big hostile offensive of prolonged duration',[48] but diluted the warning by adding:

I also told Army Commanders that I was very pleased at all I had seen on the fronts of the 3 Armies which I had recently visited. Plans were sound and thorough, and much work had already been done. I was only afraid that the Enemy would find our front so very strong that he will hesitate to commit his Army to the attack with the almost certainty of losing very heavily.[49]

As late as 18 March 1918, he recorded in his diary that, 'Cox reported Enemy has 187 divisions now on West Front: of these 80 are believed to be in reserve ... Enemy has concentrated already adequate means for a large attack here, and so we must expect an attack at short notice, and make our plans accordingly.'[50] In light of the signs of catastrophe that had been obvious to others for so long, it was a matter for concern that the alarm bells were not ringing more loudly in the Commander-in-Chief's ears.

Instead, Haig's reaction to the impending attack was a mixture of complacency and overconfidence. It is difficult to resist the conclusion that Haig's worst fears, if there was an attack, were that the Germans would take back a few miles of front, much as the British had done at Polygon Wood or Broodseinde ridge.

But the positions were not comparable. The Germans had advanced so far into France that a few miles' retreat to the east meant nothing to them — as their retreat to the Hindenburg line in 1917 had shown. For the Allies to retreat a few miles to the west at Amiens, or Hazebrouck, or Arras could mean the difference between keeping and losing the Channel ports, or between maintaining a single front and splitting the French and British armies apart.

Churchill estimated that 1 000 000 men and 3000 guns had been moved from the Russian front to the western front,[51] and that there were 110 German divisions facing the 57 British divisions early in 1918.[52] It was not something that should have slipped under Haig's radar. Even Wilson minimised the threat, writing in his diary on 20 March 1918: 'Signs of more aerodromes, etc, on our Front, and certainly the signs are cumulative of a big attack, but I still think that the Boches, while pressing us, should wait and fall on Italy later.'[53]

Haig did, however, find time to write to Lady Haig on 28 February 1918, that:

I spent some time with the Canadians. They are really fine disciplined soldiers now and so smart and clean. I am sorry to say the Australians are not nearly so efficient. I put this down to Birdwood who, instead of facing the problem, has gone in for the easier way of saying everything is perfect and making himself as popular as possible. We have had to separate the Australians into Convalescent Camps of their own, because they were giving so much trouble when along with our men and put such revolutionary ideas in their head.[54]

Wounded men with revolutionary ideas? Heaven forbid!

On 3 March 1918, Haig once again found time to return to the same theme. Someone in the New Zealand Parliament had implied that Birdwood was 'an excellent disciplinarian' and that Godley, the New Zealand commander, was not. Haig wrote a letter in Godley's defence, attaching a graphic that showed:

9 per thousand Australians in prison
1.6 per thousand Canadians, NZ, South African [in prison]
1 per thousand British ... [in prison][55]

That night, Haig copied the graphic into his diary, and added the comment:

That is to say nearly one Australian in every hundred men is in prison. This is greatly due to the fact that the Australian government refuses to allow capital punishment to be awarded to any Australian.

Before we introduced the 'suspended sentence' in February 1915, the British had 5.1 men per thousand in prison. By June that year the numbers fell to 1.2 and in August to .7 per thousand. Really the absence of crime in this Army is quite wonderful.[56]

According to Haig, once a convict, always a convict.

In that same convict spirit, all Australians would pray that it was not by hanging them that the British reduced the number of prisoners held in their gaols.

Over the winter of 1917–18, the Australian divisions came together under Birdwood's command. Unlike the British, their preoccupation was defence, not attack. Monash wrote:

> The information at our disposal led to the inevitable conclusion that, during January and February, the enemy was busy in transferring a great mass of military resources from the Russian to the Western Front. No one capable of reading the signs entertained the smallest doubt that they contemplated taking the offensive, in the spring on a large scale. The only questions were, at what point would he strike? and what tactics would he employ?[57]

CHAPTER FIFTEEN

THE GERMAN OFFENSIVE — 21 MARCH 1918

The German offensive began at 4.30 am on 21 March 1918.[1] From the outset, the Germans had the advantage. They began with a bombardment from 6000 guns. They committed 37 divisions to the attack, and held 30 more in reserve. Their total force was more than 750 000 men. Against this force, the British had 2500 guns, seventeen divisions, with only five divisions in reserve. The total British force was 300 000 men.[2] The British were outnumbered by more than 2:1.

The Germans attacked on a front of 50 miles. The start line for the offensive ran from Arras in the north, to St Quentin in the centre, to La Fère in the south. The offensive was codenamed Michael.

The Germans set themselves relatively modest objectives for Operation Michael. Prince Rupprecht's group of armies, to the north, was to 'push on towards Arras-Albert' fixing his 'left wing … on the Somme near Péronne.'[3] The German Crown Prince's group of armies, to the south, was to 'seize crossings over the Somme and over the [Somme] Canal' extending 'its right flank as far as Péronne'.[4]

Péronne was thus the central target of the attack. The distance from the start line to Péronne was about eight miles. In the light of the experience of the previous three years, this was probably ambitious enough. Whilst the Germans intended to capitalise on the success of Michael, if it was a success, the orders for Michael do not mention plans to exploit a breakthrough, nor do they refer to grander objectives. They contain nothing about taking the railhead at Amiens, separating the British from the French, or driving the British Army into the sea. It has sometimes been suggested that there was a grander strategy behind Michael.

Attention in this regard has focused on a meeting between Ludendorff, von Kuhl and von der Schulenberg at Mons on 11 November 1917. Churchill, for example, claimed that this meeting agreed that Michael was to be followed by a series of attacks in which the 'available German forces, wheeling as they advanced, were to attack the British in a north-west direction and drive them towards the coast'.[5] He made the claim whilst acknowledging that 'Hindenburg, Prince Rupprecht and the Crown Prince ... were not troubled to attend' — a matter of surprise if the meeting was intended to make important strategic and tactical decisions.[6]

The more plausible view is that the 11 November 1917 meeting did not descend to the detail that Churchill claimed. Rather, Ludendorff, by far the senior officer at the meeting, led his colleagues to agree to a plan he suggested. The thinking behind the plan was as follows: the Germans had the strength for only one major offensive; the offensive had to be made before the Americans could play a decisive role in the war; the offensive could fall on the French or the British, but not on both; defeating the British would accomplish more than defeating the French, since Britain was the moving force among the Allies; and the best ground for attacking the British was at St Quentin.

Operation Michael would not copy the pattern of the Passchendaele battles. Ludendorff believed that the tactics of Passchendaele 'only offered advantages in the case of untrained troops'.[7] If the Germans broke through, they were to continue on the offensive without the protection of a creeping barrage, and without worrying about protecting their flanks. German prisoners captured in the week after Michael began told their captors that no objectives were given, but companies were told to go as far as possible.[8] 'Wherever [the attack] penetrated it was to go on, fed from the rear and pushing out mushroom-wise to right and left, so as to envelop from the rear the enemy posts that were holding up the flanking troops'.[9]

In fact, Ludendorff avoided laying down any grand objectives for Michael. His conclusion was entirely consistent with the orders for the battle: 'We will punch a hole … For the rest, we shall see. We did it this way in Russia.'[10]

In fact, the attack brought success beyond the Germans' wildest dreams. They attacked along both sides of the valley of the Somme. Luck ran with the Germans — a heavy fog covered their advance. The attack on the north side of the Somme fell on the British Third Army, under the command of General Byng. The Third Army was holding the line in front of the old Somme battlefield. The attack on the south side of the Somme fell on the British Fifth Army, under the command of General Gough. The Fifth Army was holding the southernmost part of the British line, between the Third Army and the French. The Fifth Army reeled back in disarray. The Third Army held together, but it still fell back.

Within a week, the German advance on the Third Army had taken them as far as the old Somme battlefield, to Pozières, Thiepval, and almost to Albert — a distance of fifteen miles. The advance on the Fifth Army had taken them to the heights of Villers-Bretonneux, overlooking the Valley of the Somme to the east, and the city of Amiens to the west — a distance of 30 miles. On any scale, Operation Michael was a spectacular success.

The Fifth Army had succumbed with alarming speed. At 3.40 pm on 21 March 1918, a British colonel of artillery received a neatly written note from Major Dennes, who was commanding a forward battery:

I have fired 2,200 [artillery] rounds, and have only 200 rounds left. My S.A.A. [small arms ammunition] for Lewis-guns and rifles is also running short. Can more ammunition be sent up immediately, please?

The enemy has got through the wire in front of the battery, and is now on two sides of us. If the infantry can assist we can hold out until dark, when I will retire to rear position.[11]

By 5.30 pm, Major Dennes, polite to his last message, was dead, shot through the head.[12]

On the second day of the attack, Lieutenant Green was in a position at Roupy, near St Quentin. His was a tale of confusion, retreat and plummeting morale:

I saw a piteous band of men rise from the ground, and run rapidly towards me. A great shout went up from the Germans; a cry of mingled triumph and horror. 'Halt Eenglisch!' they cried, and for a moment were too amazed to fire; as though aghast at the folly of men who could plunge into such a storm of death. But the first silent gasp of horror expended, then broke the crackling storm. I don't remember in the whole war an intenser taste of hell. My men came along spreading rapidly ... Bayonets clashed there. Along the line men were falling swiftly as bullets hit them. Each second they fell, now one crumpling up, now two or three at once. I saw men stop to pick up their wounded mates, and as they carried them along, themselves get hit and fall with their inert burdens. Now they were near me, so I rushed out of my pit and ran with them to the line of trenches three hundred yards behind ...

Low-lying aeroplanes hovered over the advancing line, and their wireless messages soon put the German guns on us. Big black high-explosive shells began to fall on our position, making our tired flesh shudder. I now began to be amazed at the advancing contact lights. They did not merely stretch in front of us: they encircled us like a horse-shoe, the points of which seemed (and actually were) miles behind us. On the right the enemy was enfilading us with machine-gun fire …

I searched for the major commanding the troops on my left, but could not find him. By this time I was determined to act, and therefore gave the order to withdraw … The major … now appeared again, and cursed me for giving the order to retire. I was too tired to argue, and even then a gust of machine-gun fire swept above our heads. They were going to attack again.[13]

Retreat was turning into rout, not only in the Fifth Army, but also in the Third. Imaginary fears spread from man to man, driving the British to flee, often more effectively than the Germans themselves. On 25 March 1918, Captain Behrend, in the Third Army, arrived in Forceville north-east of Albert. There, he reported to General Marshall and Major Healing. He found them in the large and beautifully furnished salon of an undamaged chateau. As he left the room, having made his report, the General shouted:

'Come back!'
'How long will it take you to get to Colonel Thorp?' he asked.
'About four minutes, sir.'
'Then get off as quickly as you can and tell him to continue to retreat at once. The Germans captured Albert half an hour ago. Make for Doullens. Either the Brigade Major or I will be at the Town Hall there to give you fresh orders. Hurry up — Forceville is only six miles from Albert.'[14]

The Germans had not captured Albert. Forceville was safe, as Behrend saw for himself when he met his colonel there:

The Colonel was still standing complacently in the middle of Forceville, surveying the neatly stretched-out brigade with a proud and fatherly eye. The lorry drivers were wiping down their lorries, the gunners were cleaning their guns. Billets had already been chosen for half the brigade; the other half had found their way into the estaminets.[15]

In the confusion of the retreat, Captain Behrend was called to the telephone:

'Is that you?' Major Pargiter asked in colder tones than usual. 'You know those rum jars you kindly sent us this afternoon?'[16]

'Yes, sir," I replied, and added politely, "You mean the ones the Colonel told you not to open till we get on the move again?'

'Yes, but that's not the point.'

'No, sir?'

'The point is they don't contain rum. They contain Nut Oil for Chinese Labourers.'*[17]

At first, Field Marshal Haig greeted the news of the Michael attack with equanimity. His reaction was as though his army had sustained only a limited reverse. His diary note for 21 March 1918 was

Very severe fighting on the Third and Fifth Army fronts continued well into the evening. Our men seem to be fighting magnificently ... Having regard to the great strength of the attack (*over* 30 extra divisions having reinforced those holding the original German front line for the battle) and the determined manner in which the attack was everywhere pressed, I consider that the result of the day is highly creditable to the British troops: I therefore sent a message of congratulation to the Third and Fifth Armies for communication to all ranks.[18]

---

*   The rum, which was dark and syrupy, came in jars marked SRD, which was said to stand for 'Soon Runs Dry'. It could only be issued when the Brigade Commander certified that the weather was inclement, which, according to the certificates, it mostly was.

On the 22 March 1918, he continued in the same vein: 'All reports show that our men are in great spirits. All speak of the wonderful targets they had to fire at yesterday.'[19] Haig did, however, call on the favour of French reserves. Pétain agreed to send help, but only three divisions.[20]

Wilson, on the other hand, did not see things in such a favourable light. In his diary on 22 March 1918, he wrote: 'The Boches are pushing on in an awkward way at Croiselles, and Roisel and south of the Oise. I don't understand why we are giving ground so quickly, nor how the Boches got through our battle zone so easily.'[21]

A note of urgency crept into the diary on 23 March 1918:

I then went to Villers-Bretonneux and saw General Gough Commanding Fifth Army. [I was surprised to learn that] his troops are now behind the Somme and the River Tortille. Men very tired after two days fighting and long march back. On the first day they had to wear gas masks all day which is very fatiguing, [but I cannot make out why the Fifth Army has gone so far back without making some kind of a stand] ... [22]

Haig was confronting two problems. The lesser problem was that the Fifth Army would become separated from the Third Army. The greater problem was that the entire British force would become separated from the French.[23] His diary for the 23rd continued:

Pétain is most anxious to do all he can to support me. The basic principle of co-operation is to keep the two Armies [French and British] in touch. If this is lost and the Enemy comes in between us, then probably the British will be rounded up and driven into the sea! This must be prevented even at the cost of abandoning the north flank.[24]

There was also the danger of losing Amiens. Not only was it a large town, it was also a vital railhead. The movement of troops by rail between Paris and the Channel ports was by two lines running simultaneously, each accommodating 24 trains per day. One line followed the coast, through Étaples and Abbeville. The other was further east, running through Arras. Both lines passed through Amiens.

The Arras line was so far to the east that it was threatened by the German advance. If it was forced to close, all operations would fall on the coastal route. Moreover, if Amiens fell, there would be no rail link between Paris and the Channel ports,[25] and the German path to the Channel would be clear.

The heights at Villers–Bretonneux overlooked Amiens. If the Germans could secure Villers–Bretonneux, it would be a short step to the fall of Amiens. More significantly, allowing a breach between the British and the French Armies would mean the undoing of the strategic approach that had been the foundation of Allied resistance on the western front since the war began.[26]

Whilst these dramas were unfolding on the Somme, the Australians were 60 miles north, following developments from Flanders.[27] The diggers were in high spirits, straining on the leash that was keeping them out of the action.[28]

Indeed, Australian morale at this stage was as high as the British was low. Captain Joynt had noticed the difference between Australian and British morale when he spoke to two British officers on his return from leave late in January 1918:

They told me that they dreaded going back to France to face the huge German offensive expected. One even said, 'We are going to take a terrible beating'. This sort of talk amazed me — it was so different from the Diggers' thoughts. Australian officers were hurrying back to France to 'be in it' and the Diggers were actually looking forward to it all. For the whole of the war they had been used as attacking troops and now it was their turn to sit behind prepared defences and shoot down the oncoming enemy. I heard a Digger say, 'This will do us for a change'. The Australian morale was never so high.[29]

Churchill agreed that it would be a pleasant change to fight a battle from entrenched and fortified defensive positions. Having inspected a Canadian sector of the line in February 1918, he was filled with confidence in the strength of the defensive system. He expressed his confidence in a language no digger would use: 'Holding the conviction [that the advantage rested with the defensive] under modern conditions, I looked forward, at least so far as this sector was concerned, to the day when the Germans would taste a measure of that bitter draught our armies had been made to drink so long.'[30]

On 25 March 1918, the Australian 3rd, 4th and 5th Divisions heard that they were to be sent south.[31] The 4th Division, under General Sinclair-MacLagan, left first. Its destination was Barly, south-west of Arras. At Barly, they found the old people of the village loading their possessions onto carts, ready to evacuate. When they learned the Australians had arrived, they began, one by one, to unpack. Asked why he was unpacking the cart, an old man answered, 'Pas necessaire maintenant — vous les tiendrez.'[32] When the remark was translated to a digger, he said, 'We'll have to see the old bloke isn't disappointed.'[33]

The 4th Brigade of the Australian 4th Division was sent to occupy Hébuterne, north of Albert and overlooking the Somme battlefield. On their way, they saw:

... evidence of rout everywhere in the disordered groups of British troops retiring along every road ... They all told of the nearness of the Boche and his tremendous resources of tanks and artillery. 'Jerry's got tanks galore!' we were told over and over again. The refugees told us similar news. Nine Staff Officers were crowded on a small car hastening to the rear. They were visibly nettled by the unkind remarks of our men, but they did not slacken speed. 'Thank God we've got a Navy,' a Digger grumbled.[34]

Despite reports that the Germans had taken Hébuterne, the diggers took it with little resistance, capturing only the 'ownerless fowls and rabbits' they found in the yards, with the result that, soon, 'the "pozzies" of some platoons became carpeted with feathers'.[35] The 4th Brigade held Hébuterne, whilst the remainder of the 4th Division, and the 3rd Division went into the main battle further south, in front of Amiens.

General Monash was on leave in the south of France when the German offensive began. Cutting short his leave, he arrived in Paris on the morning of 25 March 1918, and was soon heading towards Amiens, normally a vibrant, bustling town:

> At Amiens we found everything in a state of frightful confusion. The Boche had been heavily bombing the town and civilians were evacuating it rapidly. There was great excitement. The railway square and the streets were full of war-worn, mud-spattered, excited, and starved-looking troops of all kinds, and excited officers and other ranks who had been on leave and were struggling to get back to their units in various parts of the front. At Amiens, which is an important interchange station, all the normal activities of the city seemed to have been arrested. The railway transport officers and the military authorities in the town had no news of the events at the front, had been working for several days with their staff without sleep, and were in a condition of almost mental paralysis. The ordinary supply-depots had ceased to function; we could hardly get any petrol, and it was with some difficulty that we managed to get some lunch ...
>
> At Doullens there was still greater confusion and streams of soldier stragglers pouring in from the east with the most hair-raising stories that the Boche was almost on top of them. Viewed from that particular locality it almost looked as if the whole British Army in this part of the world was in a state of rout.[36]

In other parts of the front, it was not a rout, but, after four days of non-stop fighting, it was more a case of the tired chasing the worn out, as Captain Butler, an Australian officer of the 180th Tunnelling Company attested:

> There was never any rout of the troops, as far as he knew. They were simply tired and too dead to offer any resistance. We had heard how, when the Germans got up, our men would get up too, and the two lines would stroll along at a distance from one another, each trailing its arms, the Germans as tired as our men. Someone would take a shot. Then down both sides would fall and shoot at one another for a bit, and then on again.[37]

As Monash came from Paris by car, part of 3rd Division was on trains heading south from Flanders, and part was marching. Monash set about finding someone who could give him sensible orders what to do with the division when it arrived. It was no easy task. He later wrote:

> Over three years of trench warfare had accustomed the whole Army to fixed locations for all Headquarters, and settled routes and lines of communication. The powerful German onslaught and the recoil of a broad section of our fighting front had suddenly disturbed the whole of this complex organisation. The Headquarters of Brigades, Divisions, and even Corps, ceased to have fixed locations where they could be found, or assured lines of telegraph or telephone communications, by which they could be reached. Everything was in a state of flux, and the process of getting into personal contact with each other suddenly took responsible leaders hours where it had previously taken minutes.[38]

He found no one, but, on the morning of 26 March 1918, he did find the first of the trains carrying the 3rd Division arriving at Doullens station:

During the twenty four hours between my visits to [Doullens] there had been a great change in atmosphere. Doullens was full of civilian refugees and many thousands of soldiers who had got detached from their units and were streaming in from the east. All had the wildest stories and all looked starved and broken down with fatigue and want of sleep. There must have been a great conference between the British and French High Command in the Mairie[39] at Doullens, for the town square was packed full of motor cars and brilliantly uniformed French and British officers.[40]

While searching for his division and his orders, Monash had come to Doullens at the same time as the British and the French high commands met there to appoint General Foch as *generalissimo* to co-ordinate the response to the German offensive. So also had Driver Edmunds, one of the 3rd Division artillerymen who had marched from Flanders to the Somme:

We passed through St Paul and on to Doulens, where troop trains were disgorging some more of our Infantry.

To avoid congestion, the column passed through this town at a trot. The clatter and jingle of horse artillery over the cobble stones excited the inhabitants; they cheered us on with a Vive l'Australie. It was near here we received the command, 'Eyes left'. Strictly to attention, with our whip hand extended, we passed before a very distinguished group of Allied Generals, who critically examined the passing column. I recognised Marshal Foch and General Haig before we passed on.[41]

All roads led to Doullens that day.

In the confusion, and at ten o'clock on the night of 26 March 1918, Monash eventually found the chateau at Montigny which Lieutenant-General Congreve had made his temporary headquarters. Monash received orders from Congreve and his chief of staff, Brigadier-General Hore-Ruthven.[42] Both men had won the Victoria Cross:

They were seated at a little table with their maps spread in front of them, examining them by the light of a flickering candle. As I stepped into the room General Congreve said — 'Thank heaven, the Australians at last'. Our conversation was the briefest. He said — 'General, the position is very simple. My corps at four o'clock today was holding the line from Bray to Albert, when the line broke, and what is left of three divisions in the line after four days' heavy fighting without food or sleep are falling back rapidly. German cavalry have been seen approaching Morlancourt and Buire. They are making straight for Amiens. What I want you to do is get into the angle between the Ancre and the Somme as fast as possible and stop him.[43]

The Ancre River runs into the Somme at Corbie. The river junction is about nine miles south-east of Albert, two miles north of Villers-Bretonneux and nine miles east of Amiens. The Australians had been ordered to make a stand on the ridge running through Méricourt and Sailly-le-Sec between the Ancre and the Somme.

From Doullens, Monash moved to Franvillers, on the north bank of the Ancre. From there he could see the German cavalry operating on the high ground at Morlancourt, a mile or two to the east. It was touch and go whether the diggers would arrive in time to intercept them.[44]

They did, arriving in an unlikely convoy that 'consisted of sixty motor buses, old London motor bus type, all crowded with troops, fully armed and with plenty of ammunition'.[45] It sounds a shambles, but Monash called it 'a miracle of good management'.[46]

By two o'clock in the afternoon of 27 March 1918, the buses had shuttled over 5000 troops to Monash at Franvillers. These men took up positions on the ridge. The ridge, which formed the base of a triangle completed by the confluence of the Somme and the Ancre, stood in the path of the German advance.[47]

Moreover, many of the retiring British were anxious to join with the Australians. Major Wieck wrote that:

it was simply amazing how many British units, parts of the retiring troops, reported themselves [to the 3rd Division headquarters at Franvillers] saying that they were quite ready to fight so long as they could find someone to co-operate with or take orders from. They were mostly gunners, and their support at this time gave us a most comfortable feeling.[48]

Monash posted military policemen to gather these men together and form them into units that could be turned to good use when needed.[49]

In the meantime, the diggers who had missed the buses, or could not fit on them — two brigades of artillery (among them Driver Edmunds), the divisional ammunition column, the pioneer battalion and sundry others — were marching to their positions on the ridge. All day they marched into a throng of French refugees. The *Official History*:

> As far as the eye could see ... came carts lurching with towering loads, precious mattresses, bedsteads, washstands, picture frames piled together with chairs, brooms, sauce-pans, buckets, the aged driver perched in front upon a pile of hay for the old horse; the family cow — and sometimes calves, or goat — towed behind by a rope or driven by an old woman or small boys or girls on foot. One old man, whose wife was too sick to walk, was wheeling her before him in a barrow. In this retreating stream there were also withdrawing, by order, British heavy artillery and transport. As the howitzers rumbled past the Australian infantry, 'gangs of Tommies accompanying them ... would stare ... and vary their "Hy, lookout, Jerry's coming!" with sarcastic comments such as "You're going the wrong way, Digger — Jerry'll souvenir you and your [expletive] band too"'.[50]

When Corporal Campbell marched from Doullens to Behencourt, he wrote home that:

Fritz was playing havoc with the 5th Army ... The road ... was crowded with civilians and Tommy soldiers all fleeing for their lives from the enemy. We found houses just as the people had left them, washing still on the lines and meals half eaten. Poor people! It was pitiable to see the poor old women and little children trudging along the roads, carrying their few valuables with them. However, the arrival of the Australians cheered them up a lot, because they knew that the enemy would bump troops who would not run away.[51]

If the plight of the civilians was pitiable, and the retreat a shambles, it was not for want of planning. The Second Army, for example, had a system for the local mairie[52] to notify evacuees who were to leave by roads not needed by the military and make their way to train stations whence they could be taken to safety. For the different types of supernumeraries, a different protocol had been developed:

In addition to the combatant troops of each Army, there was in each Army area a very large amount of skilled and unskilled labour employed on a great variety of work. There were army troops companies, tunneling companies, entrenching battalions, white and native labour companies, prisoner of war companies and other personnel employed by the various services and departments; there were also civilians and there might be newly-captured prisoners of war. Lists were prepared of each category showing how it was employed and who would issue orders for its withdrawal.[53]

Odds and sods like these swelled the numbers of evacuees crowding the roads that day.

An Australian Lieutenant, marching at the head of his platoon, was concerned at first that the depressing scenes of retreat would dishearten his men, but they were unfazed:

... from the little band of my command [I] heard whistling, laughter and jokes, I was vastly proud of being an Australian soldier ... At one of our halts, when a group of middle-aged Tommies from a labour battalion asked for cigarettes and said in awe-inspired voices that it was impossible to stop the Boches — as they were 'coming over in swarms,' I heard one of my platoon remark to his pal: 'Strewth, Bill, we'll get some souvenirs now.'[54]

Driver Edmunds, too, was excited at the prospect:

The Germans, with Amiens in sight, were advancing under their artillery barrage, the main thrust being down the valley of the Somme. If they could brush the Australians aside (only part of the Corps was here yet) the Channel ports would be theirs and the division of the British and French Armies accomplished. No doubt Ludendorff, the Chief of Staff of the German Command, was awaiting the events of that day with keen anticipation. Almost as soon as the barrage opened, our O.C. received his orders. We pulled out of the quarry and ascended the hill; we reached the crest, and today the memory of the panorama before our eyes from that hilltop is as vivid as on that early morning so long ago. I remember thinking what a scene, if only an artist could record his impressions on canvas from here.

We were looking up the valley of the Somme towards Hamel about a mile and a half away; our view of the battle extended from Villers-Bretonneux on the right to Hamel, then over the Somme to wooded broken ground on the left.[55]

The view Edmunds describes is the view from the Australian War Memorial, majestically situated on the heights north of Villers-Bretonneux. It is a sweeping, breathtaking view — one of the finest in all the battlefields. Standing there, looking down on the valley below, it is impossible not to admire the Germans, who, exhausted after seven days of hard fighting, had the courage and determination to mount an attack up the open ground of that forbidding hill.

By the morning of 28 March 1918, most of the 3rd Division was in position, waiting for the Germans.[56] Monash sent out patrols, probing eastwards. The patrols made contact with the enemy, who came on up the hill under the cover of brief, hurricane bombardments.[57] The German attack was easily repelled with artillery and machine gun fire.[58]

The same day, the 4th Division began arriving, taking up positions to the north of the 3rd Division, overlooking Albert.[59] By 29 March 1918, the 4th Division had completed its move, and the 5th Division was beginning to arrive. The 5th was in reserve at Senlis.[60] By the end of March, there was a strong and determined Australian front between the Germans and Amiens.[61]

Their frontal attack repulsed, the Germans paused a few days to sort themselves out, and bring up artillery. On 4 April 1918, they struck again, advancing though Hamel, on the flat ground below the Villers-Bretonneux heights. Halted there, the Germans switched the point of attack south of Villers-Bretonneux, where they captured Hangard Wood.[62]

Further north, the 4th Brigade and the New Zealanders repulsed a new attack at Hébuterne.[63] That day and the next, still to the north, the Germans attacked the 4th Division between Dernancourt and Albert. The attack, although heavy, was defeated.[64]

The tide was beginning to turn. As the advance pushed forward, the Germans were outrunning their supplies and their artillery support. Churchill quotes Ludendorff:

The enemy's line was now becoming denser and in places they were even attacking themselves; while our armies were no longer strong enough to overcome them unaided. The ammunition was not sufficient, and supply became difficult. The repair of roads and railways was taking too long, in spite of all our preparations. After thoroughly replenishing ammunition … on 4th April the Second Army and the right wing of the Eighteenth attacked at Albert, south of the Somme towards Amiens. These actions were indecisive. It was an established fact that the enemy's resistance was beyond our strength ... The battle was over by April 4.[65]

Churchill argued that Operation Michael was a failure.[66] True it was that the attack had not achieved the grand objectives that Churchill claimed were Ludenforff's aims, but judged against the objective — 'We will punch a hole ... For the rest, we shall see' —[67] the attack had been a superb success.

In the end, the German attack bore out the Allies' experience of attacking across the trench lines. The advantage did lie with the defender. The German offensive had succeeded in taking more ground than any of the Passchendaele battles, but it ultimately broke down for many of the same reasons that had caused the British to limit themselves to the bite-and-hold tactics at Messines and in the Passchendaele battles. The German infantry eventually outran its supplies of food, water and ammunition. They halted for want of artillery support. They bogged down in the churned up mud and dirt of the abandoned trenches. They were simply too tired to go on.

Indeed, Operation Michael could be seen as the Somme in reverse. Now it was the Germans who were coming on shoulder to shoulder.[68] It was their turn to push home the attack, regardless of the cost; their turn to pay 'the price of victory'.

Standing on the defensive, the British exacted a full toll, just as the Germans had at the Somme. Whatever the stories of rout and disarray, the vast majority of British soldiers stuck manfully to their task. In March and April 1918, the British fired nearly nine million 18-pounder shells, and a total of over 15 million shells, including nearly four million heavy shells.[69]

Although they were outnumbered, by their persistence, the British, Australian and French had held back the German advance long enough for it to collapse under its own weight.

On the Somme, the collapse of the advance came on the outskirts of Villers-Bretonneux.

CHAPTER SIXTEEN

VILLERS-BRETONNEUX

It was not until 11 April 1918 that Field Marshal Haig revealed the pressures and emotions that were bearing on him as he defended this great battle. He wrote a message to 'To all Ranks of the British Forces in France':

Three weeks ago today the Enemy began his terrific attacks against us on a 50 mile front. His objects are to separate us from the French, to take the Channel ports and destroy the British Army.

In spite of throwing already 106 divisions into the battle and enduring the most reckless sacrifice of human life, he has yet made little progress towards his goals.

We owe this to the determined fighting and self-sacrifice of our troops. Words fail me to express the admiration which I feel for the splendid resistance offered by all ranks of our Army under the most trying circumstances.

Many amongst us are now tired. To those I would say that victory will belong to the side which holds out longest. The French Army is moving rapidly and in great force to our support.

There is no other course open to us but to fight it out. Every position must be held to the last man: there must be no retirement. With our backs to the wall, and believing in the justice of our cause, each one of us must fight on to the end. The safety of our homes and the freedom of mankind alike depend on the conduct of each of us at this critical moment.

Thursday 11 April 1918

D. Haig. F.M.[2]

In the handwritten version of this note, there are but three minor corrections. For a man said to be inarticulate and tongue-tied, it is a superb piece of writing. Direct, simple and beautifully expressed, it shows heart, sympathy and genuine courage. Why did this man fight so hard to conceal these qualities within himself?

As well written as Haig's note was, it was also curiously belated. When the note was issued, the German attack was already coming under control. According to General Godley, the note caused considerable amusement among his men, who knew perfectly well that they had had 'their backs to the wall since March, and did not need to be told it'.[3]

Some of the British were embarrassed that Haig had let the side down by expressing emotions in public. 'Which bloody wall?' they asked.

As their advance in the valley of the Somme was showing signs of slowing, the Germans had turned their attention further north. On 9 April 1918, they had launched an attack between Armentières and Messines. Again, luck was with them, as they made windfall gains against an unmotivated Portuguese Corps that fled, almost without firing a shot in anger, and against exhausted British troops from the Somme who had recently replaced the Australian 1st and 2nd Divisions when they had been ordered south to the Somme.[4]

After this unexpected success, the German attack in the north had penetrated far enough to threaten Hazebrouck, which was only twenty miles from the coast, and was another important rail link.[5] In response to this new crisis, the Australian 1st Division, which had just arrived in Amiens, was ordered back to the train station to return north. Fortunately, the emergency arrangements for the railway at Amiens had held up well, even though the troop movements at this time were the most intense of the whole war.[6]

The 1st Division arrived back in Hazebrouck on 12 April 1918. The German attack did not fall until 17 April 1918, when the 1st Division joined the French and British in repelling the attack. The Germans were confined to limited gains west of Messines.[7]

In hindsight, the attack on Hazebrouck was seen as a feint, with the real goal of the Germans still being Amiens.[8] Three Australian Divisions now held the approach to Amiens: the 4th in the north; the 3rd in its old positions between the Somme and the Ancre, and the 5th to the south of the Somme, between the 3rd Division and the French.[9]

In these positions, the diggers had front row seats to watch the dogfights between the fighter planes overhead. Fighter planes had developed to the point that their pilots had become famous as flying aces — some with large numbers of kills to their names. The most famous of all was the 'Red Baron', Baron Manfred von Richthofen, who took his nickname from his bright red Fokker DR-1 Dridecker fighter plane. He had 80 Allied kills to his name.

In April 1918, his squadron was flying from an airstrip at Cappy, only a few miles down the Somme valley from the Australian front. On 22 April 1918, the Baron started a dogfight with a British airman, Lieutenant May. May tried to escape by flying his Sopwith Camel low and fast along the line of the Somme towards the Allied lines. A Canadian pilot, Captain Brown, was, in turn, chasing von Richthofen, and firing at his plane.

May flew low over the lines of the 3rd and 5th Divisions. Von Richthofen followed at tree-top height. Australians from both divisions blazed away with their Lewis guns as the Baron pulled back on his tri-plane to clear the spur on the north bank of the river. Suddenly, the tri-plane spiralled out of control and crashed into a field.

Von Richthofen was dead, shot through the chest. Captain Brown claimed (and the air force awarded him) the kill. Lieutenant Quinlan, an Australian who was watching from the south bank of the river, said that, 'Every Lewis gun was potting at Richthofen and everyone claimed the honour of eventually bringing him down.'[10]

Autopsy evidence showed that the exit wound of the fatal bullet was higher in the body than the entry wound. Some have interpreted this as evidence that the fatal shot was fired from the ground, not the air. If that is true, Bean believed that it was a Queenslander, Sergeant Popkin, who fired the fatal shot,[11] but Monash attributed the kill to the battery cook and the assistant cook of one of General Hobbs' artillery batteries, without naming either of them.[12]

Whatever may be the truth of the mystery of who killed the Red Baron, the downing of his plane so close to the Australian lines was a first rate opportunity to indulge the Australian penchant for looting. Joe Maxwell wrote later: 'An hour after the gallant ace had crashed and his identity had been established there were sufficient pieces of aeroplane,

Officers of the Australian Flying Corps bury Baron von Richthofen with full military honours, 22 April 1918. General Monash gave credit for downing the legendary pilot, who had 80 Allied kills to his name, to an unknown battery cook and an assistant cook. AWM P00743.039

General Glasgow, on the left, and his staff pose with Pete the dog on 25 April 1918, the day of the battle for Villers-Bretonneux. Glasgow's skill at disputing unacceptable orders politely was pivotal to this battle's success. AWM E02135

all claimed by their possessors to be a piece of Richthofen's machine, to have been assembled into an entire squadron.'[13]

The Australians buried von Richthofen with the respect and military honours that he deserved.★

Gratifying as it was to help bring down the Red Baron, the main role of the Australian divisions in these positions was the defence of Villers-Bretonneux, and, in turn, of Amiens.

On 24 April 1918, two tired British divisions relieved the Australians on the front between Villers-Bretonneux and Hangard Wood to the south. The very day of the relief, the Germans attacked the positions that these troops had taken over. For the first time in the war, the Germans attacked with tanks — thirteen of them — and a fog covered the advance of the infantry behind the tanks.

★   After von Richthofen's death, the command of his flight passed to none other than Hermann Goering, who was a decorated fighter pilot in the First War and the Commander of the Luftwaffe in the next.

The Germans went through the defenders, across the crest of the all-important heights, taking Villers–Bretonneux and Abbey Wood, and laying open the way to Amiens.[14] Three British tanks saw off the German tanks, and whippet tanks scattered some of the German infantry, but there was no effective counterattack at first, and the Germans remained in Villers–Bretonneux.

The town had to be recovered. That responsibility fell to the Australians.

The attack was to be a pincer movement. 15th Brigade, from the 5th Division, was to form one of the pincers, and 13th Brigade, from the 4th Division, the other. Emphasising the *ad hoc* nature of the preparations, these two brigades would fight under a British general, Lieutenant General Butler, who was in command of British III Corps.[15]

General Birdwood claims to have given General Hobbs (commanding the Australian 5th Division) the idea of a pincer movement.[16] General Rawlinson claims to have given the same idea to General Butler, and to have sent one of his staff officers to make sure there were no changes.[17] Success has many fathers.

In fact, as events demonstrate, the credit for the plan rests with the commanders of the Australian brigades. The 13th Brigade, under General Glasgow, would form the southern pincer. The 15th Brigade, under General Elliott, would form the northern pincer.

After a brief reconnaissance of the ground, Glasgow took up the planning of the attack with General Heneker, who was commanding the British 8th Division. They met at 2.30 in the afternoon. The attack was planned for that night. Under pressure from Generals Rawlinson and Butler,[18] General Heneker was, in turn, pressuring Glasgow to make a dangerous attack on short notice. To make things worse, he wanted to dictate how and when it should be done — quickly, and without adequate preparation. The spectre of General Gough had returned.

Heneker and Glasgow agreed that it would be a surprise attack, with no bombardment and no creeping barrage. From that point, there was only disagreement. Glasgow had chosen a different start line than General Butler:

Heneker: But you can't do that. The Corps Commander says the attack is to be made from Cachy.

Glasgow: I will not do it that way. Why, it is against all the teaching of your own army, Sir, to attack across the enemy's front. They'd get hell from the right.

Glasgow's start line would avoid this risk.

Glasgow: Tell us what you want us to do, Sir, but you must let us do it our own way.

The British also wanted also to dictate the time of the attack.

Glasgow: What about the time? You must coordinate that, Sir.

Heneker: The Corps Commander wishes it done at 8.

Glasgow: If it was God Almighty who gave the order, we couldn't do it in daylight. Here is your artillery largely out of action and the enemy with all guns in position.[19]

After more negotiation, they settled on 10.00 pm.

The painful lessons of 1916 and 1917 had taught Glasgow to resist impulsive suggestions from British officers who would not themselves be taking part in the fight. Moreover, he had developed the skills to dispute unacceptable orders politely, and with a proper military bearing.

It was not until 8.00 pm that Glasgow met Elliott for the first time to coordinate their attacks. There was precious little time for any disagreement between them, and there was none. The advantages that Monash had described, of close and constant association between divisions and commanders, and the mutual trust and confidence that close association brought, were never more apparent.

Glasgow and Elliott settled their plans in a few minutes, with Elliott agreeing to a last minute change proposed by Glasgow.[20] They passed on their orders to the battalion commanders, who in turn, passed them on to the men. None of the junior officers had even seen the ground for the attack, nor for the approach.[21]

When the 13th Brigade assembled at its start point, it was still light. The Germans in the woods to the north saw them and opened fire. Lieutenant Sadlier and Sergeant Stokes decided to deviate from orders by clearing out the machine guns in the woods. They bombed out six machine guns, the lieutenant winning the Victoria Cross and the sergeant the Distinguished Conduct Medal.[22] This cleared the way for the attack. Both brigades rushed on cheering wildly:

With a ferocious roar and cry of 'Into the bastards, boys,' we were down on them before the Boche realized what had happened. The Boche were at our mercy. They screamed for mercy but there were too many machine-guns about to show them any consideration as we were moving forward.

With a cheer that would have turned a tribe of Red Indians green with envy we 'hopped the bags' … Each man was in his glee and old scores were wiped out two or three times over.[23]

Sergeant Downing, attacking with the 15th Brigade, remembered the noise of the men cheering:

The wild cry [from the 15th Brigade] rose to a voluminous, vengeful roar that was heard by the 13th Brigade far on the right of Villers-Bretonneux. Cheering, our men rushed straight to muzzles of machine-guns, not troubling to take them in the flank. There was no quarter on either side. Germans continued to fire their machine-guns, although transfixed by bayonets … and though they were brave and far outnumbered the Australians, they had no chance in the wild onslaught of maddened men … [The Australians] killed and killed. Bayonets passed with ease through grey-clad bodies, and were withdrawn with a sucking noise.[24]

Eventually the two brigades linked up at the eastern end of the town. From there they turned back to the west and, with the assistance of two battalions of the British 8th Division who came from the north and west of the town, they mopped up the remaining Germans. When the battle was over:

> ... there was a weird silence. An extraordinary scene then took place. 'Markers' were set out as if it were an ordinary parade ground, and a thousand men fell in in two ranks, in close order, dressed by the right, and were numbered and checked by platoon commanders. The lurid glare of the burning houses in the town shone fitfully on the quiet ranks, where each man stood erect and steady with his rifle at the order, bloody, shining bayonet fixed, the flames reflected at intervals on all our faces.[25]

The battle cost the Australians 1009 casualties in the 13th Brigade, and 455 in the 15th. The battle for Villers-Bretonneux had been relatively costly, but the result had a disproportionate strategic influence on the course, and outcome, of the war.[26] General Birdwood's assessment was: 'From that day the Germans never advanced a foot. For them it was the beginning of the end. I have always maintained that this action was the great turning point of the war ...'[27]

Lieutenant Rule thought the Germans may have dropped their guard after capturing the town: 'Liquor being very plentiful and the cellars easily entered, no doubt the Huns were a muddled lot by [the time of the Australian attack].'[28] The place was littered with empty bottles when the Australians arrived, and with more by the time they left. Germans and Australians took turns at looting the houses, with many diggers taking the chance to change 'their old dirty stuff for beautiful chemises with pretty pink ribbons' or to change their underpants 'for garments never made for men'.[29]

The great German offensive, Operation Michael, was spent. Germany had gambled all her reserves in an attempt to 'break through'. It was a gambler's throw,[30] and it had not come off.

Villers-Bretonneux stands at the forefront of the honours of the 13th and 15th Brigades. By taking back the village in a highly complex, coordinated manoeuvre, made at short notice, made at night, made without any detailed reconnaissance, made without bombardment or barrage, and carried by vicious hand-to-hand fighting, they achieved a victory that could only have been won by men in the peak of training, and in the peak of morale.

By retaining Amiens, and maintaining the connection between the French and British armies, the Australians had preserved intact the grand strategy of the Allied war plan.

The battle for Villers-Bretonneux was won — on the third Anzac Day.

CHAPTER SEVENTEEN

HAMEL

By 1 May 1918, all the Australian divisions, except the 1st, had taken up positions on the extreme right of the British line, adjacent, once again, to the French.[1] The 1st Division remained in Flanders, in front of Hazebrouck.

The Australian Corps formed part of the British Fourth Army, under the command of General Rawlinson. It held the line from Cachy in the south to Ville in the north — a total of ten miles. Villers-Bretonneux lay behind the Australian lines in the south. Morlancourt lay in front of the Australian lines in the north. Hamel, also in front of the Australian lines, lay on flat country in the centre, just south of the Somme.

Sergeant Linton spent his watch on 11 June 1918 looking on as the Germans bombed Amiens:

> It makes one's blood boil, especially when one remembers that there
> is hardly a soul in the place, everybody having cleared out when a
> couple of months ago it seemed a dead cert for Fritz. But our little
> Aussie Army came to the rescue (only two Divisions — 3rd and 4th
> — for the first week of the rush after the British Bulldogs had

turned it up and were scattering in all directions, and stopped the Huns mad rush for Amiens and Paris. Possibly the above sounds rather big talk, but the French soldiers, alongside whom our chaps are now fighting, swear by the Aussies, giving them every credit for the work they did on this Sector. The Tommies name here is 'mud' and the French people that still remain around these parts (they are few and far between) boil the situation down to the following:

English Tommy (not Scots or Irish)	No bon
Frenchman	Tra bon
Australian	Tra Tra Tra bon

You just ought to hear them say it.[2]

The Australian Divisions rotated, with three in the front line, and one in reserve. In May 1918, a company of the 21st Battalion in reserve at Querrieu, five miles behind the lines, was camping in the outhouses and

Five miles behind the lines, Brewery Farm, Querrieu, was the home of the Australian 21st Battalion in May 1918. Grooms water horses in the canal. AWM E04884

In a world away from the front line diggers read, smoked and played cards.
AWM E02168

barns of Brewery Farm.[3] Most of the men slept on straw in lofts around the yard. Ladders reached from the yard to the loft windows. In the room where the farm wagons were once kept, a table and chairs had been rigged up, and a game of cards was in progress: 'strong faces, loose brown khaki clothes, dashing old hats, strong sun-browned faces intent on the game; easy, strong virile attitudes of half a dozen players and onlookers'.[4]

The first to stir in the morning were the cooks, lighting fires, making tea, porridge and bacon. Odd men woke early, climbing down the ladders with their towels to wash in the stream that flowed past the house.

Breakfast was served in mess tins and pannikins, or mess tins and mess tin lids. Parade was not until nine o'clock. In the meantime, men cleaned rifles or polished boots. A corporal called: '"Turn out the sickers". A few men, three or four, some looking really worn out, and mostly seedy, move across the yard and disappear.'[5]

The *Official History* continued:

The cooks are fidgeting around their cooker, one in a guernsey, another in singlet, and trousers — each in his hat and smoking all the while either a pipe or a cigarette. They take the chaff⁶ as a duck is supposed to take rain — let it run off their backs while the good-humoured creases around their eyes never alter.⁷

The cook of the 5th Battalion was himself a source of humour. A W Keown recounted that he called a walk with a French girl 'a promenade with a nice little bint up that there revenue of popular trees'; he translated an order for the men not to loiter in the cooks' lines as, 'Yer not allowed to hang round the virginity of the Cooks' lines'; and said that the man who had gone to the Ordnance Store had 'gone down to Audience'.⁸

The scene was rather different at General Monash's headquarters. These were situated in Bertangles, in what Monash described as a 'handsome seventeenth-century Château ... with ... pleasant grounds and spacious parks'.⁹ In fact it was a glorious house, on the scale of Versailles, not unlike

There was even time for a hair cut. AWM E00029

'The cooks are fidgeting around their cooker': slicing bacon on the left; making bully beef rissoles on the right. AWM E01064

the chateau that General Plumer occupied in 1915, where the officers 'heard nightingales sing in the garden and chatted to Plumer as he fed the ducks in his artificial pond'.[10] For Monash, as for Plumer:

> The contrast between life in such surroundings and that of the frontline troops, even when they were out at rest, was indeed stark, but staff officers and their generals had to live and work somewhere, and the château provided the space required for transport parks, telephone exchanges and wireless telegraphy centres. But it was hardly surprising that Plumer [and Monash] had to work hard to attempt to reduce the inevitable alienation that resulted.[11]

At Querrieu, the men paraded. The roll was called. The men marched out for a 'special exercise in outpost work'. They worked until midday, when they returned for lunch. They worked again for a couple of hours in the afternoon.

When they returned after work in the afternoon, a cart delivered fresh bread, and tea was served. There was jam, chocolate and a packet of biscuits. The regimental band came to play to men who sat under the apple trees to listen:

An old French miller or baker or some relic of the population of the place came out from one of the outhouses … and started to argue with an Australian driver who was letting two horses feed (while he held their reins) on the long grass of the orchard. [The old man] quivered with the rage of his argument, shook his fist in the Australian's face, gesticulated with long skinny quivering fingers — the Australian looked at him in a stolid, interested way, and made absolutely no change in his attitude or his occupation. The old miller went away … and fetched a long stick like a whip handle … as if to frighten the horses — and at last went away shaking his fist, the Australian never once having moved anything except his head, or shifted his weight from one foot to another.[12]

One hundred men of each Australian Division parade for King George V at Bertangles after the battle of 8 August 1918. The King told General Monash he hoped the captured German horses would soon learn to speak Australian. AWM E03895

Games of two-up began, with seventy or eighty in one school, and twenty or so in another. The spruiker cried: 'You come here in rags and go away in motor cars.'[13] The strange Australian argot was everywhere:

> The language in the yard is such that you'ld think there was going to be a knifing every two minutes. 'Ah [expletive] you, you lazy bastard'. 'Go to [expletive], to hell wid yer'. 'Would yer, yer bastard!' — and you look out the window and find that it is all spoken with a grin …
>
> The long-range British gun behind the village goes off with a tremendous bang. From the yard: 'Oh Jesus! Cut it out!' Another: 'Here, I'm off.'[14]

'Outpost work' was a name given to the new style of attack that the diggers were developing. They quickly became bored with sitting on the defensive, and so invented a new style of attack by which they approached German outposts quietly and under cover, and 'cut out' the outpost.[15]

The 1st Division was responsible for the first instance of cutting out an outpost. The ditches and hedgerows at Hazebrouck gave good cover for the approach, and the diggers had good success in using the technique to kill and capture Germans. They planned the attacks themselves, without input from higher command. On 11 July 1918, the 1st Division took over 1000 yards of the German line and captured 120 prisoners (including three officers) and eleven machine guns.[16]

Before the war, the popular press had often complained that German capitalism was taking over the British Empire more surely than the German military ever could. They had a name for this process: 'peaceful penetration'. This was the name that the diggers gave to the new style of attack.[17]

The technique of peaceful penetration spread, almost by osmosis, to the Divisions on the Somme. On 5 April 1918, a corporal of the 58th Battalion used the technique to capture 32 Germans near Hamel.[18]

The attacks became almost daily events. 3rd Division, for example, captured German prisoners on 41 separate occasions between 27 March 1918 and 11 May 1918.[19] There was less natural cover in the Somme, but as the crops grew over summer, the diggers took advantage of the cover they increasingly afforded.[20]

In May 1918, Field Marshal Haig promoted General Birdwood to replace General Gough as commander of the British Fifth Army. Consistent with the Australian government's policy of appointing Australian officers to commands in the Australian Corps, this was an opportunity to appoint an Australian general to command the entire Australian Corps. The choice was between Monash, who had been so successful in command of the 3rd Division, and White, who had distinguished himself as Birdwood's chief of staff and as the architect of the split that saw the birth of the new 4th and 5th Divisions from the old 1st and 2nd.

Bean and Birdwood favoured White as the new commander. Keith Murdoch (father of Rupert Murdoch, who did not hesitate to pull strings where the AIF was concerned) favoured Monash.[21] A compromise, in which Monash would take administrative command and White would command the corps, was also floated.[22] Monash was senior to White. Moreover, Haig preferred Monash and so, reluctantly, did Birdwood, although he found the choice between the two invidious, and agonising.[23]

Haig prevailed. Monash was appointed to the command of the Australian Army Corps. In addition to the command of the Fifth Army, Birdwood retained a role as administrative commander of the AIF, and White was promoted to accompany Birdwood to the Fifth Army as chief of its general staff.[24]

Captain Joynt gave the men's reaction to the change of command:

We admired Birdwood and were sorry to see him go. We did not know Monash so did not have the same affection for him as we had for Birdwood, nor did we of the older divisions think much of the

3rd Division that he commanded [whom we thought of as] 'new chums'. However, a remarkable change of opinion came over us all in the 1st Division when we heard from officers of the British division that had come up from the Somme and relieved us after Nieppe Forest, how well the 3rd Division had done in stopping the Huns opposite Amiens, and what a name that Division had made for Australia. From this moment we accepted them as our equals and were proud to have General Monash as the leader of what was now virtually the Australian Army ...

We were not sorry to see Gough go. Australian troops had suffered much by his mishandling of them, particularly after the battle of Pozières ... [25]

Monash was an astute student of tactics. He, and the 3rd Division, had fought under Plumer at Messines and at Polygon Wood. They had also taken part in the ill-fated attack on the Passchendaele ridge, and had fought stoutly in turning back the Germans in front of Amiens.

General Monash, seated, poses with his staff in the grounds at Bertangles. 'Like that great prototype (Napoleon) he ranged leagues beyond the intellectual confines of most soldiers'. AWM E03186

In 1918, Monash was 53 years of age. He had been born in Melbourne of German-Jewish parents. He was educated at Scotch College and Melbourne University, from which he graduated with degrees in engineering, arts and law. The *Official History* commented:

In his intellectual development John Monash was as catholic as Napoleon; his mind knew no horizon except that of the universe, and every item of knowledge that it daily acquired was docketed for future use. Like that great prototype [Napoleon] he ranged leagues beyond the intellectual confines of most soldiers.[26]

An engineer and a lawyer by profession, a citizen-soldier by interest, and a meticulous, logical and careful man by nature, Monash had absorbed from Plumer the lessons of thorough preparation. Before Messines, Plumer spent the afternoon of 18 May 1917 with Monash, 'going patiently and minutely through the whole of [his] plans'.[27]

Monash also held to Harington's concept of the role of the staff: 'Harington's doctrine, that all staff exists to help units and not to make difficulties for them, is the only one that can lead to success, and I am constantly preaching that doctrine myself.'[28]

Monash was ambitious, even pushy, and, like many commanders, was anxious that his superiors should have a good opinion of him and his achievements. He exercised his command from his headquarters, rarely visiting his men, but turning out large volumes of paperwork in the form of orders and checklists. His orders were voluminous and detailed — his orders for the Messines battle, which Monash called his *magnum opus*,[29] were outlined in 36 separate circulars, including one for the machine gunners that ran to seven parts.[30] Monash's orders were as long as Holmes' were short.[31]

But Monash was much more than a paper shuffler. He could expound his plans in meetings with clarity and in detail. Like Plumer, he held regular conferences of his own commanders, when questions were invited and problems solved. When the plan had been settled, however, Monash permitted no changes, no matter how tempting. 'Fixity of plan engendered a confidence throughout the whole command which facilitated the work of every Commander and Staff Officer.'[32]

In his aptitude for office-work, he challenged Brudenell White. In his reluctance to spend time visiting his men, he stood in contrast to Plumer, Birdwood, Harington and Haig.

His intellectual disposition led him to identify, and articulate, the principles on which he based his command decisions. His approach in this regard differed from that of Haig and the British high command, who were uncomfortable questioning the theoretical basis of their actions. Indeed, Monash's search for doctrine was more typical of the German military than the British.[33]

In a letter home on 14 June 1917, a week after the Messines battle, Monash affirmed his belief in the bite-and-hold approach:

I am the greatest possible believer in the theory of the limited objective. So long as we can hold and retain the initiative we can in this way inflict the maximum of losses when and where we like. It restores to the offensive the advantages which are natural to the defensive in an unlimited objective.[34]

Monash expounded the doctrine that underpinned his planning and orders in the following terms:

I had formed the theory that the true role of the Infantry was not to expend itself upon heroic physical effort, nor to whither away under merciless machine-gun fire, nor to impale itself on hostile bayonets, nor to tear itself to pieces in hostile entanglements — (I am thinking of Pozières and Stormy Trench and Bullecourt, and other bloody fields) — but, on the contrary, to advance under the maximum possible array of mechanical resources, in the form of guns, machine guns, tanks, mortars and aeroplanes; to advance with as little impediment as possible; to be relieved as far as possible of the obligation to *fight* their way forward; to march resolutely, regardless of the din and tumult of the battle, to the appointed goal; and there to hold and defend the territory gained; and to gather in the form of prisoners, guns and stores, the fruits of victory.[35]

Monash's blueprint for a battle plan stood in contrast with Haig's empty precepts that the loss of men was the 'price of victory';[36] that this was a 'serious, scientific war';[37] and that results were best achieved by 'steady, methodical step-by-step advance'.[38]

The Monash blueprint reminded the staff that its job was to minimise the price of victory — not mindlessly to pay it.

When Monash took command of the Australian Corps, the two remaining British commanders of Australian divisions, Generals Walker and Smyth, were also promoted and replaced with Australian officers. For the first time, every senior command in the Australian Corps was held by an Australian officer.[39]

The full complement from June 1918 was General Monash as corps commander; General Blamey as his chief of staff; General Glasgow in command of 1st Division; General Rosenthal the 2nd; General Gellibrand the 3rd; General Sinclair-MacLagan continued in command of the 4th Division; and General Hobbs of the 5th.[40]

This line-up remained the same until the fighting finished.

When he took his command in May 1918, Monash was anxious that the Australians should be the first to resume the offensive.[41] The tactics of peaceful penetration had advanced the northern part of the line, held by 3rd Division, but the centre of the line, at Hamel, remained where it had been in March. As the 3rd Division advanced, the German line at Hamel increasingly formed a salient from which the Germans could fire on the right flank of the 3rd Division. Monash had discussed with

Rawlinson the idea of a limited operation to straighten the line and eliminate the salient. Their early planning foundered on lack of manpower and resources.

At this time, Rawlinson and Monash received an invitation from General Elles, the commander of the Tank Corps, inviting them to see the newest tank that had just arrived in France: the Mark V. The Australians retained their low opinion of tanks, formed from the bitter experience of Bullecourt. The success at Cambrai had demonstrated that tanks could be decisive if used in suitable conditions. Monash, being open-minded to new technology, was prepared to see how the new tanks performed.

Rawlinson, Monash and Blamey saw the tank demonstration. It set them all thinking in the same direction: perhaps the tanks could be used for the proposed operation at Hamel.[42]

On 21 June 1918, Monash wrote to Rawlinson outlining a scheme to retake Hamel.[43] The operation would be primarily a tank operation. It would use one division, and be under the control of one divisional commander. The tanks would capture the ground. The infantry would follow the tanks to help reduce strong points, to mop up, and to consolidate captured ground. Artillery, machine gun and transport support would come mainly from within the Australian Corps. In short, the operation could be run on a relative shoe-string, but as Monash realised, there was a possible down side:

In view of the unsatisfactory position of Australian reinforcements, any substantial loss would precipitate the time when the question of the reduction in the number of Australian Divisions would have to be seriously considered. It is for higher authority to decide whether a portion of the present resources would be more profitably ventured upon such an operation as this, which is in itself a very attractive proposition, rather than to conserve such resources for employment elsewhere.[44]

Monash had not altogether lost his suspicion of tanks, nor had he forgotten the lessons of Bullecourt. He was adamant about one aspect of the scheme:

> Valuable training in the joint action of Tanks and Infantry can be arranged, probably in the territory west of the HALLUE VALLEY — provided that one or two Tank Companies can be detached for such a purpose. Thorough liaison prior to and during the operation between all Tank and Infantry Commanders would have to be a special feature. For this reason only Infantry not in the line can be considered as available to undergo the necessary preparation.[45]

The attack was to be carried out by the 4th Division, the very division that had suffered at Bullecourt. It would take a lot to restore their confidence in the tanks.[46] Battalion by battalion, they were bussed to a spot north-west of Amiens:

> … to spend a day at play with the Tanks. The Tanks kept open house, and, in the intervals of more formal rehearsals of tactical schemes of attack, the Infantry were taken over the field for 'joy rides,' were allowed to clamber all over the monsters, inside and out, and even to help drive them and put them through paces. Platoon and Company leaders met dozens of Tank officers face to face, and they argued each other to a standstill upon every aspect that arose.[47]

The tanks and the infantry rehearsed every part of the coming battle. According to Monash, the men gradually gained confidence in the tanks: 'The fame of the Tanks, and all the wonderful things they could do, spread throughout the Corps. The "digger" took the Tank to his heart, and ever after, each Tank was given a pet name by the Company of Infantry which it served in battle, a name which was kept chalked on its iron sides.'[48]

The contrast with Bullecourt was complete. There was time for training. The men had the opportunity to learn what the tanks could do. The tank officers had the opportunity to learn what the men would like the tanks to do. There was rehearsal. There was debate and discussion. There was none of General Gough's hurry-hurry.

But the key was command. Would the tanks command the infantry, or vice versa? Here Monash imposed two conditions. First, each tank was to be treated as an infantry weapon, and to come under the command of the infantry commander to whom it had been assigned. Second, the tanks would advance level with the infantry, close behind the creeping barrage. The second condition caused dissension among the tank commanders who believed that, because the tanks were so tall, there was a risk that they would be hit by any 'drop-shorts' in the artillery barrage.[49] Elles accepted Monash's conditions.

Monash's account of the battle preparations continued:

> The larger questions relating to the employment of the Tanks having been disposed of, the remaining arrangements for the battle presented few novel aspects. Their manner of execution, however, brought into prominence some features which became fundamental doctrines in the Australian Corps then and thereafter.[50]

This was revolutionary stuff — 'doctrines' being formulated within Haig's own command.

The elements of the 'doctrine' were hardly rocket science. They were comprehensive written orders; conferences of all senior commanders and heads of departments; Monash personally explaining every aspect of the plan; Monash confirming that everyone interpreted the plan in the same way; questions welcomed; answers given; criticisms encouraged and considered; problems raised and solved; conflicting views expressed, discussed and ironed out; and, once the plan had been settled, the resolve to adhere to it.[51]

In modern jargon, the doctrine would be expressed in terms of teamwork and mutual respect, which is, indeed, what it represented. Monash's doctrine was pure Plumer and Harington — and the reverse of the normal picture. Harrington observed:

> When lower formations were not consulted but merely ordered into action with the result that they thought that neither the stages nor the time of attack nor the place of the barrage was correct, [they] did not start in good heart. Simply the difference between the art of commanding by trust as against distrust.[52]

The painstaking preparations did engender the trust of the men. Newton Wanliss described the preparations from the troops' viewpoint:

> After the issue of Brigade orders, a strenuous time was spent by all completing the essential preparatory work for the battle. Plans and orders were given out; conference followed conference — conferences of senior officers being followed by conferences with junior officers, NCOs and men — until all thoroughly understood their parts ... Every contingency was provided for, and nothing was left to chance, with the result that everyone instinctively recognised the excellence of the staff work, and confidence reigned supreme. All were convinced of the success of the venture.[53]

The attack was fixed for 4 July 1918, in recognition of the fact that four companies of American soldiers were to take part. On the eve of the battle, when the troops were already taking up their positions for the attack, General Rawlinson passed on an order from General Haig withdrawing the American troops who were to take part in the attack. In giving this order, Haig was deferring to General Pershing's policy that American troops should only fight under American officers. It was to have been the first time American troops fought an offensive battle.[54]

Monash complained to Rawlinson in his 'best diplomatic language'. The following is a fine example: 'As always, Lord Rawlinson's charming and sympathetic personality made it easy to lay my whole case before him. He was good enough to say that while he entirely agreed with me, he felt himself bound by the terms of a clear order from the Commander-in-Chief.[55] The reward for Monash's tact came shortly afterwards when General Haig, having learned of the situation and the impact of his order, indicated that he wanted the attack to go ahead with the Americans as planned. Newton Wanliss recounted:

At 3.10 am precisely, in the semi-twilight of the early morn, our barrage opened. For miles every gun burst out simultaneously. The air was full of the tumult of high explosives, and the whole of the enemy's lines seemed one mass of fire and flame. Overhead, like gigantic warbirds, were aeroplanes; just behind the barrage waddled the tanks, and behind them the long lines of the grim Australian infantry. A ground mist facilitated our operations, and added to the enemy's troubles. In answer to his SOS signals, his artillery opened, and, in the circumstances, put up a creditable display, but it was too late, for our men were already in his lines.[56]

Monash was well pleased:

No battle within my previous experience, not even Messines, passed off so smoothly, so exactly to time-table, or was so free from any kind of hitch. It was all over in ninety-three minutes. It was the perfection of teamwork. It attained all its objectives; and it yielded great results ... The attack was a complete surprise, and swept without check across the whole of the doomed territory. Vaire and Hamel Woods fell to the 4th Brigade, while the 11th Brigade, with its allotted Tanks, speedily mastered Hamel Village itself. The selected objective line was reached in the times prescribed for its various parts, and was speedily consolidated. It gave us possession of the

The debris of war. Stretcher bearers carry a wounded man past the wreckage of an RE8 aircraft on the Hamel battlefield, July 4 1918.
AWM E04888

whole of the Hamel Valley, and landed us on the forward, or eastern slope of the last ridge, from which the enemy had been able to overlook any of the country held by us.[57]

So were the men:

So excellent had been the Corps Staff work that the battle may be said to have been won before it began, due to the care with which every contingency was provided for, the effect of surprise on the enemy, and the excellent collaboration of all arms. Only one battle in France up to date in the varied experience of the AIF was comparable to it for higher staff work efficiency, viz. Messines ... The long-coveted woods opposite our lines were now permanently ours, and the groundwork was laid for the great battle of August 8. The work of the tanks had been excellent, whilst our aeroplanes had dropped ammunition for our men during the battle.[58]

Sergeant Linton was not involved in the battle, but watched it from his tent, on the ground overlooking Hamel. He reported the gossip among the men: 'According to our chaps that were in the stunts,[59] the tanks and aeroplanes did great work. The tanks took up wire and pegs for the boys also water and food while the planes flew overhead and dropped bundles with 200 rounds of ammunition in each and so kept our machine guns in action.'[60]

Lieutenant Rule benefited from this innovation: 'That afternoon aeroplanes brought us ammunition. Flying low, they threw it out, and it slowly came down hanging to a parachute. It was very welcome; from now on we had a bit to present to the Hun planes, and next afternoon I had the time of my life [firing Lewis guns at the planes].'[61]

The attack killed or disabled 1500 Germans, and netted 1500 prisoners, two field guns, 26 mortars and 171 machine guns. On the Allied side, there were fewer than 800 casualties, mostly walking wounded. The tanks had been a huge success. It was due to them that so many Germans had surrendered. Only a few machine gun posts stood their ground to the last.[62]

The prisoners were looted of their possessions. Lieutenant Rule described what happened:

What a harvest for our boys. Talk about 'ratting'; as each Hun advanced with his hands above his head, several of our lads would dive at him, and, before the astonished Hun knew what was happening, hands were in every pocket, and he was fleeced of everything but his name and his clothes. When I saw the harvest that was being gathered, I felt inclined to pick a few pockets myself, but officers were not supposed to do such things, so I decided to use my head. Near Ramsay Woods a new reinforcement was working like a cat on a tin roof, pulling cigars out of a Hun's pocket. In a ferocious manner I asked him if he was not aware of the order that all loot had to be handed over to an officer to be sent back to headquarters. He meekly handed them over. I smoked cigars all day, and the rest of the platoon tormented the youngster for falling to the joke.[63]

After the battle, Haig paid Monash and Blamey the compliment of publishing the text of their orders for the Hamel battle as an example for the whole British Army. The publication attributed the success of the attack:

(a) To the care and skill as regards every detail with which the plan was drawn up by the Corps, Division, Brigade, and Battalion Staffs.

(b) The excellent co-operation between the infantry, machine gunners, artillery, tanks and RAF.

(c) The complete surprise of the enemy, resulting from the manner in which the operation had been kept secret up till zero hour.

(d) The precautions which were taken and successfully carried out by which no warning was given to the enemy by any previous activity which was not normal.

(e) The effective counter-battery work and accurate barrage.

(f) The skill and dash with which the tanks were handled, and the care taken over the details in bringing them up to the starting line.

(g) Last, but most important of all, the skill, determination and fine fighting spirit of the infantry carrying out the attack.[64]

One of the innovations introduced in this attack was the use of aeroplanes to drop ammunition to the machine gunners. Previously this ammunition had to be man-handled on the battlefield. Casualties among ammunition carriers were always substantial. A large canvas in the shape of a V (for Vickers) marked the drop zone for the flyers.[65]

In the days leading up to the attack, the artillery invariably used a combination of gas shells and smoke shells, so that it became instinctive for the enemy to put on their gas masks whenever there was a bombardment. During the attack itself, only smoke shells were used. The result was that the enemy wore gas masks during the battle, but the attackers did not. The masks obscured the enemy's view and hampered their freedom of action, whilst the men attacking had no such inconvenience.[66]

The battle was not, of itself, a large gain or a huge victory. It was more significant because it vindicated Monash's tactics. The team-based approach; the co-operation of all arms to make things easier for the infantryman to do his work; the exploitation of technological innovation — with tanks, aircraft and artillery all being used in new and imaginative ways; the strict timetable; and the immutable plan had all been proven to be effective.

Field Marshal Haig may not have known it, but a distinct philosophical approach was evolving in his own armies.

After the battle for Hamel, the Australians continued with peaceful penetration to drive back sections of the German lines, step by step, relieving the pressure on Villers-Bretonneux.[67]

Congratulations were received from all quarters. Georges Clemenceau came personally to thank the diggers. Although his city was still under siege, and being bombed periodically, the mayor of Amiens entertained twenty representatives for lunch to celebrate 14 July 1918 — and, as it transpired, the last Bastille Day in that war.[68]

After the battle, the 4th Brigade held a sports day at Querrieu Château. Thousands attended. The bands played, including the band of the 132nd United States Infantry, which arrived to tumultuous applause. There were running races, swimming races and sideshows. In true Australian style, there was a tote; and 'a certain number of privates were allowed to act as bookmakers'.[69]★

★ Punters will note the care with which it is recorded that it was private soldiers and not officers who acted as bookmakers.

Lieutenant Rule's 14th Battalion also withdrew from the front line to rest in Querrieu, but his men indulged in sport of a different stamp:

> The sheiks of the battalion were not long in getting hold of the social news; the main item appeared to be that four ladies of easy virtue had come on a visit to Querrieu and would be 'at home' to their friends. The ladies handed out refreshments for all they were worth, until some brass hats bundled them out of town.[70]

In Querieu, there was entertainment for all.

CHAPTER EIGHTEEN

8 AUGUST 1918

The planning for the 8 August 1918 battle began at a meeting on 21 July 1918, chaired by General Rawlinson, and attended by the Canadian, General Currie, General Butler of III Corps, General Kavanagh of the Cavalry Corps, General Monash and by senior representatives of the tank and air forces.[1]

The attack was to be a joint effort between the Australians and the Canadians, attacking on the south side of the Somme, with some assistance from the British III Corps, which held the front immediately north of the Somme. It fell to Monash to formulate and expound the plan of the battle.

Monash's plan was built on the concept of leap-frogging that had been used at the Messines battle. It was to be a bite-and-hold operation with a difference. In accordance with normal practice, the attacking troops stopped their advance before they reached the enemy's artillery. This often allowed the enemy to withdraw his guns at his leisure.[2] The difference here would be that the troops who would leap-frog the leading troops would press forward with a view to destroying or capturing the whole of the enemy's defensive system.[3] Monash planned to advance 9000 yards on the first day:

Phase A — Set-piece attack with barrage	3000 yards
Phase B — Open-warfare advance	4500 yards
Phase C — Exploitation	1500 yards
Total distance to final objective	9000 yards

All the maps were marked with lines of different colours to indicate the three objectives: Phase A by a green line; Phase B by a red line; and Phase C by a blue line. Nine thousand yards is just over five miles.

The planning for Phase A was adapted from the approaches developed in the 1917 battles and at Hamel. The main modification was to extend each divisional frontage from 2000 yards to two miles. There were four reasons for this; the weather was dry and the going easy; the enemy's defences were relatively new and primitive; four battalions of tanks would be taking part in the infantry advance, allowing a reduction of infantry numbers; and the manner in which the enemy's infantry and guns were distributed along his front.[4]

Monash compensated for the reduction in the density of men in the attack by increasing the intensity of the artillery coverage. He regarded this as the most important factor.

The first objective of 3000 yards was selected from aerial photographs to include the whole mass of the enemy's forward artillery, all of which was to be put out of action by the first phase. This task fell to the 1st and 2nd Australian Divisions. They were allowed 143 minutes to complete Phase A. An interval of a further 100 minutes was allowed for the succeeding two divisions to advance and deploy ready for Phases B and C.

The advance from the green line marking the objective of Phase A to the red line that marked the objective of Phase B involved a totally different tactical approach — open warfare — something not seen on the western front since the trenches were dug more than three years before.[5]

Open warfare would mean that the headquarters would also be mobile, so that Divisional headquarters would lose touch with Brigade and Brigade with Battalion. The decisions would have to be made by those actually doing the fighting — the subordinate leaders would have to take the initiative.

Open warfare also meant that the artillery would need to be mobile, increasing the reliance on ordnance of smaller natures. These had the advantage in open warfare because they were horse-drawn and could move over rough country. They could also be aimed over their sights.[6]

These two innovations also represented the two main risks of the operation. The alternative of a classic bite-and-hold operation would have meant stopping on the blue line until the heavier artillery could be brought forward, and made ready to fire — maybe, delaying Phase B by 48 hours, and allowing time for the enemy to reinforce his position.[7]

With the River Somme being the line of demarcation between the Australians and the British III Corps, it was important for the British to advance sufficiently quickly along the north bank of the river to take the high ground north of the Chipilly bend of the river. Failure to do this would leave the Australian left flank exposed, which was a matter of concern for Monash. He had no such concern for his right flank where he trusted the Canadians to do their part.[8]

The task of carrying out Phase B fell to the 5th Australian Division in the south and the 4th Australian Division in the north. Monash allocated mobile artillery to each of these divisions ready to take part in the Phase B advance.

The object of Phase C, marked with a blue line on the maps, was to exploit the gains of Phases A and B. Phase C would not go ahead unless Phases A and B had succeeded. The physical goal of Phase C was about a mile east of the objective of Phase B. This final advance fell to the second line brigades of the 4th and 5th Divisions. If they did attack, they would be supported by 36 of the same sort of tanks that had been successful at Hamel.[9]

Since there would be no creeping barrage for Phases B and C, only rough time estimates were made for completing those phases. In all 2½ hours were allowed to secure the green line; 6 hours to secure the red line; and 8 hours for the blue line. Starting at dawn, it should all be over by midday.[10]

Monash also devised a new scheme for the order in which the troops would leave the trenches, so as to equalise roughly how long each man had to march. In effect, there was a double leap-frog, one when leaving the trenches before the battle, and one during the battle when switching over from Phase A to Phase B.[11]

The balance of the plan was devoted to ensuring the infantrymen would not have to fight their way into the enemy trenches, but would be protected by the 'very ample resources in mechanical aids which the foresight and confidence of Fourth Army Commander, General Rawlinson, entrusted' to Monash.[12]

Surprise was the key element. It had been achieved at Cambrai and Hamel, but in precious few other Allied attacks. The recent series of peaceful penetration attacks had lulled the Germans into the belief that small time patrols were as much as the Allies on that front could manage.

The object was to maintain secrecy while the front was converted from a state of passive defence to a state in which it was capable of attacking on the largest scale. An elaborate scheme was formulated to disguise the move into the lines of the French and Canadian divisions. Troop movements were disguised. False rumours were spread.[13]

It was not so easy to disguise the other preparations for battle, especially now that aerial photography was in use. Normal work continued as before, but the preparations for the attack were all done under cover of darkness. This created difficulties for the artillery, which had to bring up more than 600 guns and place them in their battle positions, fully camouflaged before first light. In the French summer, first light is early indeed.[14] The artillery moved over 10 000 tons of ammunition by these night carries.

Registering the guns was a problem, since any trial and error process would give away the element of surprise. To avoid this, the guns had been calibrated at a test range miles behind the front.[15] Monash reported that, 'this great advance in art of gunnery contributed in the most direct manner to the result that when these 600 guns opened their tornado fire upon the enemy at day break on 8th August, the very presence in this area of most of them remained totally unsuspected'.[16]

To disguise the tanks, they were forbidden to travel anywhere that they might leave trackmarks that could be picked up on aerial photographs. The tanks themselves moved slowly, and in small groups. Their arrival at the battle was disguised by using aeroplanes to fly overhead at low altitude — which effectively covered the noise of the tank engines.[17]

On 1 August 1918, the British relieved the 5th Australian Division north of the Somme. The 5th Division went into reserve to train with the tanks.

On 2 and 3 August 1918, the 4th Australian Division moved from reserve to Hangard Wood, to relieve the French, taking up the southern part of the Australian line, next to where the Canadians would be. On 2 and 4 August 1918, the 2nd and 3rd Divisions side-stepped, taking up their positions for the attack.

The Canadians, those other Colonials, who were similar in so many ways to the Australians — not least in their long experience in attacking roles — began to slip into their positions on the nights of 4, 5 and 6 August 1918.

In a night raid on 4 August 1918, the Germans captured an Australian outpost, including a sergeant and four men who knew the plan for the attack. It looked as though the plan would be blown. Intelligence reports later captured from the Germans showed that the men had revealed nothing: 'The report went on to praise their soldierly bearing and loyal reticence, and held up these brave Australians as a model to be followed by their own men, adding that such a demeanour could only earn the respect of the enemy.'[18]

In response to the concern that the plan had been blown, the arrival of the 1st Division was accelerated. On 6 August 1918, the 1st Division arrived in Amiens from Hazebrouck. At last, all five Australian divisions would fight together under the same Australian commander.[19] The 1st Division left the train at Amiens and marched overnight to Corbie, where it halted for the night at the point where the Somme joins the Ancre.[20]

The effect of these moves was to reduce the Australian front from eleven miles to a little over 7000 yards, around four miles, extending from the Somme in the north to the Péronne railway in the south, whilst introducing the Canadians in the south.[21]

On 7 August 1918, Sergeant Linton with his donkey saw many things that suggested that Monash's orders for secrecy were being ignored for the sake of getting things ready for the battle:

> ... kept busy carting up ammunition for the big stunt, which, as far as we can hear, is to come off tonight. One of our Heads reckons he's got the 'good oil' and says the first barrage opens at 11 pm tonight ... All <u>our</u> Divisions are going over, the first Division having arrived here yesterday from up north.
>
> Big siege guns drawn by Caterpillar tractors have been passing here for days, and the motor transports on the road, carting up ammunition, are countless; night and day they are going for their lives. The motors take our stuff up as close as it is safe for them to go and then we pick it up and take it as far as we can with the old donks.[22]

It was the afternoon of 7 August 1918. W D Joynt described the scene:

> It was obvious a big offensive was about to take place. All the roads leading forward were crammed with movement, troops, tanks, artillery — we realized later, all endeavouring to get into position before dawn. Aeroplanes were flying overhead and we were told afterwards that this was to drown the noise of the moving transport and tanks.

That afternoon, the troops not yet in the know were let into the secret of what was in store:

We lay 'doggo' all next day in the cover of the village waiting for orders. Lieutenant-General Monash's Special Order of the Day was read to the troops:

Corps Headquarters

August 7th, 1918

To the Soldiers of the Australian Army Corps

For the first time in the history of this Corps, all five Australian Divisions will tomorrow engage in the largest and most important battle operation ever undertaken by the Corps.

They will be supported by an exceptionally powerful Artillery, and by the Tanks and Aeroplanes on a scale never previously attempted. The full resources of our sister Dominion, the Canadian Corps, will also operate on our right, while two British Divisions will guard our left flank.

The many successful offensives which the Brigades and Battalions of the Corps have so brilliantly executed during the past four months have been but a prelude to, and the preparation for, this greatest and culminating effort.

Because of the completeness of our plans and dispositions, of the magnitude of the operations, of the number of troops employed, and of the depth to which we intend to over-run the enemy's positions, this battle will be one of the most memorable of the whole war; we shall inflict blows upon the enemy which will make him stagger, which will bring the end appreciably nearer.

I will entertain no sort of doubt that every Australian soldier will worthily rise to so great an occasion, and that every man, imbued with the spirit of victory, will, in spite of every difficulty that may confront him, be animated by no other resolve than grim determination to see through to a clean finish, whatever his task may be.

The work to be done tomorrow will perhaps make heavy demands upon the endurance and staying powers of many of you; But I am confident that, in spite of excitement, fatigue, and physical strain, every man will carry on to the utmost of his powers until the goal is won; for the sake of AUSTRALIA, the Empire and our cause.

I earnestly wish every soldier of the Corps the best of good fortune, and a glorious and decisive victory, the story of which will re-echo throughout the world, and will live forever in the history of our homeland.

JOHN MONASH

Lieut.-General

Cmdg. Australian Corps[23]

Zero hour was 4.20 on the morning of 8 August 1918. Lieutenant Maxwell was waiting with his platoon on the forming-up point:

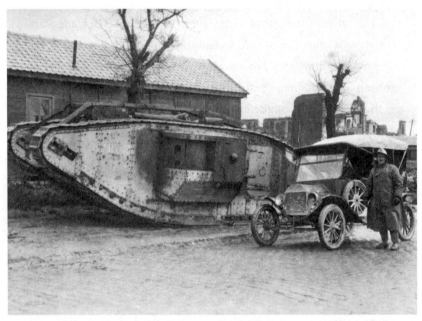

A strange wartime pair, a tank named Henry and a T-model Ford owned by the YMCA, Bapaume 1918. AWM P01322.010

With fifteen minutes to go our tank waddled through the night, moving at a snail's pace through the mist wreaths. It pulled into position and I opened the steel door. Out rolled a British second lieutenant, slightly drunk, with a water-bottle still filled with whisky. I relieved him of this oil-fuel and after taking a swig myself passed it along to the troops.

'Here, I say, old bean,' he protested, alcoholically. 'Don't be too awfully [expletive]. It's almost time this little war commenced, what!'

A strained silence, the bark of a gun a fraction of a second before schedule, then out of the night roared the voice of thousands of guns, crashing and smashing everything in their path. Along our line appeared the glow of dozens of matches as the men each lit a 'fag'. Sixty yards in front rose a wall of earth, kicked up by bursting shells. The flame of the explosives lit the smoke and dust with a blood-red glare ... A heavy mist muffled us.[24]

The troops advanced into a thick haze. The haze was the combination of a heavy fog, the dust stirred up by the shells and the smoke bombs used to provide artificial camouflage. The haze became so thick that the men mistook one another for Germans. Some shot their own comrades in the confusion.[25]

The battle ran ahead of the clock. Phase A was completed by 7.00 am. Phases B and C were ready to begin punctually at 8.20 am. Their objectives, the red and blue lines were each captured half an hour ahead of schedule.[26] The only negative was on the left, where the British allowed the Germans to remain in occupation of Chipilly spur, leaving Germans overlooking the ground that had been gained, and able to bomb it with artillery situated on the spur,[27] as Driver Edmunds described:

In the darkness before the dawn of August 8th our artillery barrage opened ... Thousands of gun flashes stabbing the darkness, each flash reflected, rippling along under the clouds as far as I could see to right and left, while behind the German lines coloured signal flares were frantically fired into the air. You could not imagine anyone surviving in that avalanche of shells, yet the majority did, and were prisoners in a very short time. The morning proved ideal for attacking troops. Before the mist lifted, long columns of prisoners were marching in. As we advanced close to the river, the attack across the river [at Chipilly spur] seemed to lag a little. It was wooded, broken ground, unsuitable for tank and actually we had infantry fighting on our left rear, but not for long if the Germans were captured. They retreated to avoid being cut off. Our tanks were ranging far and wide this side, it was ideal tank country. Among other things captured that day was the big gun used for shelling Amiens; we used to call it the Amiens express, as the shells whistled over each day. I believe it came to Australia; a 'souvenir de guerre'.[28]

Monash was scathing of the failure at Chipilly spur. He quoted the official reasons: the enemy had resisted strongly; fighting had been fierce; and no progress could be made. According to Monash, these were nothing but code for 'faulty staff coordination, or faulty local leadership'.[29] It was no wonder Monash was angry — the failure to take Chipilly spur left sixteen field guns and many machine guns free to fire into the left flank of the advancing men.[30] But he saved his anger for later. When dealing with the set-back, Monash was 'cool and resourceful'.[31]

The timetable for the advance was dictated by the artillery plan. Newton Wanliss wrote:

Our heavy artillery was still playing on the western end of the village, and whilst 'A' Company men were waiting for it to lift before resuming their advance, the enforced leisure was profitably employed in routing prisoners out of their dugouts and in 'souveniring', i.e. acquiring the spoils of war. The souvenirs obtained here both in number and in value exceeded anything of which the 14th [Battalion] men had experience.[32]

One innovation at this battle was the 'Contact Patrol' where a two-seater plane, with pilot and observer flew low over the battlefield, jotting down observations and positions on a map. The plane flew back to headquarters and dropped the map and reports in a field nearby 'wrapped in a streamer of many colours. It was then brought by cyclists into the Staff Office'. It was ten minutes from observation to delivery of the message.[33]

Another innovation was the use of armoured cars, both for reconnaissance, and as mobile scavengers, moving quickly to take advantage of opportunities that presented themselves in Phases B and C of the battle.[34]

For a week before the attack, 'giant planes' had flown up and down the front, so that the enemy would become used to the noise, and not notice the noise of the tanks when they finally arrived.[35] Once again, the tanks advanced under the close protection of the creeping barrage — another example of the benefits of cooperation between different arms that Monash instigated.[36]

After so long bound to the trenches, the troops were surprised to see once more the signs of open warfare. Newton Wanliss again: 'A stirring incident about this time, which created a great impression, was the trotting through the infantry of a battery of field artillery, which went into action alongside of them. Such incidents had been seen in army manoeuvres in Egypt, but it was an absolute novelty as far as practical warfare in France was concerned.'[37]

The 13th Battalion noticed the same thing, which obviously came as a surprise to the Germans as well. Captain Thomas White recounted:

During this advance, our Field Artillery, having quickly hooked up, passed through us as they hurried forward to occupy new positions just behind the green line, and crowds of intensely delighted prisoners came streaming back, openly marveling at all they saw.

On the second F.U.P. [forming up point — it was the first objective, the green line], we waited until 8.30 am, at which time the barrage which had been protecting 3rd Division digging in, was lifted to allow us to leapfrog them and to proceed to the Second Objective, the Red Line ...[38]

A further manifestation of open warfare was the task given to Sergeant Denning and his section of engineers for the 8 August battle. He was asked to report to British Artillery headquarters at Corbie, and there given eight trucks, seven filled with bridge and road building materials and one for the men and equipment. When the attack came. Denning remembered:

We were kept busy as we followed along, repairing bridges and filling up shell holes along the road. Fortunately we had a good supply of all materials necessary and sufficient manpower to do the job. As we progressed, prisoners were being marched back in hundreds. Despite the smoke fumes, fog and congestion of troops, we made good progress ... We were again on the advance and prisoners were coming in droves. The village was nothing but a smouldering ruin. The roadways were blocked by the fallen buildings and were being cleared as quickly as possible by a large party of Pioneers.[39]

This was true open warfare: not a trench in sight; the infantry on the move; and the engineers and pioneers clearing the way for them.

And in the open fields, even the Light Horse had found a part to play, near the redline, or second objective, 7500 yards from the start point. Sergeant Downing recounted:

Our artillery was following. Australian batteries trotted into position in a ravine behind us. On the opposite hill, about a mile away, Germans were swarming around a train. It slowly drew away, then, gathering speed, disappeared, leaving great puffs of steam. A second train began to move, then stopped. Men on horseback were riding round it. It disgorged a crowd of men. Our cavalry had it. Australian Light Horse patrols were riding swiftly all over the country.[40]

Monash often complained that the media did not give his achievements the full measure of adulation he thought they deserved. This battle was no exception:

The tactical value of the victory was immense, and has never yet been fully appreciated by the public of the Empire, perhaps because our censorship at the time strove to conceal the intention to follow it up immediately with further attacks. But no better testimony is needed than that of Ludendorff himself, who calls it Germany's "black day," after which he himself gave up all hope of a German victory ...

'August 8th was the black day of the German army in the history of the war. This was the worst experience I had to go through ... Early on August 8th, in a dense fog that had been rendered still thicker by artificial means, the British, mainly with Australian and Canadian Divisions, and French, attacked between Albert and Moreuil with strong squadrons of Tanks, but for the rest with no great superiority. They broke between the Somme and the Luce deep into our front. The Divisions in line allowed themselves to be completely overwhelmed. Divisional Staffs were surprised in their Headquarters ... The situation was uncommonly serious. If they continued to attack with even comparative vigour, we should no longer be able to maintain ourselves west of the Somme ... Owing to the deficit [of men] created our losses had reached such proportions that the Supreme Command was faced with the necessity of having to disband a series of Divisions, in order to furnish drafts ...'[41]

General Rawlinson was unstinting with his praise, even if Monash did have to share the glory with the Canadians: 'While everyone did splendidly, I think the spirit of the Colonial Infantry was probably the decisive factor.'[42] Rawlinson agreed with Ludendorff that, 'The result of this victory should have a far-reaching effect on the Boche morale.'[43]

Two more events completed a satisfying week for General Monash. By serendipity, on 11 August 1918, under a beech tree spreading its branches over the garden of the Red Château in Villers-Bretonneux, there met a group of old, white-haired, gentlemen. They sat in chairs on the grass, enjoying the warm afternoon weather. Maps were strewn carelessly around them.

They were Field Marshal Haig, General Rawlinson, General Currie, General Kavanagh (of the Cavalry Corps), General Godley, General Monash, General Montgomery, General Budworth, General Laurence (Haig's chief of staff), Sir Henry Wilson, Georges Clemenceau, the French finance minister Katz, General Blamey (Monash's chief of staff) and the Australian divisional Generals Glasgow, Rosenthal, Gellibrand, Sinclair-MacLagan and Hobbs. They were taking time out to congratulate one another on their success.[44]

One well-aimed bomb could have made up for Ludendorff's black day on 8 August.

After this meeting, Monash and his five divisional generals had tea with Sir Henry Wilson. Monash told Wilson that this was the first time he and his five divisional generals had ever been together in the same room![45]

In characteristic style, however, Haig had already put pen to paper claiming the credit for the 8 August battle. At 10.30 on the morning of the attack, he had taken the time to write to Lady Haig: 'Our attack started at 4.20 this morning and seems to have taken the enemy completely by surprise ... I hear. Two of our armoured cars being sent on to round up German Corps Headquarters! Who would have believed this possible even 2 months ago?'[46]

Most men emerging from the narrow scrape that Haig had experienced would be pleased beyond words just to be able to thank their lucky stars in this way — but not Haig. He could not resist going that little step further, and adding two sentences of self-justification that must have bemused even his wife: 'How much easier it is to attack, than to stand and wait an enemy's attack! As you well know, I feel that I am only the instrument of that Divine Power who watches over each one of us, so all the Honour must be His.'[47]

Over four years of cataclysmic warfare, Haig had stood, at a safe distance, watching while his offensive tactics killed almost one million of his own men and wounded two million more.[48] In the face of that carnage, had it not occurred to him to question the tactics, or to question the wisdom of the Divine Power who had apparently suggested them to him?

Monash had to rush away from the picnic under the beech tree at Villers-Bretonneux. The next day, he was entertaining the King at the chateau at Bertangles. He had arranged for the King to inspect one hundred men from each of the Australian divisions, as well as a collection of guns and other war trophies which the men had hauled into position in the gardens of the chateau for the King's amusement and approval. The King's favourites were the German transport horses. He told Monash he hoped they would soon learn to speak Australian.[49]★ In the middle of all this, John Monash was honoured to go down on bended knee before his monarch, and arise as Sir John Monash.[50]

The results of the battle were worth the knighthood. The British advanced eight miles on a front of 15 000 yards. They captured more than 400 guns. The Germans suffered 27 000 casualties, including 12 000

★   A surprising number of Englishmen and women seem to find this simple skill beyond their reach.

A battle won well. King George V rewards General Monash with a knighthood in front of other generals and captured German ordnance.
AWM E02839

prisoners.[51] The British suffered 9000 casualties. 'As far as the Australians were concerned, the battle was a picnic compared to many of their previous experiences in France', commented Newton Wanliss.[52]

The high number of German prisoners suggested surprise, or demoralisation, or a combination of the two. The 13th Battalion was so swamped with prisoners that it used two Light Horsemen to round up the prisoners and shepherd them to the rear. The Horsemen also carried messages, making things easier for the runners.[53]

The tactics of the battle had been almost faultless. Surprise had been achieved. All arms — aircraft, artillery, tanks, infantry, armoured cars — had been coordinated so as to allow the infantry to arrive at the enemy trenches fit and ready to fight. Moreover, the tactics were not simple stereotypes. With the combination of bite-and-hold, open warfare and exploitation, they had been tailored to meet the circumstance of the day. The marriage of the skills of the infantryman with the latest mechanical innovations was coming together. A theoretical or doctrinal approach had been developed that explained how a battle should be planned and executed, and why.

Of course, Haig was not the one to recognise the changes that were taking place in his command, nor to document them. On 22 August 1918 he wrote in his diary:

> Tonight I issued a Note to Army Commanders asking them to bring to the notice of all subordinate leaders the changed conditions under which operations are now being carried out. 'It is no longer necessary to advance step by step in regular lines as in 1916-17 battles. All units must go straight for their objectives, while reserves should be pushed in where we are gaining ground.[54]

The order added, 'Risks which a month ago would have been criminal to incur, ought now to be incurred as a duty.'[55] This amazing order begs the questions whether any subordinate officers still adhered to the step-by-step advance in regular lines as late as 1918, and, if so, how on earth had they survived? For them and them alone, Haig's note must have come as a distinct relief.

The rest of the infantry had long ago abandoned the step-by-step advance in regular lines. Since the Somme, the officers in the field had modified their approach time and again to suit conditions encountered on the ground. Examples abound of mechanical innovations that were developed to take the pressure off the step-by-step advance in regular lines: the mines at Messines; the tanks at Cambrai; the creeping barrage at Broodseinde ridge; the pincer movement at Villers-Bretonneux; the creeping barrage combined with tanks and smoke at Hamel; and the combination of creeping barrage and open warfare on 8 August 1918.

In fact, it could fairly be said that these successful battles shared the absence of three elements: there was no step-by-step advance in regular lines; there was no miraculous breakthrough; and there were no glorious cavalry charges that chased the Hun back to the Rhine.[56] Experience had taught that all of these techniques were unsuitable for the situation encountered in the Great War. Experience had also taught that innovation paid dividends.

While Haig saw the good in some of the innovations, he still thought the old ways were best. In September 1918, he wrote to his wife: 'Too many men are being sent to air Service, Tanks & such fancy jobs, & not enough to the infantry who can win the War!'[57]

Just as the victory they had dreamed of over four thankless years seemed within the Allies' grasp, the War Cabinet became weak at the knees. They gave little encouragement to Haig, and less to the 8 August attack. When General Wilson reported the advance to the War Cabinet on 8 August 1918 — 'Gentlemen, there was an attack this morning and many prisoners and guns have been taken' — the Cabinet responded to a man, '*There*, I told you so, I *knew* we'd be surprised again.' When told it was an Allied attack, their response was to ask why it had been made.[58]

Churchill visited Haig on 21 August 1918. As Minister for Munitions, and as an inveterate experimenter, Churchill was full of schemes, but Haig was not interested:

His schemes are all timed for completion in next June! I told him we ought to do our utmost to get a decision this autumn. We are engaged in a 'wearing-out battle' and are outlasting the Enemy. If we have a period of quiet, he will recover, and the 'wearing-out' process must be recommenced [In reply, I was told that the General Staff in London calculate that the decisive period of the war cannot arrive until next July].[59]

Now that Wilson had replaced Robertson as Chief of the General Staff, the opinions of the General Staff were no longer identical with those of General Haig, so Haig had to endure rough weather coming from that direction as well. Wilson enraged Haig on 1 September 1918 by sending him the following telegram:

HW Personal

Just a word of caution in regard to incurring heavy losses in attacks on Hindenburg line as opposed to losses when driving the enemy back to that line. I do not mean to say that you have incurred such losses, but I know the War Cabinet would become anxious if we received heavy punishment in attacking the Hindenburg Line WITHOUT SUCCESS. Wilson[60]

Although the telegram was marked 'Personal' it seems certain that it was sent on the instructions of Lloyd George, if not the War Cabinet as a whole.[61] Haig certainly regarded it as coming from Lloyd George. It was insurance taken out to save the prime minister if the attack on the Hindenburg line failed.[62] Whilst Lloyd George wanted to meddle in Haig's battle plans by expressing his anxiety about casualties, he was not prepared to take responsibility if the plans went awry. He would, of course, take the credit for every success.[63]

In his diaries, Haig called the politicians 'a wretched lot of weaklings',[64] and replied to Wilson with an uncharacteristic attempt at sarcasm: 'With reference to your wire re. casualties in attacking the Hindenburg Line. What a wretched lot! And how well they mean to support me!! What confidence!'[65]

Haig was justified in being upset. The preoccupation of the War Cabinet was to avoid another Somme or Passchendaele.[66] The amazing thing is how long it took the members of the War Cabinet to realise that a military victory was on the cards in 1918, and to seize the credit for that.[67]

Haig pushed on after the 8th August battle without support or encouragement from the War Cabinet, as always, sticking resolutely to his task; ignoring obstacles in his way; and scorning the doubts, apprehensions and reservations of others. John Buchan wrote of Haig at this time:

When the last great enemy attack came he took the main shock with a quiet resolution; when the moment arrived for the advance he never fumbled. He broke through the Hindenburg line in spite of the doubts of the British Cabinet, because he believed that only thus could the War be ended in time to save civilization. He made the decision alone — one of the finest proofs of moral courage in the history of war.[68]

This was a lonely time for Haig. He had ignored the discouragement of the proud and intellectual London elite to steer his own course through 1918. He had stood firm during the reverses of Operation Michael. Now that victory seemed imminent, he could, like the cooks at Querrieu, shake off the chaff like water off a duck's back, but he would not have been human if the good-humoured creases around his eyes had not thinned a little after the rough treatment he received from London during the low times of Operation Michael.[69]

Moreover, Haig was magnanimous in victory. He did not gloat that his way had been vindicated, nor that the rest had been proven wrong. And, perhaps, Haig did this for good reason — no-one could say that the result would have been different if another path had been taken. When great minds differ on a choice between two competing options, in most cases, both options would be a sound choice.

CHAPTER NINETEEN

MONT ST QUENTIN AND PÉRONNE

After the success of the 8 August battle, peaceful penetration once again became the watchword of the diggers, with the troops at the front taking every opportunity to advance the line.[1] By 21 August 1918, the Australian Corps found itself holding a frontage on both sides of the River Somme, about 22 miles in front of Amiens and 11 miles short of Péronne.[2]

The front was about ten miles long. The 4th and 5th Divisions, together with the British 32nd Division, held the line south of the river. The 3rd Division held the line north of the river. The 1st and 2nd Divisions were in reserve.[3]

The rain which had turned Passchendaele into the sea of mud that defeated the Allied offensive in 1917 had not returned in 1918. There is barely a mention of rain in the accounts of the battles on and after 8 August 1918; indeed most comment that the weather was fine, and the going good.

All the same, autumn was imminent, and the weather could turn at any time. With the help of the weather gods, there might be eight or nine weeks of campaigning before winter closed down the fighting for the year.

In the time available, one option was to shepherd the Germans back into defensive positions for the winter. By 1919, when the Americans would have arrived in force, it would be an easy matter to push the Germans back to the Rhine. This was the policy that Lloyd George and the War Cabinet favoured.[4]

The disadvantage of this policy was that the Germans were now retreating more or less in disarray. The winter pause would give them an opportunity to build a decent defensive line, reinforce their depleted battalions, refit and rearm, and to repair their shattered equipment and morale.[5]

The optimists — including Haig, Rawlinson and Monash — thought there might a chance to deal a serious blow to the Germans before winter. With luck, they would force the Germans further east at the winter break. With a great deal of luck, they might even force an end to the war.

Some of those who took the optimistic view also believed that the German morale had suffered a dramatic about-face with the failure of Operation Michael and the success of the 8 August battle. Others believed that German morale might actually have stiffened as the German Army recovered from the shock of 8 August,[6] but those who held this view still wanted to strike hard while the iron was hot.[7]

This policy of pressing the attack had two difficulties. The physical and military obstacles in the path of the Allied troops, if they wanted to strike again before winter, were formidable. Moreover, the Allied troops were themselves nearing the end of their endurance. Although their morale generally remained high, it was perfectly understandable that they were exhausted after the dramatic campaigns of 1918.

However peaceful Sergeant Denning and his men found life on the Somme, they could not escape the war:

We were camped near the Somme and were enjoying life, letting the waters of the river gently massage our weary limbs, naked but for our 'cold meat' tickets. We were enjoying ourselves immensely when Fritz

Diggers put a shell hole to good use. AWM E03925

dropped a salvo of shells into the river just near us. The explosions temporarily almost emptied the river at the spot, causing quite a tidal wave. We decided to postpone our swim until another day.

The Advance was proving very successful. Our troops moved further and further forward despite obstinate opposition. I actually heard a band playing back in the distance and it was rumoured that the Germans were asking for terms.[8]

Lieutenant Maxwell described the feelings of his men, after so long in one another's company, after so frequently screwing up their courage and strength for another supreme effort, and with no end of the ordeal in sight:

We had been in the thick of the fighting since 8 August and the strain was beginning to tell. It seemed that the end was yet far off. We began to reflect that it was merely a matter of time when we would all be killed off and a new generation would take up the struggle. A man who was wounded was damned lucky to be out of it. Out of nearly 300 who left Australia in B Company not half a dozen remained. It was with these gloomy thoughts that many a man sat waiting for zero before the new thrust. He began to realize that it was all a wild gamble in human lives … Personally at this juncture I was utterly sick of the war and everything associated with it.[9]

There were five obstacles in the path of the Allies if they wanted to make another major advance before winter. In the order in which the Allies would encounter them, the obstacles were: first, the Somme valley; second, the original Somme battlefield, which was still scarred and barren from the fighting there in 1916; third, the 'line of the Somme', which had two elements — the River Somme, as it broadened and turned south at Péronne, and the Canal du Nord,[10] a half-finished canal, that extended the line of the River Somme north from Péronne; fourth, Mont St Quentin, a majestic hill which commanded both Péronne and the line of the Somme; and fifth, that familiar symbol of German strength and resistance, the Hindenburg line.

From Amiens and Villers-Bretonneux to Péronne, the Somme valley is a country of exquisite beauty. The advance from Villers-Bretonneux initially took the diggers down into the valley at Hamel. From Hamel, the river flows in an east–west direction. The advance on 8 August had followed the river upstream, along the line of the valley. Here, the river twists and turns between expansive marshes, thick woods and commanding spurs, like Chipilly.

Small tributaries flow into the Somme from the north and south. The valleys of these tributaries are, in turn, well wooded, with hedges and copses forming good cover on both sides of their hills. The largest of the tributary valleys stretches from Herleville to Chuignes, before it enters the Somme at Bray. In all of this country of rivers, marshes and wooded valleys, the advantages of cover, concealment and broken ground rested with the defensive.

The old Somme battlefields remained much as they had been left when the battle passed over them. There were old trenches, rusted barbed-wire entanglements, disused fortifications, and a clutter of battlefield debris.[11]

At Péronne, the Somme takes a southerly turn and the topography of the river changes. From Péronne to Amiens, it is a narrow, gentle river. From Péronne, upstream (that is, to the south of Péronne), it becomes a broad stretch of water, often 1000 yards wide. The river alternates between channels and marshes. A canal, used for inland shipping, runs along its banks. North from Péronne, work had begun to extend the canal in a northerly direction. The unfinished Canal du Nord and the Somme river south of Péronne were together called the line of the Somme. They were a formidable obstacle for an army seeking to cross them, especially when, as had happened here, the Germans had been careful to destroy all the bridges as they fell back.

The line of the Somme near Péronne was dominated by Mont St Quentin. A hill, more than a mountain, Mont St Quentin lies about a mile north of Péronne. Crops grow from its base almost to its summit. The summit is covered in woods. As in Australian wheat paddocks, there are few, if any, trees where the crops are grown on the sides of the hill. Assaulting troops had to find what protection they could in the sunken roads and the folds in the hill.

Mont St Quentin and the line of the Somme were the last serious obstacles before the first trenches of the Hindenburg line, but the leap from the Somme to the Hindenburg line was not a short hop — it was about fourteen miles from Péronne to the Hindenburg line.

On 21 August 1918, General Monash called a conference to set in train the next step in the process. This was to be an attack on the tributary valley that ran from Herleville to Chuignes. This attack was to be led by the 1st Division, under the command of General Glasgow, and by the 32nd British Division, under the command of General Lambert, attacking side-by-side.[12]

The initial attack was set for 23 August 1918. If it was a success, the 2nd and 5th Divisions were under orders to stand by to take up the offensive a day or two later, 'in order to commence immediately the process of keeping the enemy on the run, and hustling him clean out of the river bend and across the line of the Somme'.[13]

Again, the plan for an attack in three phases:

Phase	Nature of attack	Objective
1	Set-piece attack with barrage	The village of Herleville
2	Open-warfare advance	1000 yards past Herleville
3	Exploitation	Clearing the Cappy bend of the river

In the first phase, under normal artillery barrage, the 32nd British Division would attack the town of Herleville on a 1000 yard frontage, and two brigades of the 1st Australian Division would advance to a line on the far (or eastern) side of the Chuignes Valley on a frontage of 4500 yards. The second objective was a further 1000 yards on from the first. It was also a task of the 1st Division. The third phase was an exploitation phase, to be undertaken by the reserve brigade of the 1st Division, but only if the first two objectives had been achieved. It involved the seizure of the entire Cappy bend of the river.

The phased nature of the plan was similar to the plan that had succeeded in the 8 August battle. In this case, with some participants new to Monash's planning process, the conference was a long one. Monash thought the extra time taken was well spent:

The regular battle conferences were in the Australian Corps an innovation from the time the command of it devolved upon me. They proved a powerful instrument for the moulding of uniformity of tactical thought and method throughout the command. They brought together men who met face to face but seldom, and they permitted of an exhaustive and educative interchange of views.

They led to a development of 'team-work' of a very high order of efficiency.[14]

There was nothing new about conferences in the military context. Haig held weekly Army Commanders' Conferences 'at each Army H.Q. in turn, and these took place punctually, with a proper agenda and recorded minutes, except when great battles were on'.[15] What is striking about those conferences is how rarely Haig records that they took place, let alone that they actually achieved anything. Another difference of note is that Haig abandoned his conferences when big battles were on. That was the time when Monash made the greatest use of his.

Haig certainly does not write about his weekly conferences as an important element of his command, or of his style of leadership.

Of course, conferences are not the only method of instilling teamwork, or of leadership. Monash, Plumer and Harington put great faith in conferences because they were a means for a free and open interchange of views, doubts and reservations without fear of recriminations or criticism.

Not all conferences are like that — it will be recalled that, when White remonstrated with Haig after Pozières, Haig's chief of staff gave him a warning shake of the head, no doubt to signify that White was straying into risky territory. Even John Terraine, Haig's greatest apologist and supporter, reluctantly conceded that Haig had three defects: his 'mental texture', meaning his lack of interest outside military subjects; his inarticulateness; and his relationship with his staff and subordinates:

Neither category [staff and subordinates] would feel themselves in a strong position to argue with him, and having no dialectical proficiency, he felt no inclination to seek debate. One detects in him a certain gaucheness with those who were his superiors or equals in rank ... He, for his part, developed an unstinting admiration for [the members of] his Command. Concerning himself, he had no doubts.[16]

A person with these qualities would never feel comfortable in a free-ranging exchange of views, especially one in which his juniors were encouraged to criticise his decisions or opinions. It is hardly to be expected, therefore, that Haig would follow Plumer or Monash in using such a debating chamber as the preferred method of fine-tuning his plans. Moreover, the juniors, if they were at all sensitive, would be reluctant freely to express dissenting views.

It is not necessarily a criticism of Haig that he was disinclined to engage in debates. There is more than one way of skinning a cat. Nor is there any necessary reason why a committee should reach a better decision than an individual — indeed, many committees do worse than individuals.

There is, however, an issue when the individual decision-makers make decisions without explaining to the others affected by the decisions how and why they made them. This is particularly so in an inherently team activity, like an army. Without an explanation for the decision, those affected by the decision may not understand the reasoning behind it, or the reasons why it was preferred to the other available options.

Moreover, without the process of debate, the decision will not be informed by the criticisms and suggestions for improvements which other intelligent and sympathetic minds will (nearly) always make.[17] Unless the decision-maker is especially talented, his decisions will (nearly) always be the worse for this omission.

In fact, there is evidence that Haig discouraged the expression of dissenting views. One of his aides-de-camp from 1917 to 1919, Captain Morton, said that Haig 'hated being told any new information, however irrefutable, which militated against his preconceived ideas or beliefs' and that Haig's Intelligence Chief, General Charteris, 'always concealed bad news, or put it in an agreeable light'.[18]

Monash gave two reasons why the battle conference was valuable: by giving his instructions to all subordinates collectively, and not individually, he created a responsive spirit that was competitive; and by giving all instructions at once, every commander knew not only what every other commander was going to do, but also what he was ordered to do, and could consider the effect of that on his own actions.[19]

The first two phases of the battle for Chuignes went off without a hitch. The third phase was delayed in starting and was held back by the congregation of a large number of retreating Germans in Garenne Wood. The mobile artillery moved forward and enveloped the Wood. This led to the collapse of the resistance. The last of the Germans were swept off the plateau into the Cappy valley.

The victory meant that the Germans had left behind the last of the 'inhabitable' land, and been driven back onto the broken country of the Somme battlefield. North of the river, the British 3rd Division, completing a larger advance that had begun on 21 August 1918, succeeded in taking the township of Bray. The combined result of these two setbacks was that the Germans decided to abandon all the country west of the line of the Somme.[20]

The victory at Chuignes was another feather in the cap of General Glasgow. Following his success leading the 13th Brigade at Villers-Bretonneux, he had been promoted to command of the 1st Division, a promotion that was more than justified by the results at Chuignes.[21]

Monash was particularly proud when his men captured enemy guns and materiel. He was in for a special treat at Chuignes, where the booty included a 15-inch bore naval gun, manufactured by Krupp, which had been used to bombard Amiens. The gun was mounted on a railway carriage and housed in a special installation that included the carriage, platform and concrete foundations weighing over 500 tons. The barrel of the gun was 70 feet long. It fired a projectile weighing nearly a ton over a range of 24 miles. It was loaded mechanically and aimed electronically.[22]

It could fire only 28 rounds per day. It fired continually from its first installation on 2 June 1918 until 28 June 1918, by which time its barrel had worn out (after firing only 350 rounds). Krupp made a new barrel, which was fitted on 7 August 1918. The gun fired only 35 more rounds. On 9 August 1918, it was dismantled and the barrel disabled with explosives.

Monash inferred from these facts that 8 August was indeed the black day of the German Army, and that their preparations to retreat began almost as soon as the outcome of that battle had become apparent.[23]

After the success of the Chuignes battle, the object of reaching the Hindenburg line before winter seemed more attainable than it had before. Monash resolved to continue to harry the Germans in their retreat, denying them time to rest or build fortifications. He sent the 1st and 4th Divisions to rest. He asked the 1st, 3rd and 5th Divisions to continue the task at hand, and they, though tired, were keen to finish the task. However, a setback that no amount of enthusiasm could overcome threatened to stop the Australians. General Rawlinson had decided that the Fourth Army, north and south of the Somme, had done enough to earn a month's break to rest and refit.[24]

With the scent of the fox in his nostrils, Monash was not about to give up the chase. With his lawyer's training, he read the order to pause very closely. It contained the formal and standard instruction that, 'Touch must be kept with the enemy'. This was enough for Monash. Nothing in the order said how close the touch should be. Monash took full advantage of the loophole — and 'loophole' was exactly what he called it.[25]

Peaceful penetration was resumed with a vengeance. When the patrols advanced, they found the defences unoccupied. For three days from 27 August 1918 until 29 August 1918, they chased the Germans back over the Somme at Péronne.[26]

When the Germans had retreated to the Hindenburg line at the beginning of 1917, the retreat had been orderly and controlled. They had gone at their own pace, carefully removing all gear of value, and destroying what they could not carry. This time, the retreat was pell-mell. Whilst discipline held throughout, and the machine gunners maintained their usual composure, the Germans were not dictating the timing or execution of this retreat. They left guns, artillery ammunition and stores in their wake. Divisional headquarters were abandoned where they stood. Six hundred prisoners were taken.[27]

Monash countered the machine guns by novel use of his mobile artillery. He put the artillery under the command of the infantry commanders, allowing them to direct fire at any machine gun nest that was holding up the advance. He also insisted that the artillery include 20 per cent smoke shells in what they fired. The smoke shells had the effect of blinding the machine gunners.

Even in these last few weeks of fighting, further innovations were coming to the fore. Aeroplanes were used to follow the German retreat and spot targets using a system of flares fired from friendly forces on the ground to help the pilots distinguish friend from foe.[28] The Bangalore torpedo, a British invention which was used to blow up barbed-wire entanglements, was tried for the first time. Another invention was a device which was light to carry, easy to assemble, quick to deploy, and allowed men to run over the top of barbed wire. An American invention, it was chicken-wire.[29]

In open warfare, however, the wire entanglements were no longer the main problem. The roads and bridges were. No one could advance unless there were roads and bridges which could carry the traffic. The roads were crowded, and the traffic was taking a heavy toll. The repair gangs were stretched to the limit.[30]

On 29 August 1918, the Australians reached the line of the Somme. They had outpaced the tanks and their artillery. For the moment, they were on their own. They found that the Germans had destroyed every bridge and crossing of the river.[31]

Monash's solution was to attack the one feature that dominated the line of the Somme: Mont St Quentin. Speed was the key to his plan. He had to take the hill before the Germans had the time to man and fortify it. Already, it was 'ringed around with line upon line of barbed wire entanglements' from the 1916 battles.[32]

It was time for another conference. This one was held late in the afternoon of 29 August 1918. In addition to Monash and his staff, it was attended only by the infantry commanders: General Lambert, commanding the British 32nd Division, and Generals Rosenthal, Hobbs and Gellibrand commanding the Australian 2nd, 3rd and 5th Divisions. No artillery or tank officers were present. Having been left behind in the rush of the advance, they could play no part in the attack. The plan was made to attack the Mont without them — only mobile artillery would be involved. If nothing else, it deserved marks for audacity.

The three Australian divisions were ordered to continue their eastward advance across the Canal du Nord. The 32nd British Division was to take up a position in the bend where the Somme turns south, and make a demonstration there to convince the Germans that it was to be the main point of crossing.

Three Battalions of the 2nd Division would go first. On the night of 30 August 1918, the 2nd Division had secured a crossing of the river at Ommiécourt, and was setting about repairing it to make it suitable for foot traffic. Using this crossing, the centre battalion would go straight for the top of the Mont. The other two battalions were to fan out left and right in the hope of developing flank attacks on the Mont. The total force of the three battalions was only 70 officers and 1250 men. The remaining two brigades of the 2nd Division were to wait in reserve.

Both the 5th and 3rd Divisions were to attempt to forge other crossings, with the first to succeed allowing the other first use of the bridge to cross.

On the afternoon of the next day, 30 August 1918, General Monash explained his plan of attack to General Rawlinson. Rawlinson, who had tried and failed to apply the brakes to the Monash juggernaut only a few days before, reacted with amused approval: 'And so you think you're going to take Mont St Quentin with three battalions! What presumption! However, I don't think I ought to stop you! So, go ahead, and try — and I wish you luck!'[33]

The plan was not in the *Field Service Regulations*. It did not follow Monash's own formula for an attack which used all modern means to

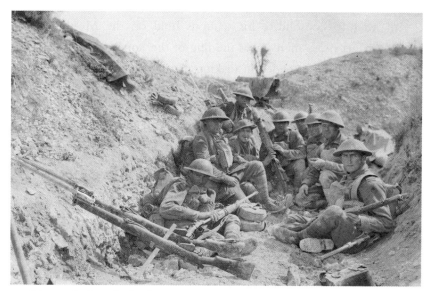

Diggers had to find what protection they could in the sunken roads and folds of the hill Mont St Quentin, 1 September 1918. 'The capture of Mont St Quentin by the Second Division is a feat of arms worthy of the highest praise'. AWM E03138

protect the infantryman as he advanced on the enemy trenches. About the only precept it did follow was General Haig's recent direction that 'Risks which a month ago would have been criminal to incur, ought now to be incurred as a duty.'[34] It was a gamble, but it might just succeed. Stranger things had happened. Perhaps Monash could succeed with a hurry-hurry attack, where Gough had failed.

In favour of the attack were the disorganisation of the Germans following their headlong retreat, and the surprise that another major attack so soon after the last would bring.

The attack began at 5.00 am on 31 August 1918. The attacking battalions crossed the river and made for their targets. By 7.00 am the centre battalion had passed through the ruins of the village on top of the Mont and crossed the main road north-west out of Péronne. Later, they fell back to positions in old trenches on the west side of the Mont. From here, they successfully drove off five German counterattacks before nightfall.[35]

In order to consolidate his tenuous hold on the Mont, Monash needed to get more men across the line of the Somme. The balance of 2nd Division had succeeded in making the bridge at Feuillères passable for guns and vehicles. The original crossing at Ommiécourt and a third crossing at Buscourt were open for foot traffic. Monash gave General Hobbs the order for the 5th Division to cross the river and advance in support of the 2nd Division.[36]

The crossing at Buscourt would have driven back men who were less determined. Private Bert Bishop was there:

During the afternoon we crossed the river. Tracks through the marshes we negotiated safely. We came near the river crossing.

'If I'd known about this I wouldn't have come,' growled Pojo. Past the shambles of Buscourt, we entered a small copse of trees, from whence we could glimpse what was going on. Groups of infantry from every whichway were slowly making their way to a certain spot. The spot was a bridge, or rather what had once been a bridge. The concrete piers still stood, but all the top of the structure had been blown away. German artillery on Mont St Quentin was firing over open sights straight down on the stricken structure. Planks connecting the piers were allowing groups of infantry to run the gauntlet.

As planks were ready, infantry scrambled across. Sometimes they started but had to come back as a shell blew away planks they needed, and at times a plank loaded with infantry was smashed. Some men dragged themselves over, some crawled back and some were blown into the river. More planks were positioned, more troops rushed across. A shell landed in our little copse, then another. We got behind little tree trunks.

At last it was our turn. As we rushed to the bridge a shell exploded before us. Three casualties, the bridge was still there. Slipping on mud and blood, holding with one arm to anything in reach, we forced ourselves across. I saw the water beneath. It seemed there was as much blood as water. My platoon crossed without further casualties. A forward aid post was hard at work under the protection of the bank. On the left as we reached the other side was something we'd never seen before. Tidily stacked was a pyramid-shaped object. The pyramid was built of legs and arms tossed out of the AMC workshop.[37]

After a long and difficult march overnight, the 5th Division was in position to attack on the morning of 1 September 1918. They attacked across the crest of the hill. Things were more than tough. Private Bishop wrote:

Two men were alive enough to be arguing. One had told the other to 'cheer up, laddie, you'll soon be dead'.

'Cheer up? There's one thing would make me cheer up. I think it would even make me happy.'

'Well, what is it?'

'If the bastard who planned and ordered this stunt was in it with us I'd be laughing my head off.'

Other men were talking. They were angry. Things were said that I never expected to hear Aussies say. If they could have got their hands on the heads responsible for our attack the heads would have been torn to pieces. We were all in a very ugly mood.[38]

The diggers were putting General Monash on the same pedestal as General Gough.

In tough bayonet fighting, the 5th and 6th Brigades of the 2nd Division carried the line 600 yards east of the top of the Mont, whilst the 14th Brigade of the 5th Division pushed down into the western half of Péronne.[39]

The 3rd Division, meanwhile, had pushed north along the Bouchavesnes spur capturing the high ground north of the Mont and capturing ground near Cléry before resuming the general eastwards direction of the advance.[40]

It was not until the night of 3 September 1918 that the outcome of the battle was finally secured. That night, the high ground at Flamicourt, behind Péronne, also fell.

The capture of Mont St Quentin, by an old-fashioned infantry advance, up a steep hill, across open wheat fields, without adequate artillery support, without tanks and with a minimum number of men was one of the last miracles of the diggers' war. Monash boasted that General Rawlinson called it the 'finest single feat of the war'. Rawlinson gave special credit to General Rosenthal, but most to the men of the 2nd Division, who achieved the feats of rushing the top of the Mont on the first morning of the battle, and holding it until it was fully secured. Rawlinson wrote:

> The capture of Mont St Quentin by the Second Division is a feat of arms worthy of the highest praise. The natural strength of its position is immense, and the tactical value of it, in reference to Péronne and the whole system of the Somme defences, cannot be over-estimated. I am filled with admiration at the gallantry and surpassing daring of the Second Division in winning this important fortress, and I congratulate them with all my heart.[41]

Monash was happy with this, except that he thought it downplayed the role of the 5th Division.[42]

Lieutenant Maxwell had a different take on who had been the bravest man on the mountain:

> In the assault on Mont St Quentin nobody was cooler or more courageous than Padre Tugwell of the 17th. In the thick of the shell-fire he calmly made tea and distributed it to the tired troops. It was men like Tugwell and old Father Clune who really had influence over the men. Religion in the army resembled to a great extent the rum issue — much depended on the man who dispensed it. Men, dog-tired after nights without sleep, attended

services conducted by these chaplains, not from an excess of religion, but from the downright respect in which they held these two men's men.[43]

Monash had now reached the end of his supply lines. In order to advance further, he needed somehow to restore a workable railhead in Péronne and, ideally, on the eastern side of the line of the Somme. He also needed to repair the roads serving the railhead. He embarked upon a program of rail and road building in and around Péronne, gradually clearing the traffic congestion.[44]

This enforced break allowed the men to catch their breath, and return their units to some kind of order. The German retreat continued, but the main thrust for it now came from attacks being made by the French and British on other parts of the line.

Monash called the 1st and 4th Divisions forward from their resting positions. They relieved the 3rd and 5th Divisions. The British 32nd Division, which had served with the Australians with distinction for almost four weeks, returned to their own people. The Australian line was shortened and moved further north. There was little pressure from the Germans, and increasing evidence that their resolve was waning. Normally so bullish, Monash wrote, 'We could well afford to approach the immediate future with greater deliberation.'[45]

Poor Monash: the quality of the accommodation in which he found himself living was declining alarmingly. The chateau at Bertangles 'whose spacious halls and spreading parks had formed so pleasant a habitation for the whole of my Corps headquarters'[46] was now far behind. Monash's digs went from 'château to humbler dwelling house, and thence into bare wooden huts, and later still into mere holes hollowed out in the sides of quarries or railway cuttings'.[47]

Following the period of consolidation, work resumed on attacking the Hindenburg line. By now it was mid-September, and winter was rapidly approaching. There was only limited time to prepare an attack on a formidable position.

The first move was a standard set-piece battle, under a classic creeping barrage on 18 September 1918. The set-piece advance would take the front line to where it had been in March 1918. In addition, there was an exploitation phase of between 1500 and 2000 yards, which, if it went ahead, would take the outpost line of the Hindenburg line.[48]

Monash described the mechanics of the attack behind the creeping barrage:

The barrage is nothing more nor less than a steady shower of shells, bursting over the very heads of the leading lines of Infantry, and striking the ground some 80 to 120 yards in front of them. This shower is usually so dense that three to four shells per minute fall on every 20 yards of frontage. It is so intense a fire that no enemy, however courageous, could remain exposed to it. It falls on one line for three or four minutes, while the Infantry lie down flat. Suddenly, the barrage "lifts" or advances 100 yards. At a signal from the platoon or company commander the whole line rises and rushes at top speed to catch up to the barrage, again to throw itself flat upon the ground.

So long as no enemy are encountered, these successive rushes may go on without check for hundreds of yards. If during the course of any rush, trenches or strong points are met with and they contain enemy who do not immediately surrender, prompt use must be made of rifle and bayonet. But it is the primary business of the leading line of Infantry to push on and not to delay by engaging in close combat. The second and third lines of Infantry are there to 'mop up' ... Where Tanks co-operate that is also their special business, and when it has been attended to they go forward at top speed to rejoin the line.[49]

The 18 September 1918 battle began at 5.30 am. The 1st and 4th Divisions, being most recently rested, made the attack. They attained all the objectives of the set-piece by 10.00 am. They pushed on. The 1st Division, under General Glasgow, made its way to the outpost line. The 4th Division, under General Maclagan, pulled up 500 yards short. The 4th Division rested while the artillery was brought up. At 11.00 pm, they advanced again, advancing to what 'appeared certain death, for the enemy, firing phosphorous tracer bullets from numerous machine-guns skimmed [their] trenches with innumerable balls of fire'. Charging the last yards 'yelling like fiends', they took their part of the outpost line.[50]

The casualties tell the tale. The 1st Division, which attacked with 2845 men, suffered 490 killed or wounded, but captured 1700 prisoners with unknown numbers of Germans killed or wounded. The 4th Division, which attacked with 3048 men, suffered 532 killed or wounded, but captured 2543 prisoners with unknown numbers of Germans killed or wounded. Also captured were upwards of 80 guns — the icing on the cake for Monash.[51] On the figures alone, it was a huge victory.

This was the last battle of the war for the 1st and 4th Divisions. They did not exactly ride off into the sunset, but it was close. Monash again: 'Their labours ended, the troops were taken by motor bus and railway to a coastal district lying to the south-west of Amiens, there to rest and recuperate in the contemplation of a noble past devoted to the service of the Empire.'[52]

After months of continuous fighting, the Australian numbers had grown dangerously thin. The 1st and 4th Divisions were not sent to rest in anticipation of the end of the war. They were resting and refitting for 1919. Of the remaining three Divisions, the 3rd and 5th were in better condition than the 2nd for serious fighting, and, in any event, Monash had promised the 2nd Division a rest until towards the end of September.

The next obstacle was the attack on the Hindenburg line. It was expected to be serious fighting. The task loomed as too big for the Australians on their own.[53]

To address this problem, Rawlinson asked Monash to take into his Corps two American divisions. Monash agreed. At two more conferences, of extra length and detail because of the involvement of the Americans, Monash explained his plan for an attack on the Hindenburg line. This was not to be a surprise attack, but it was to be powerful one. The force of five divisions was the largest force that Monash commanded, and he had generous resources at his disposal. There was a 60-hour bombardment.[54]

The plan for the attack was similar to the plan for the 8 August battle. The 2nd Division would remain in reserve. The attack would be made on a frontage of 7000 yards. The two American Divisions, the 27th and the 30th, would handle the set-piece part of the attack: an advance of 3500 yards. The 3rd and 5th Australian would then leap-frog them for the exploitation phase: a further advance of 4000 yards.[55]

As the days became shorter, dawn and the start times for the attacks came later. This attack was fixed for 5.50 am on 29 September 1918. The timetable required the Americans to take the first objective by 9.00 am and the Australians to leap-frog them at 11.00 am on their way to the exploitation objectives.[56]

By eleven o'clock, it was evident that things were not going well. The attack had halted at the obstacle of the Canal du Nord. The attack had been aimed at a section where the canal went underground through a long tunnel, called the Bellicourt Tunnel. The Germans had used the tunnel as a vast garrison. The Americans had crossed it without 'mopping up' thoroughly. After they had passed on, the Germans emerged from the tunnel, and were creating havoc in the rear of the advance.[57]

It fell to the Australians to recover the situation. Monash had to abandon his carefully made plan, and improvise. His solution was, first, to ensure contact between both Australian divisions — Gellibrand and Hobbs had already done this; second, to close the battle down for the day, holding the positions already gained; and, third, to call up the 2nd

'If I'd known about this, I wouldn't have come'. Diggers pose near the ruins of a bridge near Péronne. AWM E03196

Division from its reserve position. Allowing for the delay in transport, the 2nd Division would not be ready to enter the front line until the evening of 1 October 1918.[58]

In the meantime, on 30 September 1918, the 3rd and 5th Divisions fought on together. The 3rd Division advanced 1000 yards in a north-easterly direction, in wet conditions and by dint of more hand-to-hand fighting. The 5th Division maintained its position on the left of the 3rd. During the night of 30 September 1918, the Germans evidently decided to cease their attempts to retain the contested territory. By nightfall on 1 October 1918, the operation had been completed with all objectives finally gained.[59]

This was the last battle of the war for the 3rd and 5th Divisions — they 'had so reduced their fighting strength, that a very drastic re-organisation had become necessary', wrote Monash.[60] '… in the course of the next few days, [they] followed the First and Fourth Australian Divisions into the grateful rest area which had been provided to the west and south-west of Amiens, and before they were called upon for further front-line service hostilities had ended.'[61]

And so there was one.

The 2nd Division, on its own, was back in the front line and under orders to attack the heavily fortified Beaurevoir line. On 3 October 1918, they captured the line, and went beyond it in an exploitation phase, capturing 1000 prisoners and many machine guns. On 4 October 1918, they continued to harass the enemy, taking 800 prisoners and five guns.[62] The ground was not easily gained, as Lieutenant Maxwell described:

I had never seen such wire entanglements as confronted us. Belt upon belt of it barred our way to the Beaurevoir line. Our artillery made no impression on it. From the enemy came a hail of machine-gun fire. Several men tried to walk over the wire, but a moment later their bullet-riddled bodies were strung up on it. The whole of our advance was held up. Our Lewis gunners did splendid work — one after another was hit, but others immediately took up the gun and poured volley after volley through the red-hot barrels. The enemy realized our predicament and those who had lost heart returned to reinforce the machine-guns and open upon us with rifle-fire. Directly in front I could see the steam from an enemy gun. It had fired with such continuous rapidity that the water-jacket for cooling the barrel was boiling. Its crew worked furiously to break our assault. I managed to crawl beneath the first two belts of wire without being discovered. A young Lewis gunner (Bonzer was his [nick]name, and he lived up to his name in the Australian vernacular) crawled beside me. Our only chance was to make a dash and trust to luck. Bonzer wiggled ten yards to my left and, balancing his gun on the bottom strand of wire, fired a burst. His aim was accurate and the German gunner, throwing up his arms, fell backwards. The wire was so thick that after the first leap I was able to retain my balance as I leapt from ream to ream. Before another German could manipulate the gun I had landed amongst them.

I had fired my revolver at each bound and it was now empty. When the Germans before us shouted 'Kamerad', I was the most pleased and relieved man in France.[63]

'Bonzer' was awarded the Distinguished Conduct Medal for his gallantry. Maxwell was awarded the Victoria Cross, which he added to the Military Cross and Distinguished Conduct Medal he had previously won.[64]

Monash made one last demand of the 2nd Division. At dawn on 5 October 1918, with a dashing bayonet charge, it took the village of Montbrehain, and held it against counterattack all day. Monash summarized: 'By the night of October 5th the Corps had, by the victory at Montbrehain, advanced its line to a point six miles east of the Bellicourt Tunnel, and had thereby confirmed the irretrievable collapse of the whole of the Hindenburg defences.'[65]

That night, the 30th American Division relieved the 2nd Division in the front line.

For the diggers, the fighting was over.

CHAPTER TWENTY

VICTORY

The Armistice came into effect at 11 am on 11 November 1918. Private Harney, a soldier from the Australian outback, saw it this way:

I remember that just before the news of the Armistice came, we were on the big last attack down the Bellicourt line. The Americans were just coming in then. They were taking over, and I had to stop behind to help them. And there we attacked, and that's when I saw the whole thing of the war — well, to me, the stupidity of it.

… here were the Germans, all along the line. Some of them were wandering about with dazed looks on their faces — these people that I'd always reckoned were supermen. Lying on the ground they'd be, with their legs broken, and I'd shout out to some of the chaps: 'Any of you chaps know English? Come and pick up your mates! We can't carry them back'.

They'd come and they'd salute me — blimey! I'd never been saluted in my life — and they'd pick up these chaps and take them back, and there I saw one thing, a most terrific thing. There was a chap, a big, tall man, you know, and he had his jaw shot away, and he's got a bloke with a broken leg — he's got this chap on his back. He's staggering along the road, and when they saw me, they had to put up one hand. It made me very near cry to think of it. I used to go up and pat them on the back, and then they'd point to the big bottle that they had; it was full of coffee and cognac, and I'd have a drink of this cognac, and give them some, and then they'd sit down and pull out their postcards and show you their photos of their wives and their children and the farms they were in. And when I saw all these things, I thought, well blimey, what's it all about? It's a terrible thing, war. It's all right for people that are victorious, to march in, but think of the defeated people going back, the horror of it all. It makes you think, you know, the kindliness of people in the war, the horror of war, the sorrow for the afflicted, the vanquished, the people that were vanquished. How great they fought and yet how much they lost.[1]

Field Marshal Haig saw it the same way:

We heard this morning that the Kaiser is in Holland. If the war had gone against us no doubt our King would have had to go ... [Remember] John Bunyan's remark on seeing a man on his way to be hanged, 'But for the Grace of God, John Bunyan would have been in that man's place'.[2]

And life went on, as Lieutenant Colonel Lushingham recalled:

Very early on the last morning Shadbolt was watching the men dragging the heavy howitzers into a little clearing in the wood. The day was grey and overcast and the raindrops from a recent shower were dripping sadly off the trees. Above them a few pigeons, disturbed by the movements and cries of the men, circled and wheeled. A dispatch rider rode up and handed him a message form. 'Hostilities will cease at 11 am to-day. A.A.A. No firing will take place after this hour.' He sat down on the stump of a tree. In any case, the order did not affect him. The enemy was already out of range, and they could move no further.

This then, was the end ... This was the very end. What good had it all been? To serve what purpose had they all died? For the moment he could find no answer. His brain was too numb with memories.

'Mr. Straker?'

'Sir.'

'You can fall out the men for breakfast. The war is over.'

'Very good, sir.'

Overhead the pigeons circled and wheeled.[3]

MAJOR BATTLES FOUGHT

Year	Battle	Division 1st	2nd	3rd	4th	5th
1915	Gallipoli	■	■			
1916	Fromelles					■
	Pozières and Mouquet Farm	■	■		■	
1917	Bullecourt	■	■		■	■
	Messines			■		■
	Menin Road	■	■			
	Broodseinde Ridge	■	■	■		
	Polygon Wood				■	■
	Passchendaele			■	■	
1918	Villers-Bretonneux				■	■
	Hamel				■	
	8 August 1918	■	■	■	■	■
	Mont St Quentin and Péronne		■	■		

SHORT BIOGRAPHIES

À Court Repington, Colonel Charles

Formerly of the Rifle Brigade, Colonel Charles À Court Repington became famous as the military correspondent of the *Times* newspaper. Educated at Eton and Sandhurst and passing the Staff College, he had an impeccable military pedigree. Throughout the war he remained an ardent proponent of the western front school of thought. He was equally ardent as antagonist of Sir Henry Wilson — the legacy of the roles each had played when Repington's wife divorced him for adultery that led to the end of Repington's military career.

Asquith, Rt Hon Herbert

Prime Minister of England from 1911 until 6 December 1916.

Bean, Charles

Australia's official correspondent during the First World War, and subsequently its official historian. Born in Bathurst, New South Wales and educated in England, he was a journalist on the *Sydney Morning*

Herald before the war. An eye-witness to many of the events he describes in the *Official History*, Bean offers a particular insight into the lives and thoughts of the diggers.

Behrend, Captain Arthur

The adjutant of a British artillery brigade, and in *As From Kemmel Hill*, he gives a lively account of the chaos of 1918.

Birdwood, Field Marshal Lord

Birdwood commanded Australian troops from Gallipoli until 1918. He retained an administrative role after Monash was appointed to command of the Australian Corps in 1918. He was popular with the Australians under his command. With General White as his chief of staff he formed a team equivalent in cohesion and ability to the similar team of Generals Plumer and Harington.

Bishop, Private Bert

A private soldier, and a member of the 55th Battalion, his *The Hell, the Humour and the Heartbreak: A Private's View of World War 1* is a fine account. Bert Bishop was awarded the Military Medal in September 1918.

Blamey, General

General Monash's chief of staff from 1918.

Blunden, Edmund

Author of *Undertones of War*.

Boraston, Colonel J H

Field Marshal Haig's private secretary, and the author of *Douglas Haig's Command 1915-1918* and *Sir Douglas Haig's Despatches*. A fervent supporter of Haig and his command.

Bridges, Major-General Sir William

Commanded the Australian Division at Gallipoli. Died of wounds received during the battle.

Buchan, John

Famous as the author of *The Thirty-Nine Steps* and a member of Parliament, he was given charge of the Department of Information when it was formed in February 1917. He was a strong supporter and admirer of Field Marshal Haig. As Lord Tweedsmuir, he later served as Governor-General of Canada.

Butler, Captain

An Australian officer of the 180th Tunnelling Company.

Butler, Lieutenant-General

The commander of British III Corps, under whose command the 13th and 15th Australian Brigades fought at Villers-Bretonneux.

Byng, General Hon Sir Julian

Originally a cavalry officer, Byng was appointed to the command of the British Third Army in June 1917.

Campbell, Corporal Wally

From Argyle, New South Wales, Wally Campbell served in various Australian transport units.

Campbell, Sergeant Harold

Brother of Wally, Harold Campbell was a member of the 3rd Australian Battalion. He was killed in action on 7 October 1917 at Broodseinde ridge.

Churchill, Rt Hon Sir Winston

Famous for his leadership during the Second World War, Churchill played a less dominant rôle in the First. Blamed for the failure in the Dardanelles, he resigned from the Cabinet and spent two years in relative oblivion, including a period when he actually commanded a battalion on the western front. He was restored to the Cabinet in 1917, first as Minister of Munitions and, later, as Secretary of State for War.

Clayton, Lieutenant-Colonel Sir Hector

A Sydney solicitor, whose role in the war was limited by injuries received at Gallipoli.

Clemenceau, Georges

'Tiger' Clemenceau was the Prime Minister of France from November 1917 until 1920. He figured strongly in the tumultuous events of 1918.

Cooper, Duff

Wrote a partial biography of Field Marshal Haig at the request of Haig's family. An admirer of Haig's. Held important Cabinet offices in the Second World War.

Currie, Lieutenant-General Sir Arthur

The Commander of the First Canadian Division in 1915 and 1916, he was appointed the Commander of the Canadian Army in June 1917, a position he held with distinction until the end of the war. A favourite of Haig's, but unpopular with his own men.

Denning, Sergeant Roy

A carpenter by trade, Sergeant Denning enlisted as an engineer with the Australian 1st Division at Victoria Barracks, in Sydney, on 9 September 1914.

Donnell, Sister Anne

Sister Donnell enlisted in May 1915, and saw service in Egypt and France. Her *Letters of an Australian Army Sister* are a compelling record of her service.

Douglas, Sister Grace

A nursing sister posted to No. 1 AGH.

Downing, Sergeant Walter

Walter Downing was a solicitor from Victoria. His book, *To the Last Ridge*, is one of the best accounts of the diggers' experiences.

Duffell, Gunner William

Gunner Duffell served with the 2nd and 22nd Batteries of the 1st Australian Field Artillery Brigade.

Edmonds, General Sir James

A general of the British Army who became the British Official Historian of the First World War.

Edmonds, Lieutenant Charles

An English lieutenant, who wrote a memoir which he called *A Subaltern's War: being a memoir of the Great War from the point of view of a romantic young man, with candid accounts of two particular battles, written shortly after they occurred, and an essay on militarism.* British to his bootstraps.

Edmunds, Driver George

An Australian Artillery driver.

Elles, General Hugh

Commander of the Tank Corps.

Ellis, Captain Alexander
A member of the 29th Battalion, who also wrote *The Story of the Fifth Australian Division*.

Elliott, Brigadier-General Pompey
The colourful commander of the Australian 15th Brigade.

Elliott, Sir James
A New Zealand doctor, who served on hospital ships plying between Le Havre and England.

Evans, Sergeant
A sergeant in the Australian 13th Battalion.

French, Field Marshal Sir John
Commander-in-Chief of the British Expeditionary Force until displaced in distasteful circumstances by Field Marshal Haig.

Geddes, Sir Eric
An English businessman seconded by Haig to bring order to the railway system that supplied the Western front.

Gellibrand, Major-General Sir John
Rose to be commander of the Australian 3rd Division.

Gibbs, Sir Philip
An English war correspondent, whose reports from France, although clear and concise, are disappointing because they were written under the cloak of such heavy censorship.

Glasgow, Brigadier-General William
Rose to be commander of the Australian 1st Division.

Godley, Lieutenant-General Sir Alexander

An English general, commanding the New Zealand Army before the war, he became Commander of II Anzac until the Australian Corps was formed, when her took command of the New Zealanders. An aloof man, he was not popular with his men.

Gough, General Sir Hubert

English commander of the Reserve Army, later the 5th Army, under whom the Australians fought at the Somme and Passchendaele battles. A favourite of General Haig for his hurry-hurry attitude. Hated by the diggers, also for his hurry-hurry attitude. His impetuosity in command needlessly cost many Australian lives. The diggers disliked serving under his command. He was finally dismissed (or degummed) as commander of the Fifth Army after the reverses of March 1918, although many believed that, on that occasion, he had not done too much wrong and was made a scapegoat.

Graves, Robert

Author of *Goodbye to All That*.

Haig, Field Marshal Earl

Commander-in-Chief of the British forces in France from December 1915, Haig has become a figure of controversy. Some suggest he is the epitome of the British 'donkey' general, who carelessly sent good men to their deaths through poor planning and organisation. Others suggest that he is the epitome of a courageous high commander, who took the difficult decisions that duty forced on him courageously, and with great forbearance.

Haking, Lieutenant-General Sir Richard

As commander of the British XI Corps, Haking commanded men of the Australian 5th Division in the attack on Fromelles. The planning for the attack was so inept that the Australians nicknamed the General 'Butcher' Haking.

Haldane, Lord

Minister for War from 1905 to 1912, Haldane had been responsible for the reforms that had transformed the BEF after the Boer War. Although he was not a member of Lloyd George's Cabinet, he continued to play an influential role in the war.

Hankey, Lord

As the Secretary of the British Cabinet, Lord Hankey exerted a steadying hand and a pervasive influence on the policy that guided Britain's prosecution of the war. He was a supporter of Lloyd George against what he regarded as the excesses of Haig and Robertson. He was an astute observer, and recorder, of events at the centre of the British government.

Harington, Lieutenant-General Sir Charles (Tim)

General Plumer's chief of staff, and with Plumer, one of the architects of the victory at Messines. The author of *Plumer of Messines*, written in unconcealed admiration of Plumer.

Harney, Private Bill

Bill Harney was the epitome of an Australian bushman. A ringer and a drover before the war, he came from a life in the backblocks of Queensland and the Northern Territory to fight with the Australian 9th Infantry Battalion.

Henderson, Chaplain Kenneth

Chaplain to the Australian 12th Infantry Brigade in France. Before the war, he was a lecturer in philosophy at that fine institution, St Paul's College, at the University of Sydney — the oldest college in the oldest university in Australia.

Henry, Lieutenant-Colonel Max

A member of the Australian Army Veterinary Corps.

Hobbs, Lieutenant-General Sir Talbot

A citizen soldier, by profession an architect, on 1 January 1917, he was appointed to the command of the Australian 5th Division, in which role he continued for the rest of the war.

Holmes, Major-General William

A citizen soldier, the Secretary of Sydney's Metropolitan Sewerage and Drainage Board in civilian life, he was appointed to the command of the Australian 4th Division after the Somme battle, in which role he continued until he was tragically killed by a chance salvo on 2 July 1917.

Howell, Gunner Arthur

A signaller in the 23rd Artillery Battery, Gunner Howell was awarded the Military Medal for bravery when acting as a runner during the battle at Pozières.

Hubbard, Sister

A nursing sister posted to No. 2 AGH.

Hughes, Rt Hon Billy

Prime Minister of Australia from October 1915 until after the war. Whilst he was Prime Minister, he was successively a member of the Labor Party and the Nationalist Party, however, he drew the line at joining the Country Party.

Jacka, Captain Albert

The first Australian to be awarded the Victoria Cross in the First World War, for valour at Gallipoli, Bean claimed Jacka should also have been awarded the same decoration for his actions at Pozières in 1916 (for which he was awarded the Military Cross) and at Bullecourt in 1917 (for which he was awarded a bar to his Military Cross).

Joynt, Captain Donovan

A member of the 1st Division, he took part in the battles at Pozières, Second Bullecourt and Passchendaele. He was awarded the Victoria Cross for valour during the advance up the Somme on 23 August 1918. His books, *Breaking the Road for the Rest* and *Saving the Channel Ports 1918* are both good reads.

Kavanagh, General

Commander of the Cavalry Corps.

Keown, Private Albert

A private soldier who served in the Australian 5th Battalion. Author of *Forward with the Fifth*.

Kiggell, General Sir Launcelot

Field Marshal Haig's chief of staff during the Passchendaele battle, reputed to have wept after seeing the muddy conditions of the Passchendaele battlefield, saying, 'Good God, did we really send men to fight in that?'

King George V

The King of England throughout the war, King George did not hesitate to use his position to shape the course of the war or to influence army appointments.

Kitchener, Field Marshal Earl

Legendary figure, who had made his reputation in Egypt and Sudan, he was appointed Secretary of State for War at the outbreak of the war. Appreciating that the war would not be over quickly, he set about recruiting a huge new army, dramatically expanding the British forces in Europe with the famous slogan 'Your Country Wants You'. Kitchener was killed in June 1916 when HMS *Hampshire* struck a German mine and sank whilst transporting Kitchener to a conference in Russia.

Knyvett, Captain Hugh

Author of *"Over There" with the Australians*, a book published in New York, in which he describes himself as 'Anzac Scout, Intelligence Officer, Fifteenth Australian Infantry'.

Lawrence, Lieutenant Cyril

Cyril Lawrence was an engineer. During his time in France he was promoted from sergeant to lieutenant. His diary entitled *Sergeant Lawrence goes to France* is a treat. He was awarded the Military Cross for bravery during the Battle of Menin Road.

Lawrence, General Sir Herbert

Field Marshal Haig's chief of staff during the reverses of March and April 1918.

Lethbridge, Captain Harold

A country doctor who served as a surgeon in France and England.

Liddell Hart, Sir Basil

A well-known British historian of the First World War.

Linton, Sergeant John

A member of the Australian 3rd Divisional Ammunition Column.

Lloyd George, Rt Hon David

Prime Minister of England from 7 December 1916 until 1922. He was frustrated by the insistence of Field Marshal Haig and the rest of the General Staff on concentrating the battle on the western front. He came into such serious conflict with Haig that he would have sacked him. Only the absence of an obvious replacement stayed his hand. Lloyd George did, however, sack the Chief of the General Staff, Field Marshal Robertson, over his insistence on maintaining the focus on the western front.

Looker, Sister Effie
A nursing sister posted to No. 2 AGH.

Lucas, Sister Eileen
A nursing sister posted to No. 2 AGH.

M'Cay, Major-General Hon Sir James
Commander of the 5th Australian Division from its formation in Egypt until January 1917. His command included the disastrous battle of Fromelles which decimated the 5th Division.

Mackay, Major-General Iven
A battalion commander at Pozières, he finished the war in command of the 1st Brigade.

MacNaghten, Lieutenant-Colonel Charles
A colourful Englishman who fought in the Australian Army with great personal bravery on Gallipoli. Educated at Eton and Cambridge, and a solicitor by profession, he was popular with his men, not only for his courage, but also for his unorthodoxy, which led him into amusing escapades.

Mair, Sergeant William
A member of the 54th Battalion, originally from Argyle New South Wales. He served under General Holmes in the Australian Naval and Military Force which invaded New Guinea in 1914, and later served in France.

Mann, Leonard
Author of *Flesh in Armour,* an autobiographical novel.

Manning, Frederic
Author of *The Middle Parts of Fortune* and *Her Privates We.*

Mannix, Archbishop Daniel

Controversial Catholic Archbishop of Melbourne, whom Bean accuses of opposing the conscription referenda out of support for the Roman Catholic victims of the Easter troubles in Ireland in 1916.

Masefield, John

Served in the British Army during the Somme battle. Later became the Poet Laureate. He wrote about his experiences on the Somme in *The Old Front Line.*

Maxwell, Lieutenant Joseph

A machine gunner awarded the Victoria Cross for valour in the attack on Beaurevoir on 18 October 1918. This was the climax of a twelve-month period in which Maxwell was also awarded the Distinguished Conduct Medal and the Military Medal and bar. In his autobiography, *Hell's Bells and Mademoiselles,* Maxwell is more frank about his wartime experiences than many others.

Monash, Lieutenant-General Sir John

Not brilliantly successful at Gallipoli, Monash was sent to England to train the 3rd Australian Division. He commanded that division from the battle at Messines until he was promoted to command of the Australian Corps in May 1918. His mercurial command and his innovative use of tactics played a great part in driving the Germans out of the Somme valley.

Morrow, Private Edgar

A private soldier in the 28th Battalion.

Muller, George

A mate of Sergeant Roy Whitelaw.

Murdoch, Keith

A young Australian war correspondent who did not hesitate to use his position and influence to secure what he regarded as appropriate outcomes for the AIF. He supported, for instance, the appointment of Monash over White as the commander of the Australian Corps. Father of Rupert Murdoch.

Murray, Lieutenant-Colonel Harry

'Mad Harry' Murray was the most decorated Australian soldier in the First World War. He was awarded the Victoria Cross for valour in February 1917, at Gueudecourt. He was also a made a Commander of the Order of St Michael and St George and awarded the Distinguished Service Order and bar, the Distinguished Conduct Medal and the French Croix de Guerrre. He was mentioned in despatches four times. He rose from the ranks to command the 4th Australian Machine Gun Battalion.

Partridge, Eric

Author of *Frank Honywood, Private: A Personal Record of the 1914-1918 War; A Dictionary of Slang and Unconventional English;* and *Songs and Slang of the British Soldier.*

Pershing, General John

Commander-in-Chief of the American forces in France. He was criticised for the slowness with which he established the American Army in France.

Plumer, General Sir Herbert

A rotund and avuncular general. With his chief of staff, General Harington, he was the architect of the victory at Messines, which was the example on which later successes were modelled. Sir John Monash was an admirer of Plumer and Harington, and made no secret of the fact that he followed their methods. One of the most influential generals of the war.

Popkin, Sergeant C B

The Queensland machine gunner whom Bean credits with killing the Red Baron.

Rawlinson, General Sir Henry

Commanded the British First Army from December 1915, until he was appointed the command the British Fourth Army in February 1916. In February 1918, he was promoted to the Supreme War Council. He was recalled to the command of the Fourth Army after General Gough was degummed. The Australian Corps fought under his command during the battles in the latter half of 1918, when they drove the Germans out of the Somme valley.

Remarque, Erich Maria

Author of *All Quiet on the Western Front*.

Robertson, Field Marshal Sir William

Rose from the ranks to become a field marshal — the only man in the British Army to do so. Appointed Chief of the Imperial General Staff in 1915, he was a stout supporter of Field Marshal Haig against the proponents of a second front. For this he was replaced as Chief of the Imperial Staff by General Wilson in 1918, his ardent and unflinching support of Haig eventually costing him his job.

Rosenthal, Major-General Sir Charles

An architect by profession, and an artillery officer in his military life, he was promoted to command of the 2nd Division in May 1918, a position he held until the end of the war.

Rule, Captain Edgar

A member of the 14th Australian Battalion, the same Battalion as Albert Jacka, Rule rose through the ranks, ending the war as a captain, having been awarded the Military Cross and Military Medal. His *Jacka's Mob* is a readable account of his experiences and those of the 14th Battalion.

Sadlier, Lieutenant Clifford
Was awarded the Victoria Cross for valour in the lead-up to the attack on Villers-Bretonneux.

Sassoon, Captain Siegfried
English officer, famous for the publication of his wartime memoirs under the title *The Complete Memoirs of George Sherston*.

Shaddock
Field Marshal Haig's butler.

Sinclair-MacLagan, Major-General Ewen
Promoted to succeed General Holmes as the commander of the 4th Division following Holmes' death in July 1917, Sinclair MacLagan commanded that division until the end of the war.

Stokes, Sergeant
Was awarded the Distinguished Conduct Medal for bravery in the lead-up to the attack on Villers-Bretonneux.

Terraine, John
Historian. Author of *Haig the Educated Soldier* and *The Western Front 1914-1918*. A strong supporter of Haig.

Tighe, Captain Chaplain
Following his return from service in Flanders, Captain Chaplain P. F. Tighe S.J., A.I.F, as he called himself, gave a public lecture recounting his experiences entitled *From the Nile to the Somme* at Manresa Hall in North Sydney on 28 March 1917. It is a curious blend of tough, hard fact, and reassurance — perhaps a Jesuit trait?

Von Richthofen, Baron Manfred

A German fighter pilot, known as the Red Baron, after the bright red colour of his tri-plane. He was accredited with killing 80 Allied airmen before he was shot down and killed on 22 April 1918, possibly by Australian machine gunners.

Wanliss, Newton

The author of *The History of the 14th Battalion* who had the sad duty of reporting the death of his own son, who was a member of the battalion. He left others to describe his son, adding only these bare biographical details: Capt. Harold Boyd Wanliss, DSO, Orchardist of Lorne, Victoria. Born at Ballarat Victoria on 11 December 1891. Dux of Ballarat College and winner of the College 'Rhodes' medal; dux of his year at Hawkesbury Agricultural College (NSW) KIA September 26, 1917. Captain Wanliss — so obviously an outstanding young man — was killed at Polygon Wood.

White, Captain Thomas

An officer of the 13th Battalion. Wrote *The History of the Thirteenth Battalion AIF* and *Diggers Abroad: Jottings by a Digger Officer.*

White, Lieutenant-General Sir Brudenell

Chief of staff to General Birdwood, both in his command of I Anzac Corps and later in the command of the Fifth Army. Reputed to be the finest soldier Australia produced in the war, he was unfortunate not to be given the command of the Australian Corps that was given to Monash in 1918.

Wigram, Clive

The Machiavellian secretary of King George V.

Wilson, Field Marshal Sir Henry

A controversial and engaging man, Field Marshal Wilson stood outside the western front school of thought. Originally playing a high-level liaison role with the French, he was appointed Chief of the General Staff in 1918, when Lloyd George sacked Robertson. Entering Parliament after the war, he was murdered by Irish terrorists on the doorstep of his London home in June 1922.

Woodward, Captain Oliver
A captain in the 1st Australian Company, he participated in the mining of the Messines Hill and in blowing the mines at the start of the Messines battle.

CHRONOLOGY

Date	Event
4 August 1914	War breaks out.
11 August 1914	General Haig criticises General French to King George V. He says French is unfit to command the BEF.
1 November 1914	First Australian contingent leaves Australia.
3 December 1914	First Australian contingent arrives in Egypt.
1 February 1915	Second Australian contingent arrives in Egypt.
1 March 1915	General Rawlinson writes to Clive Wigram, the private secretary of King George V, describing the notion of 'bite-and-hold' tactics.
25 April 1915	Anzac Day — the English, French, New Zealanders and the 1st Australian Division land on Gallipoli.
1 June 1915	Planning for Messines battle begins.
30 July 1915	At a dinner party at General French's headquarters, General Haig explains his formula for winning the war to Lord Haldane.
1 August 1915	Australian 2nd Division lands on Gallipoli.

1 September 1915	Defeat at the Battle of Loos incites Haig to denounce French.
29 September 1915	Haig denounces French to Kitchener.
9 October 1915	Haig denounces French to Haldane.
17 October 1915	Haig denounces French to Robertson.
24 October 1915	Haig denounces French to King George V.
1 December 1915	Australians resume training in Egypt.
1 December 1915	Preparations begin for the Somme battle.
8 December 1915	Asquith sacks French.
19 December 1915	Asquith promotes Haig to command the BEF.
20 December 1915	Withdrawal from Gallipoli is successfully completed.
February and March 1916	The 1st and 2nd Australian Divisions are 'split' to create the 4th and 5th Divisions, with the 1st and 2nd Divisions and the New Zealand Division making up I Anzac Corps under General Birdwood, and the 4th and 5th Divisions making up II Anzac Corps under General Godley.
March and April 1916	I Anzac Corps arrives in northern France.
5 March 1916	I Anzac Corps leaves its desert camps en route for France.
1 April 1916	I Anzac Corps first enters the front line, near Armentières.
25 April 1916	The first anniversary of Anzac Day is celebrated privately by the diggers, and by a grand service in Westminster Abbey.
1 June 1916	Australians undertake trench raids.
1 June 1916	II Anzac Corps first enters the front line.
1 July 1916	The Somme battle begins. The British Army (not including any Australians at this stage) suffers an unmitigated disaster, losing almost 60 000 killed, wounded or captured on the first day.
2 July 1916	Australians undertake trench raids.

19 July 1916	The 5th Australian Division suffers 5533 casualties at the Battle of Fromelles, under the command of General Sir Richard 'Butcher' Haking. The authorities cover up the extent of the loss.
20 July 1916	The Australian 1st Division takes over positions in the front line at Pozières.
23 July 1916	The 1st Division attacks Pozières, taking a foothold in the ruins of the village.
25 July 1916	The 2nd Division replaces the 1st in the front line. The 1st Division has sustained 5285 casualties.
29 July 1916	The 2nd Division attacks towards the windmill at Pozières. Haig criticises their effort.
29 July 1916	The War Cabinet, through Robertson, asks Haig if the casualties on the Somme are likely to produce a commensurate result.
1 August 1916	Haig replies to the War Cabinet — 'Principle on which we should act — *Maintain our offensive*'.
4 August 1916	The 2nd Division finally takes Pozières ridge.
6 August 1916	The 4th Division replaces the 2nd Division in the front line. The 2nd Division has suffered 6846 casualties during its stint at the front. General Gough orders the 4th Division to advance towards Mouquet Farm and Thiepval.
15 August 1916	The 1st Division replaces the 4th Division. The 4th Division has suffered 4649 casualties.
22 August 1916	The crazy rotation continues. The 2nd Division replaces the 1st. This time in the front, the 1st has suffered 2650 casualties.
26 August 1916	The 2nd division reaches Mouquet Farm, but cannot hold it. It suffers 1268 casualties by the time the 4th Division replaces it.
15 September 1916	The 4th Division is finally relieved, having driven the salient to its farthest extent. Its losses on

returning to the front are 2409 more casualties. Total Australian casualties in 45 days on the Somme front are 24 139. The gain is small — Pozières ridge and the ridge behind it.

1 December 1916 to February 1917	Northern France experiences a particularly harsh winter.
1 December 1916	Generals Hindenburg and Ludendorff replace General Falkenhayn as the German commander on the western front.
February and March 1917	The Germans retreat to the Hindenburg line.
March 1917	The Russian Tsar is deposed and replaced by a provisional government.
6 April 1917	The United States declare war on Germany.
9 April 1917	The British attack the Germans at Arras.
11 April 1917	The 4th Division attacks the Hindenburg line at Bullecourt. The attack, let down by the failure of the planned tank attack, ends with the loss of some 3000 casualties, including 1300 taken prisoner.
May 1917	Sixteen mutinies rock the French Army.
3 and 4 May 1917	The 1st and 2nd Divisions once again attack Bullecourt.
12 May 1917	The 5th division relieves the 1st and 2nd, weathering a strong German counterattack and maintaining a foothold in the supposedly impregnable Hindenburg line. Australian casualties at second Bullecourt (which lasted from 3rd to 17 May 1917) were around 7000, compared to around 3000 at first Bullecourt.
7 June 1917	Messines battle begins. The British and Australian 3rd and 4th Divisions, under Generals Plumer and Harington, achieve a resounding victory.

19 June 1917	The War Policy Committee meets to consider General Haig's plans for the Passchendaele (or Third Ypres) battle. Policy Committee members want to avoid a repeat of the Somme disaster, but Haig and Robertson persuade them to persist with attacking tactics.
16 July 1917	The War Policy Committee gives limited approval for an attack towards Passchendaele.
31 July 1917	British troops attack from Ypres towards Passchendaele. General Gough commands the attack. Although the attack has far reaching ambitions of clearing the Belgian coast of German defenders, it founders within sight of the city walls of Ypres, mostly due to the impossibly muddy conditions.
28 August 1917	General Plumer replaces General Gough in command of the Passchendaele battle.
20 September 1917	The Menin Road battle, a true bite-and-hold operation, succeeds in driving back the Germans to Polygon Wood. The 1st and 2nd Divisions attack side-by-side, suffering some 5000 casualties.
26 September 1917	The 4th and 5th Divisions attack Polygon Wood, succeeding in taking the Wood with the help of a superbly coordinated rolling barrage.
4 October 1917	The 1st, 2nd and 3rd Australian Divisions and the New Zealand Division attack side-by-side, taking Broodseinde ridge in a strong display of hand-to-hand fighting. Australian casualties — some 6500.
6 October 1917	Whilst the Menin Road, Polygon Wood and Broodseinde Ridge battles were all fought in fine weather, the rain now sets in again, creating appallingly boggy conditions.
12 October 1917	The 3rd and 4th Australian Divisions, the New Zealand Division and five British Divisions attack

the Passchendaele ridge through shocking conditions of wet and mud. The attack proves a bridge too far, failing once again in the mud of Flanders.

November 1917	The Russian Revolution signals the end of Russian resistance. The Russians sue for peace, freeing the Germans to switch many fine divisions from the Russian front to the western front.
November 1917	Lloyd George establishes the Supreme War Council as a means of curtailing Haig's offensive ambitions on the western front. Lloyd George also limits the supply of reinforcements to the western front. He is anxious to avoid a repeat of Passchendaele and the Somme. The Supreme War Council advocates the establishment of a central Allied Reserve to cover the weak spot in the front line where the French Army met the British Army. Haig and Pétain combine to sabotage the proposal.
1 October 1916	First referendum to introduce conscription on Australia is defeated.
20 November 1917	The Cambrai battle proves the offensive value of the tank.
1 December 1917	Second referendum to introduce conscription on Australia is defeated.
1 November 1917	It is decided to form a single Australian Army Corps. Initially, the Corps is to comprise only 1st, 2nd, 3rd and 5th Divisions, but, eventually, all five Australian divisions are included.
18 February 1918	Lloyd George sacks Robertson as Chief of the Imperial General Staff. He would also have sacked Haig, if there had been another general good enough to replace him. General Wilson replaces General Robertson as Chief of the Imperial General Staff.

21 March 1918	The German offensive, Operation Michael, strikes at the British Third and Fifth Armies, driving the Fifth Army (under General Gough) far back along the line of the River Somme.
23 March 1918	Haig appreciates that the Michael attack might either separate the Third Army from the Fifth, or the French Army from the British.
24 March 1918	Pétain tells Haig that, if it comes to the crunch, he will order the French Army to separate from the British and fall back to defend Paris. This undermines the fundamental tenet of the French and British alliance: that of maintaining contact between the two armies at all costs.
25 March 1918	Haig calls Wilson to France to help solve the crisis. The Australian 3rd, 4th and 5th Divisions are ordered south to the Somme to help halt the German advance.
26 March 1918	At a crisis meeting of the top French and British commanders and politicians held at Doullens, Haig agrees to submit to the 'advice' of General Foch, provided that Pétain does likewise. This device maintains a single command, and upholds the strategy that the French and British have followed throughout the war. Foch orders that both the French and British armies to make a stand in front of Amiens. They are to concede no more ground to the Germans. Wilson orders Haig to replace General Gough with General Rawlinson.
27 March 1918	The Australians begin to take positions facing the Germans east of Villers-Bretonneux.
28 March 1918	The 3rd Division is in position and the 4th Division was arriving.
29 March 1918	The 3rd, 4th and 5th Divisions are in position facing the Germans east of Villers-Bretonneux.

4 April 1918	The 3rd, 4th and 5th Divisions halt the German advance.
9 April 1918	The Germans attack towards Hazebrouck, north of the Somme, and meet with unexpected success. The Australian 1st Division, which had been ordered south to the Somme, was sent back north to Hazebrouck to deal with this new threat.
11 April 1918	Haig belatedly issues his 'Backs to the wall' message.
17 April 1918	The German attack on Hazebrouck is repulsed.
22 April 1918	Baron Manfred von Richthofen, the Red Baron, is shot down over the Somme, whilst flying over the Australian lines. It is suggested that an Australian machine gunner may have fired the fatal shot.
24 April 1918	German forces take Villers-Bretonneux, exposing the way to the railhead at Amiens and to the Channel itself. Unless Villers-Bretonneux can be retaken, Allied war strategy will be in tatters. The task of retaking Villers-Bretonneux is given to the Australian 15th Brigade (from the 5th Division) and the 13th Brigade (from the 4th Division). They must attack at night, without support from tanks and artillery, and they must act fast. A pincer movement is selected. The attack takes place at 10.00 pm. In vicious hand-to-hand bayonet fighting, the Australians drive the Germans out of Villers-Bretonneux by early the next morning — the morning of the third Anzac Day. From that day forward, the Germans do not advance one pace.
May 1918	The Australians begin the tactic of 'peaceful penetration', in which they cut off and capture small segments of the German lines by stealth attacks, made under cover of the local crops and trees.

May 1918	General Monash takes command of the Australian Corps. For the first time, the diggers are fighting in a single corps under the command of Australian officers. Now, at last, the diggers control their own fate.
4 July 1918	The Australian 4th Division, with the assistance of a few Americans, win the Hamel battle. The battle is an example of the correct method of coordinating the different elements of the force — artillery, aircraft, tanks, infantry all play their part. The battle is won in 93 minutes.
8 August 1918	The Australians and the Canadians lead the major attack that eventually forces the Germans into surrender. Monash develops a revolutionary battle plan that reintroduces the almost-forgotten notion of open warfare. The victory is won within twelve hours, with an advance of eight miles on a front of 15 000 yards. The Germans suffered 27 000 casualties, including 12 000 prisoners.
23 August 1918	The 1st Division, together with the 32nd British Division advanced along the River Somme, taking Chuignes and the entire Cappy bend of the river.
29 August 1918	The Australians advance to the line of the Somme.
31 August 1918	General Monash launches his most daring attack — crossing the River Somme to take Mont St Quentin and Péronne. There is no available artillery. There are no tanks. The target is a bald hill, covered with wheat fields. Yet, in three days it is taken.
29 September 1918	Having secured the crossing of the Somme, Monash now attacks the Canal du Nord, using the 3rd and 5th Divisions in their last battle of the war. In a difficult battle, in which the diggers are forced to

	change and improvise their plans, they advance sufficiently to lay open the way to a final attack on the Hindenburg line.
5 October 1918	There is only one Australian division left in the front line: the 2nd Division. All the others have been sent to rest and refit. Monash makes one last demand of the 2nd Division: an attack on Montbrehain. The attack succeeds. When the Americans relieve the 2nd Division on the evening on 5 October 1918, the fighting was over for the diggers.
11 November 1918	Armistice Day. The war is over.

ENDNOTES

Chapter 1 — The Legacy of Gallipoli

1 Bean, *Anzac to Amiens*, p. 25.

2 ibid., p. 48.

3 ibid., p. 41–42.

4 The difference between a battalion, a brigade, a division, a corps, an army and the Army is explained later.

5 Bean, *Anzac to Amiens*, p. 181.

6 ibid., p. 134.

7 Birdwood, *Khaki and Gown: An Autobiography*, Ward, Lock & Co. Limited, London, 1941, pp. 241, 267.

8 ibid., p. 288.

9 Bean, *Anzac to Amiens*, p. 134.

10 ibid., p. 174.

11 ibid., p. 134–5.

12 ibid., p. 169.

13 When he left his dugout at Quinn's Post on the last day of the evacuation of Gallipoli, Lieutenant Basil Holmes left a full bottle of whisky with a note on which he had written, 'For a Good Turk': H Broadbent, *The Boys Who Came Home: Recollections of Gallipoli*, Australian Broadcasting Commission, Sydney, 1990, p. 126. Basil Holmes was my paternal grandmother's younger brother.

14 According to Eric Partridge, the famous lexicographer, 'digger' was a word that other nationalities used to describe the Australian soldiers: '...others called them ['diggers'], though they themselves used the word to address other combatants and even civilians, and among themselves, they employed it in such a phrase, as, "Hullo, Digger, what are you doing there?": E Partridge, *Frank Honywood, Private*, Melbourne University Press, Melbourne 1987, p 71.

15 Bean, *Anzac to Amiens*, p. 183.

16 J Maxwell, *Hell's Bells and Mademoiselles*, Angus & Robertson Limited, Sydney, 1933, p. 23.

17 I D Chapman, *Iven G. Mackay Citizen and Soldier*, Melway Publishing Pty Ltd, Melbourne,1975, p.9.

18 ibid., p. 12.

19 ibid., p. 69.

20 ibid., p.94.

21 E J Rule, *Jacka's Mob*, Angus & Robertson Limited, Sydney, 1933, p. 32.

22 B Bishop, *The Hell, the Humour and the Heartbreak. A Private's View of World War 1*, Kangaroo Press, Sydney, 1991, p. 23.

23 ibid., p. 24.

24 Bean, *Anzac to Amiens*, p. 75.

25 *Official History*, vol. I, p. 130n.

26 ibid., p. 130n.

27 ibid., p. 130n.

28 A Donnell, *Letters of an Australian Army Sister*, Angus & Robertson Ltd, Sydney, 1920, pp. 79, 83.

29 F E Trotter, *Tales of Billzac being excerpts from a digger's diary*, Robert McGregor & Co, Brisbane, 1923, p. 5. 'Baksish' was a term used to ask for a small gift of money.

30 *Official History*, vol. III, p. 32.

31 *Official History*, vol. II, p. 128–130.

32 Lord Birdwood, *Khaki and Gown: An Autobiography*, Ward, Lock & Co. Limited, London, 1941, reprinted, 1942, p. 263.

33 ibid., p. 284, 299.

34 Bean, *Anzac to Amiens*, p. 166.

Chapter 2 — Splitting the Divisions

1 *Official History*, vol. III, p. 36.

2 ibid., p. 43.

3 The chart is found in: A Rawson, *British Army Handbook 1914–1918*, Sutton Publishing, London 2006, p. 161. The descriptions which follow are taken from Monash, *Australian Victories*, p. 1–19; and from A D Ellis, *The Story of the Fifth Australian Division*, Hodder and Stoughton, London, p. 3–16

4 Limbered wagons were horse-drawn, articulated wagons, generally used to tow a gun of some sort.

5 *Official History*, vol. III, p. 41.

6   Lord Birdwood, *Khaki and Gown: An Autobiography*, Ward, Lock & Co. Limited, London, 1941, reprinted, 1942, p. 299.

7   E J Rule, *Jacka's Mob*, Angus & Robertson Limited, Sydney, 1933, p. 34.

8   Charge you with a crime against military discipline.

9   E J Rule, *Jacka's Mob*, Angus & Robertson Limited, Sydney, 1933, p. 5.

10   ibid., p. 35.

11   ibid., p. 34.

12   N Wanliss, *The History of the Fourteenth Battalion, A.I.F.* The Arrow Printery, Melbourne, 1929, p. 95.

13   Bean, *Anzac to Amiens*, p. 189.

14   *Official History*, vol. III, p. 39; Bean, *Anzac to Amiens*, pp. 91–92.

15   Bean, *Anzac to Amiens*, p. 190; *Official History*, vol. III, pp. 44–47.

16   *Official History*, vol. III, p. 37.

17   ibid., pp. 37–38.

18   ibid., p. 57.

19   ibid., p. 56.

20   ibid., p. 58.

21   ibid., p. 57.

22   Hankey, *Supreme Command*, p. 501.

23   Haig, *War Diaries*, p. 385.

24   *Official History*, vol. III, p. 60.

25   ibid., p. 58.

26   Monash, *Letters*, p. 102.

27   J Maxwell, *Hell's Bells and Mademoiselles*, Angus & Robertson Limited, Sydney, 1933, p. 25. Joe Maxwell was later awarded the Victoria Cross, the Military Cross and the Distinguished Conduct Medal.

28   *Official History*, vol. III, p. 58.

29   P F Tighe 'Lecture "From the Nile to the Somme" given at Manresa Hall, North Sydney, 28 March, 1917', Mitchell Library, 940.9341/T.

30   R and L Denning, *Anzac Digger: An Engineer in Gallipoli and France*, Australian Military History Publications, Sydney, 2004, p. 25.

31   *Official History*, vol. III, p. 62.

32   Bean, *Anzac to Amiens*, p. 192.

33   ibid., pp. 192–193.

34   *Official History*, vol. III, p. 68.

35   C E W Bean, *Two Men I Knew: William Bridges and Brudenell White Founders of the AIF*, Angus and Robertson, Sydney, 1957.

Chapter 3 — Arrival in France

1   *Official History*, vol. III, p. 66.

2   M Campbell and G Hosken, *Four Australians at War: Letters to Argyle 1914–1919*, Kangaroo Press, Sydney 1996, p. 65.

3   *Official History*, vol. III, p. 69.

4   B Bishop, *The Hell, the Humour and the Heartbreak. A Private's View of World War 1*, Kangaroo Press, Sydney, 1991, pp. 52–3.

5   *Official History*, vol. III, p. 69.

6   P Yule (ed.), *Sergeant Lawrence goes to France*, Melbourne University Press, Melbourne, 1987, p. 4.

7   P Wilson (ed.), *So Far From Home*, Kangaroo Press, Sydney, 2002, p. 61.

8   *Official History*, vol. III, p. 69–70.

9   A D Ellis, *The Story of the Fifth Australian Division*, Hodder and Stoughton Limited, London, p. 56.

10 N Wanliss, *The History of the Fourteenth Battalion, AIF: being the Story of the Vicissitudes of an Australian Unit during the Great War*, The Arrow Printery, Melbourne, 1929, p. 105.

11 A Tiveychoc (a nom de plume), *There and Back: The Story of an Australian Soldier 1915–1935*, Returned Sailors and Soldiers' Imperial League of Australia, Sydney, 1935, p. 123.

12 W D Joynt, *Breaking the Road for the Rest*, Hyland House, Melbourne, 1979, p. 70.

13 *Official History*, vol. III, p. 71. A kepi is the familiar French military cap.

14 A W Keown, *Forward with the Fifth The Story of Five Years' War Service Fifth Inf. Battalion, AIF*, The Specialty Press Pty Ltd, Melbourne, 1921, p. 153.

15 P Yule (ed.), *Sergeant Lawrence goes to France*, Melbourne University Press, Melbourne, 1987, p. 4.

16 *Official History*, vol. III, p. 72.

17 ibid.

18 E J Rule, *Jacka's Mob*, Angus & Robertson Limited, Sydney, 1933, pp. 39–40.

19 *Official History*, vol. III, p. 73

20 N Wanliss, *The History of the Fourteenth Battalion, AIF being the Story of the Vicissitudes of an Australian Unit during the Great War*, The Arrow Printery, Melbourne, 1929, pp. 101, 104.

21 J Maxwell, *Hell's Bells and Mademoiselles*, Angus & Robertson Limited, Sydney, 1933, p. 26.

22 *Official History*, vol. III, p. 73.

23 40 Men, 8 horses.

24   M Henry, 'Notes of a Veterinary Officer with the A.I.F. (1914–1919)' (1931) VIII *Australian Veterinary Journal* 43, pp. 47–48.

25   A D Ellis, *The Story of the Fifth Australian Division*, Hodder and Stoughton Limited, London, p. 56.

26   P Yule (ed.), *Sergeant Lawrence goes to France*, Melbourne University Press, Melbourne, 1987, p. 5.

27   A D Ellis, *The Story of the Fifth Australian Division*, Hodder and Stoughton Limited, London, p. 58; A. A Tiveychoc (a nom de plume), *There and Back: The Story of an Australian Soldier 1915–1935*, Returned Sailors and Soldiers' Imperial League of Australia, Sydney, 1935, p. 124.

28   *Official History*, vol. III, p. 74.

29   H R Clay, *Letters and Memoirs of the late Sergeant Harold Richard Clay*, T J Higham, Melbourne, 1928, p. 60.

30   *Official History*, vol. III, p. 76.

31   ibid., pp. 76–78.

32   ibid., p. 78.

33   ibid., p. 85.

34   P Yule (ed.), *Sergeant Lawrence goes to France*, Melbourne University Press, Melbourne, 1987, p. 9 and 16–17.

35   *Official History*, vol. III, p. 86.

36   P Yule (ed.), *Sergeant Lawrence goes to France*, Melbourne University Press, Melbourne, 1987, p. 16.

37   ibid.

38   J Maxwell, *Hell's Bells and Mademoiselles*, Angus & Robertson Limited, Sydney, 1933, pp. 26–27.

39   R and L Denning, *Anzac Digger: An Engineer in Gallipoli and France*, Australian Military History Publications, Sydney, 2004, p. 44.

40   *Official History*, vol. III, p. 85.

41   M Campbell and G Hosken, *Four Australians at War: Letters to Argyle 1914–1919*, Kangaroo Press, Sydney 1996, p. 68.

42   P Yule (ed.), *Sergeant Lawrence goes to France*, Melbourne University Press, Melbourne, 1987, p. 9.

43   S Sassoon, *Memoirs of an Infantry Officer*, in *The Complete Memoirs of George Sherston*, Faber and Faber 1937, 1972 reprint, p. 364.

44   Red wine, white wine.

45   A W Keown, *Forward with the Fifth The Story of Five Years' War Service Fifth Inf. Battalion, AIF*, The Specialty Press Pty Ltd, Melbourne, 1921, p. 156.

46 P Yule (ed.), *Sergeant Lawrence goes to France*, Melbourne University Press, Melbourne, 1987, pp. 17–18.

47 R and L Denning, *Anzac Digger: An Engineer in Gallipoli and France*, Australian Military History Publications, Sydney, 2004, p. 47.

48 Monash, *Letters*, pp. 111–12.

49 Lord Birdwood, *Khaki and Gown: An Autobiography*, Ward, Lock & Co. Limited, London, 1941, reprinted, 1942, p. 304.

50 A W Keown, *Forward with the Fifth The Story of Five Years' War Service Fifth Inf. Battalion, AIF*, The Specialty Press Pty Ltd, Melbourne, 1921, p. 157.

51 I Chapman, *Iven G Mackay Citizen and Soldier*, Melway Pubishing Pty Limited, Melbourne, 1975, p. 71.

52 *Official History*, vol. III, p. 79.

53 A M Henniker, *Transportation on the Western Front 1914–1918*, The Imperial War Museum, London, originally released 1937, pp. 176, 322.

54 ibid., pp. 103–105.

55 A typical supply train was for two divisions and contained:

Item	Wagons
2 packs of supplies as above, 2x15 wagons per division	30
Coal or coke, 1 wagon per division	2
Mails, 1 wagon per division	2
Ordnance, 1 wagon per division	2
Mechanical transport spares, etc., 1 wagon per division	2
1 van per division	2
Total Wagons	**40**

See ibid., pp. 103–105.

56 ibid., pp. 280, 327.

57 M Henry, 'Notes of a Veterinary Officer with the A.I.F. (1914–1919)' (1931) VIII *Australian Veterinary Journal* 43, pp. 47–48.

58 A short-barrelled cannon used for shelling troops behind cover at relatively short range.

59 O H Woodward, *The War Story of Oliver Holmes Woodward*, published privately, p. 39.

60 A Rawson, *British Army Handbook 1914–1918*, Sutton Publishing, London 2006, p. 276.

61 Enfilade fire is fire from a flank. If a gun can be sited on the flank, to fire straight down a trench line, it delivers an enfilade fire along the trench line which is especially deadly. To avoid the effects of enfilade fire, trenches were dug

in a castellated pattern, in which, say, ten metres of the trench would run east-west; the next ten metres would run north-south; the next ten metres would run west-east; the next section east-south; and so on.

62 A Rawson, *British Army Handbook 1914–1918*, Sutton Publishing, London 2006, p. 246.

63 ibid., p. 246–8.

64 Parapets and parados are both defensive walls. The parapet is in front of the defender, closer to the enemy. The parados is behind the defender. The parados (which is higher than the parapet) protects the defender from being silhouetted against the horizon or background if he shows his head or shoulders above the parapet.

65 *Official History*, vol. III, p. 89.

66 A W Keown, *Forward with the Fifth The Story of Five Years' War Service Fifth Inf. Battalion, AIF*, The Specialty Press Pty Ltd, Melbourne, 1921, p. 156.

67 Bean, *Anzac to Amiens*, p. 202. There is a photograph of the *estaminet* at Spy Farm in the *Official History*, vol. III, facing p. 108. See also *Official History*, vol. III, p. 136.

68 A G Howell, ' Signaller at the Front', Hesperian Press, Perth, 2001, pp. 6, 8.

69 ibid.

70 O H Woodward, *The War Story of Oliver Holmes Woodward*, published privately, pp. 35–7.

71 B Bishop, *The Hell, the Humour and the Heartbreak. A Private's View of World War 1*, Kangaroo Press, Sydney, 1991, p. 60.

72 S Sassoon, *The Complete Memoirs of George Sherston*, Faber and Faber, London, 1937, reprinted 1972, p. 279.

73 O H Woodward, *The War Story of Oliver Holmes Woodward*, published privately, p. 39.

74 G Corrigan, *Mud Blood and Poppycock*, Cassell Military Paperbacks, London 2003. p. 87–88.

75 E J Rule, *Jacka's Mob*, Angus & Robertson Limited, Sydney, 1933, p. 42.

76 Bean, *Anzac to Amiens*, p. 206.

77 R H Knyvett '"Over There" with the Australians, Charles Scribner's Sons, New York, 1918, p. 175.

78 Bean, *Anzac to Amiens*, p. 211.

79 G Franki and C Slatyer, 'Mad Harry', Kangaroo Press, Sydney, 2003, p. 51.

Chapter 4 — The Somme

1 Bean, *Anzac to Amiens*, p. 212, 214.

2 General Haig's *Second Despatch*, p. 20.

3 ibid., p. 21.

4 A M Henniker, *Transportation on the Western front 1914–1918*, The Imperial War Museum, London, originally released 1937, p. 122.

5 General Haig's *Second Despatch*, p. 22.

6 Churchill, *World Crisis*, p. 1041.

7 Hankey, *Supreme Command*, p. 495.

8 Churchill, *World Crisis*, pp. 1045–6.

9 Keegan calls it a 'catastrophe, the greatest loss of life in British military history': J Keegan, *The First World War*, Pimlico, London, 1998, p 317–318.

10 General Haig's *Second Despatch*, p. 27.

11 *Official History*, vol. III, p. 328.

12 ibid.

13 This description of the raid is taken from N Wanliss, *The History of the Fourteenth Battalion, AIF*, The Arrow Printery, Melbourne, 1929, p. 111ff.

14 The word 'knobkerrie' derives from Afrikaans and, ultimately, from the Hottentot word for stick or club. The use of the word in the war may have been a legacy of the Boer War.

15 The casualty figures are given in N Wanliss, '*The History of the Fourteenth Battalion, AIF*, The Arrow Printery, Melbourne, 1929, at p. 121–4.

Chapter 5 — Fromelles

1 Bean, *Anzac to Amiens*, p. 223.

2 From R Haking, 'Company Training', London 1913, quoted in R McMullin, *Pompey Elliott*, Scribe Publications, Melbourne, 2002, p. 205.

3 *Official History*, vol. III, p. 350.

4 ibid., p. 346.

5 ibid., p. 443.

6 R McMullin, *Pompey Elliott*, Scribe Publications, Melbourne, 2002, p. 210–211; *Official History*, vol. III, p. 346.

7 *Official History*, vol. III, p. 346.

8 ibid., p. 348.

9 ibid., p. 347.

10 ibid.

11 ibid., p. 348

12   ibid., p. 349–50

13   ibid.

14   A D Ellis, *The Story of the Fifth Australian Division*, Hodder and Stoughton
      Limited, London, no date, p. 94–5.

15   Bean, *Anzac to Amiens*, p. 223–4.

16   A D Ellis, *The Story of the Fifth Australian Division*, Hodder and Stoughton
      Limited, London, no date, p. 94.

17   A Tiveychoc (a nom de plume), *There and Back: The Story of an Australian Soldier
      1915–1935*, Returned Sailors and Soldiers Imperial League of Australia, Sydney,
      1935, p. 169–72.

18   One German who took part in the battle was Adolf Hitler: R McMullin, *Pompey
      Elliott*, Scribe Publications, Melbourne, 2002, p. 222.

19   M Campbell and G Hosken, *Four Australians at War: Letters to Argyle 1914–1919*,
      Kangaroo Press, Sydney, 1996, p. 88–9.

20   *Official History*, vol. III, p. 362.

21   A D Ellis, *The Story of the Fifth Australian Division*, Hodder and Stoughton
      Limited, London, no date, p. 96.

22   ibid., p. 96–97.

23   ibid., p. 97.

24   ibid., p. 99.

25   ibid., p. 100–101.

26   ibid., p. 102.

27   ibid., p. 99.

28   Bean, *Anzac to Amiens*, p. 234.

29   ibid., p. 235.

30   A G Butler, *The Australian Army Medical Services in the War of 1914–1918*,
      Australian War Memorial, Canberra, 1940, vol. II, p. 48.

31   R H Knyvett *'Over There' with the Australians*, Charles Scribner's Sons, New York,
      1918, p. 179.

32   R McMullin, *Pompey Elliott*, Scribe Publications, Melbourne, 2002, p. 224.

33   ibid., p. 224.

34   *Official History*, vol. III, p. 437.

35   W H Downing, *To the last Ridge*, Duffy & Snellgrove, Sydney, 1998, p. 13.

36   A D Ellis, *The Story of the Fifth Australian Division*, Hodder and Stoughton
      Limited, London, no date, p. 111.

37   ibid., p. 112.

38   *Official History*, vol. III, p. 443.

39 ibid., p. 446.

40 ibid., p. 445.

41 Bean, *Anzac to Amiens*, p. 237. The site of the battle is marked by the War Grave Cemetery at VC Corner, said to be the burial place of 410 of the 1299 Australian soldiers killed in the battle. It is unique among the cemeteries on the western front because it has no headstones.

42 *Official History*, vol. III, p. 442.

43 Bean, *Anzac to Amiens*, p. 236.

44 T Travers, *The Killing Ground The British Army, The Western Front & the Emergence of Modern War 1900–1918*, Pen & Sword Military Classics, Barnsley, South Yorkshire, 1987, p. 30, note 37. A British author who discounts the 'donkey' thesis claims that, when the christened Haking 'Butcher', they may not have intended it to be pejorative — 'after all, to Australians "bastard" is almost a term of affection": G Corrigan, *Mud, Blood and Poppycock*, Cassell, London, 2004, p. 202. It is true that Australians do, sometimes, use the word 'bastard' as a term of affection, but, when Australians use that word, or the word 'butcher', to describe General Haking, they mean to insult. Moreover, Tim Travers' reference indicates that the British called Haking by the same nickname.

Chapter 6 — Pozières and Mouquet Farm

1 E Partridge, *Frank Honywood, Private A Personal Record of the 1914–1918 War*, Melbourne University Press, Melbourne, 1987.

2 M Campbell and G Hosken, *Four Australians at War*, Kangaroo Press Pty Ltd, Sydney, 1996, p. 96.

3 *Official History*, vol. III, p. 449.

4 ibid., p. 448–449.

5 Meaning roughly, 'The milk is walking'.

6 A bastardised version of the French 'Bonjour Madame', meaning 'Good-day, madam'.

7 T A White, *The History of the Thirteenth Battalion AIF*, Tyrrells Ltd, Sydney, 1924, p. 64.

8 R and L Denning, *Anzac Digger: An Engineer in Gallipoli and France*, Australian Military History Publications, Sydney, 2004, p. 49.

9 Bean, *Anzac to Amiens*, p. 239. There was a legend that, when the 'Leaning Virgin' fell the war would end. It finally fell to British artillery fire in April 1918. Adherents of the *post hoc ergo propter hoc* school of causal reasoning will be asking themselves why the British did not think of blowing it up sooner.

10   *Official History*, vol. III, p. 468.

11   Bean, *Anzac to Amiens*, p. 264.

12   General Haig's *Second Despatch*, p. 21–22; see also Bean, *Anzac to Amiens*, p. 219.

13   ibid., p. 23.

14   ibid., p. 23–4.

15   ibid., p. 24.

16   *Official History*, vol. III, p. 456.

17   General Haig's *Second Despatch*, p. 32.

18   *Official History*, vol. III, p. 468.

19   ibid., p. 468.

20   ibid., p. 473.

21   I D Chapman, *Iven G Mackay Citizen and Soldier*, Melway Publishing Pty Ltd, Melbourne,1975, p. 73.

22   Bean, *Anzac to Amiens*, p. 242.

23   F C Trotter, *Tales of Billyac, being Extracts from a Digger's Diary*, Robert McGregor & Co., Brisbane, 1923, p. 16.

24   *Official History*, vol. III, p. 485.

25   ibid., p. 483.

26   ibid., p. 494.

27   M Campbell and G Hosken, *Four Australians at War*, Kangaroo Press Pty Ltd, Sydney, 1996, p. 98.

28   I D Chapman, *Iven G Mackay Citizen and Soldier*, Melway Publishing Pty Ltd, Melbourne,1975, p. 75.

29   A G Howell, *Signaller at the Front: The War Diary of Gunner Arthur G Howell*, Hesperian Press, Perth, 2001, p. 18.

30   K T Henderson, *Khaki and Cassock*, Melville & Mullen Pty Ltd, Melbourne, 1919, p. 17–19.

31   I D Chapman, *Iven G Mackay Citizen and Soldier*, Melway Publishing Pty Ltd, Melbourne,1975, p. 75.

32   Bean, *Anzac to Amiens*, p. 243.

33   ibid., p. 244.

34   G Mant (ed.), *Soldier Boy: The Letters of Gunner W J Duffell, 1915–1918*, Kangaroo Press, Sydney,1992, p. 54.

35   E J Rule, *Jacka's Mob*, Angus & Robertson Limited, Sydney, 1933, p. 63.

36   Bean, *Anzac to Amiens*, p. 244.

37   I D Chapman, *Iven G Mackay Citizen and Soldier*, Melway Publishing Pty Ltd, Melbourne,1975, p. 75.

38   Bean, *Anzac to Amiens*, p. 246.

39   ibid., pp. 246–7.

40   ibid., p. 247.

41   ibid., pp. 248–9.

42   A W Keown, *Forward with the Fifth*, The Specialty Press Pty Ltd, Melbourne, 1921, p. 174.

43   E J Rule, *Jacka's Mob*, Angus & Robertson Limited, Sydney, 1933, p. 61.

44   Bean, *Anzac to Amiens*, p. 249.

45   Haig, *War Diaries*, pp. 210–11.

46   *Official History*, vol. III, p. 643.

47   Haig, *War Diaries*, p. 211.

48   C E W Bean *Two Men I Knew: William Bridges and Brudenell White Founders of the AIF*. Angus and Robertson, Sydney, 1957, p. 79. It goes without saying that Bean was a huge admirer of White.

49   *Official History*, vol. III, p. 644.

50   Brigadier General, General Staff.

51   Haig War Diary, p. 211.

52   Lord Birdwood, *Khaki and Gown: An Autobiography*, Ward, Lock & Co. Limited, London, 1941, reprinted, 1942, p. 307–308.

53   D Cooper, *Haig*, Doubleday, Doran & Company, Inc, New York, 1935, p. 111.

54   Haig, *War Diaries*, p. 213.

55   ibid., pp. 213–14.

56   ibid., *War Diaries*, p. 214.

57   Bean, *Anzac to Amiens*, p. 253.

58   ibid., pp. 253–5.

59   ibid., p. 255.

60   *Official History*, vol. III, p. 699.

61   ibid.

62   ibid., p. 256.

63   ibid.

64   ibid., p. 724.

65   ibid.

66   J Maxwell, *Hell's Bells and Mademoiselles*, Angus & Robertson Limited, Sydney, 1933.

67   Bean, *Anzac to Amiens*, p. 257.

68   E J Rule, *Jacka's Mob*, Angus & Robertson Limited, Sydney, 1933, p. 70.

69   Bean, *Anzac to Amiens*, p. 259; W D Joynt, *Breaking the Road for the Rest*, Hyland House, Melbourne, 1979, p. 93.

70   G Franki and C Slatyer, *Mad Harry: Australia's most Decorated Soldier*, Kangaroo Press, Sydney, 2003, p. 62.

71   Bean, *Anzac to Amiens*, p. 261.

72   Haig, *War Diaries*, p. 218–19.

73   J Masefield, *The Old Front Line*, Pen & Sword Military Classics, Barnsley, South Yorkshire, 1917, reprinted 2003, p. 120.

74   Bean, *Anzac to Amiens*, p. 262.

75   ibid.

76   ibid., p. 263.

77   *Official History*, vol. III, p. 858.

78   A G Butler, *The Australian Army Medical Services in the War of 1914–1918*, Australian War Memorial, Canberra, 1940, p. 73.

79   Bean, *Anzac to Amiens*, pp. 264–5.

80   J Luvaas, *The Education of an Army: British Military Thought, 1815–1940*, Cassell, London, 1965, p. 326.

81   General Haig's *Second Despatch*, p. 40.

82   Bean, *Anzac to Amiens*, p. 268.

83   J H Boraston, *Sir Douglas Haig's Command 1914–1918*, Constable, London, 1922.

84   Churchill did not think much of the book, which he condemned in not so gentle terms. 'It is marred by small recriminations, by an air of soreness, by a series of literary sniffs and snorts, which combine to produce an unpleasant impression on the mind of the general reader': Churchill, *World Crisis*, p. 926.

85   ibid., p. 1057; *Official History*, vol. III, p. 945.

86   Haig, *War Diaries*, p. 211

87   W D Joynt, *Breaking the Road for the Rest*, Hyland House, Melbourne, 1979, p. 93.

88   General Haig's *Second Despatch*, p. 51.

89   D Cooper, *Haig*, Doubleday, Doran & Company, Inc, New York, 1935, p. 118.

Chapter 7 — Wounded

1   *Official History*, vol. III, p. 862.

2   A G Butler, *The Australian Army Medical Services in the War of 1914–1918*, Australian War Memorial, Canberra, 1940, vol. II, pp. 48 and 73.

3   P F Tighe 'Lecture "From the Nile to the Somme" given at Manresa Hall, North Sydney, 28 March, 1917' Mitchell Library, 940.9341/T, p. 19.

4   E Morrow, *Iron in the Fire*, Angus & Robertson Limited, Sydney, 1934, pp. 45–46.

5   P Wilson (ed.), *So Far From Home*, Kangaroo Press, Sydney, 2002, p. 103–04. Sergeant Evans was injured in August, 1917.

6   C Huxtable, *From the Somme to Singapore*, Kangaroo Press, Sydney, 1987, p. 36. Huxtable also served in the Second World War, when he had the misfortune to become a prisoner of war of the Japanese at Singapore.

7   High explosive.

8   J S Linton, *A Soldier's Tale: One Man's War 16 February 1916–12 June 1919*, J S Linton, Kalamunda WA, 1997, p. 40.

9   A shell that exploded prematurely, killing or wounding the members of the battery attempting to load or fire the gun.

10 W S Oliver, *The Great White Father: The biography of a Great Australian*, Bill Oliver, Temora NSW, 2003, pp. 88–109.

11 Regimental Aid Post.

12 A G Butler, *The Australian Army Medical Services in the War of 1914–1918*, Australian War Memorial, Canberra, 1940, p. 346.

13 A M Henniker, *Transportation on the Western front 1914–1918*, The Imperial War Museum, London, originally released 1937, p. 57–8.

14 ibid., p. 66.

15 ibid., p. 66.

16 ibid., pp. 379–80.

17 R H Knyvett, *'Over There' with the Australians*, Charles Scribner's Sons, New York, 1918, pp. 271–80.

18 C Huxtable, *From the Somme to Singapore: A Medical Officer in Two World Wars*, Kangaroo Press, Sydney, 1987, p. 22.

19 J Bassett, *Guns and Brooches: Australian Army Nursing from the Boer War to the Gulf War*, Oxford University Press, Melbourne, 1992, p. 56.

20 ibid.

21 ibid., p. 57.

22 ibid., p. 56–7.

23 A disease of the feet, caused by exposure to cold and wet conditions.

24 J Bassett, *Guns and Brooches: Australian Army Nursing from the Boer War to the Gulf War*, Oxford University Press, Melbourne, 1992, p. 56.

25 ibid., p. 57.

26 ibid., p. 57.

27 ibid., p. 57.

28 ibid., p. 57.

29 ibid., pp. 57–8.

30 ibid., p. 60.

31 ibid., p. 58.

32 M Tilton, quoted in C Harrison-Ford (ed.), *Fighting Words: Australian War Writing*, Lothian Publishing Company, Melbourne, 1986, pp. 131–2.

33 E Morrow, *Iron in the Fire*, Angus & Robertson Limited, Sydney, 1934, p. 48.

34 ibid., p. 49.

35 A G Butler, *The Australian Army Medical Services in the War of 1914–1918*, Australian War Memorial, Canberra, 1940, p. 495.

36 ibid., pp. 320–23.

37 ibid., chapter XII.

38 ibid., pp. 312–13.

39 ibid., pp. 316–17.

40 ibid., p. 325.

41 M Campbell and G Hosken, *Four Australians at War*, Kangaroo Press, Sydney, 1996, p. 90.

42 A recurrent fever, transmitted by lice.

43 J Elliott, *Scalpel and Sword*, AH and AW Reed, Dunedin, 1936, pp. 163–5.

44 ibid., p. 166.

45 ibid., p. 167.

46 G Mant (ed.), *Soldier Boy*, Kangaroo Press, Sydney, 1992, p. 116.

47 K T Henderson, *Khaki and Cassock*, Melville & Mullen Pty Ltd, Melbourne, p. 95.

48 E Morrow, *Iron in the Fire*, Angus & Robertson Limited, Sydney, 1934, p. 53.

49 ibid., p. 51.

50 W S Oliver, *The Great White Father: The biography of a great Australian*, Bill Oliver, Temora NSW, 2003, pp. 121–2.

51 ibid., p. 122.

52 J Bond, *The Army that Went with the boys*, Salvation Army National Headquarters, Melbourne, 1919, p. 89.

53 R H Knyvett, *'Over There' with the Australians*, Charles Scribner's Sons, New York, 1918, p. 285.

54 W S Oliver, *The Great White Father: The biography of a great Australian*, Bill Oliver, Temora NSW, 2003, p. 124.

55 A G Howell, *Signaller at the Front, the War Diary of Gunner Arthur G. Howell MM*, Hesperian Press, Perth, 2001, p. 58.

56 P Wilson (ed.), *So Far From Home*, Kangaroo Press, Sydney, 2002, p. 132.

57   K T Henderson, *Khaki and Cassock*, Melville & Mullen Pty Ltd, Melbourne, pp. 35–6.

58   Adapted from ibid., p. 36–9. Chaplain Henderson lost two brothers on Gallipoli. In civilian life, Chaplain Henderson lectured in philosophy at that wonderful institution, St Paul's College in the University of Sydney.

59   There are huge memorials containing the names of men with no known graves, amongst them Thiepval (73,357 names); Menin Gate (54,900 names); Tyne Cot — so named because the British thought the local houses looked like cottages on the Tyne: G Corrigan, *Mud Blood and Poppycock*, Cassell Military Paperbacks, London 2003. p. 358 — (34,927 names); Villers Bretonneux (more than 11 000 names); Pozières (1,374 names); Messines Ridge (840 names); and VC Corner, at the site of the Fromelles battle (410 names). The tombs of the unknown soldiers also commemorate those with no known graves.

60   J Maxwell, *Hell's Bells and Mademoiselles*, Angus & Robertson Limited, Sydney, 1933, p. 229.

61   A G Butler, *The Australian Army Medical Services in the War of 1914–1918*, Australian War Memorial, Canberra, 1940, p. 299.

62   For an account of the role of the Dental Service, see L G Wilson, 'Dental Services in the British and Australian Armies', 1935, vol. 7, *The Dental Journal of Australia*, p. 227.

63   A G Butler, *The Australian Army Medical Services in the War of 1914–1918*, Australian War Memorial, Canberra, 1940, p. 496–7.

64   J S Linton, *A Soldier's Tale*, Published privately, Perth, 1997, p. 100. For a more balanced account of the dental services provided during the war: see L G Wilson, 'Dental Services in the British and Australian Armies', *The Dental Journal of Australia*, 1935, vol 7, p. 227.

65   E J Rule, *Jacka's Mob*, Angus & Robertson Limited, Sydney, 1933, p. 111.

66   ibid., pp. 113–14.

67   I D Chapman, *Iven G Mackay Citizen and Soldier*, Melway Publishing Pty Ltd, Melbourne, 1975, pp. 93–4.

68   M Henry, 'Notes of a Veterinary Officer with the AIF 1914–18', 1932, vol. VIII, *The Australian Veterinary Journal*, pp. 84–85.

69   ibid., p. 51.

70   I M Parsonson, *Vets at War*, Army History Unit, Canberra, 2005, p. 86.

71   M Henry, 'Notes of a Veterinary Officer with the AIF 1914–18', 1932, Volume VIII. *The Australian Veterinary Journal*, p. 50.

72   I M Parsonson, *Vets at War*, Army History Unit, Canberra, 2005, p. 78.

73   M Henry, 'Notes of a Veterinary Officer with the AIF 1914–18', 1932, Volume VIII. *The Australian Veterinary Journal*, p. 53.

74   I M Parsonson, *Vets at War*, Army History Unit, Canberra, 2005, p. 83.

Chapter 8 — Breaking the Deadlock

1   D Cooper, *Haig*, Doubleday, Doran & Company, Inc, New York, 1935, p. 59.

2   ibid.

3   Haig, *War Diaries*, p. 289.

4   *Official History*, vol. III, p. 79.

5   Churchill, *World Crisis*, vol. III, pp. 927–8.

6   Hankey, *Supreme Command*, p. 555.

7   Bean, *Anzac to Amiens*, p. 214; Churchill, *World Crisis*, vol. III, p. 950ff.

8   Hankey, *Supreme Command*, p. 555.

9   Lloyd George succeeded Asquith as prime minister on 7 December 1916.

10   Hankey, *Supreme Command*, p. 514.

11   Indeed, Duff Cooper wrote of Haig that, 'Singleness of purpose is the clue to his character and the key to his greatness': D Cooper, *Haig*, Doubleday, Doran & Company, Inc, New York, 1935, p. 348.

12   General Haig's *Final Despatch*, p. 326.

13   Churchill, *World Crisis*, vol. III, p. 942.

14   General Haig's *Final Despatch*, p. 324.

Chapter 9 — Bullecourt

1   I D Chapman, *Iven G. Mackay Citizen and Soldier*, Melway Publishing Pty Ltd, Melbourne, 1975, p. 81.

2   Lord Birdwood, *Khaki and Gown: An Autobiography*, Ward, Lock & Co. Limited, London, 1941, reprinted, 1942, p. 317.

3   I D Chapman, *Iven G. Mackay Citizen and Soldier*, Melway Publishing Pty Ltd, Melbourne, 1975, p. 82.

4   A W Keown, *Forward with the Fifth*, The Specialty Press Pty Ltd, Melbourne, 1921, p. 193.

5   F H Semple, quoted in B Gammage 'The Broken Years Australian Soldiers in the Great War' Penguin Books, Melbourne 1974, p. 174–175.

6   G. Chapman (ed.), 'Vain Glory', Cassell and Company Limited, London, 1937, p. 383.

7   W H Downing, *To the last Ridge*, Duffy & Snellgrove, Sydney, 1998, p. 34–35.

8   I do not understand.

9   Sleep with me.

10 After the war.

11 Piccaninnies not good. The story comes from R and L Denning, *Anzac Digger: An Engineer in Gallipoli and France*, Australian Military History Publications, Sydney, 2004, p. 67.

12 I do not understand you, sir.

13 J Maxwell, *Hell's Bells and Mademoiselles*, Angus & Robertson Limited, Sydney, 1933, p. 196.

14 Bean, *Anzac to Amiens*, p. 346.

15 ibid., p. 316–17.

16 ibid., p. 320.

17 General Haig's *Second Despatch*, p. 40.

18 Churchill, *World Crisis*, p. 942.

19 N Wanliss, *The History of the Fourteenth Battalion, AIF Being the Story of the Vicissitudes of an Australian Unit during the Great War*, The Arrow Printery, Melbourne, 1929, pp. 320–1.

20 A G Howell, *Signaller at the Front The War Diary of Gunner Arthur G Howell*, Hesperian Press, Perth, 2001, p. 18.

21 Bean, *Anzac to Amiens*, p. 328.

22 ibid., p. 330.

23 N Wanliss, *The History of the Fourteenth Battalion, AIF Being the Story of the Vicissitudes of an Australian Unit during the Great War*, The Arrow Printery, Melbourne, 1929, pp. 191–3.

24 ibid., p. 193.

25 Bean, *Anzac to Amiens*, p. 330.

26 Meaning an officer of the 14th Australian Battalion.

27 T A White, *The History of the Thirteenth Battalion, AIF*, Tyrells Limited, Sydney, 1924, p. 93.

28 N Wanliss, *The History of the Fourteenth Battalion, AIF Being the Story of the Vicissitudes of an Australian Unit during the Great War*, The Arrow Printery, Melbourne, 1929, p. 197.

29 Bean, *Anzac to Amiens*, p. 331.

30 N Wanliss, *The History of the Fourteenth Battalion, AIF Being the Story of the Vicissitudes of an Australian Unit during the Great War*, The Arrow Printery, Melbourne, 1929, p. 198.

31 ibid., pp. 198–9.

32 ibid., pp. 199–200.

33   ibid., p. 198.

34   Bean, *Anzac to Amiens*, p. 332.

35   N Wanliss, *The History of the Fourteenth Battalion, AIF Being the Story of the Vicissitudes of an Australian Unit during the Great War*, The Arrow Printery, Melbourne, 1929, p. 202.

36   Bean, *Anzac to Amiens*, p. 333.

37   N Wanliss, *The History of the Fourteenth Battalion, AIF Being the Story of the Vicissitudes of an Australian Unit during the Great War*, The Arrow Printery, Melbourne, 1929, pp. 209, 211.

38   ibid., p. 189.

39   A M Henniker, *Transportation on the Western front 1914–1918*, The Imperial War Museum, London, originally released 1937, p. 305ff.

40   N Wanliss, *The History of the Fourteenth Battalion, AIF Being the Story of the Vicissitudes of an Australian Unit during the Great War*, The Arrow Printery, Melbourne, 1929, p. 208.

41   E J Rule, *Jacka's Mob*, Angus & Robertson Limited, Sydney, 1933, p. 185.

42   ibid.

43   ibid., p. 164–5.

44   Bean, *Anzac to Amiens*, p. 336.

45   ibid., p. 338–40.

46   W D Joynt VC, *Breaking the Road for the Rest*, Hyland House, Melbourne, 1979, p. 116.

47   Bean, *Anzac to Amiens*, pp. 343–4.

48   ibid, p. 344.

49   W D Joynt VC, *Breaking the Road for the Rest*, Hyland House, Melbourne, 1979, p. 118.

Chapter 10 — Messines

1   A Behrend, *As From Kemmel Hill. An Adjutant in France and Flanders, 1917 & 1918*, Eyre & Spottiswoode, London, 1963, p. 11.

2   ibid., p. 12.

3   ibid.

4   E J Rule, *Jacka's Mob*, Angus & Robertson Limited, Sydney, 1933, p. 190.

5   Quoted in IFW Beckett and S J Corvi (eds), *Haig's Generals*, Pen & Sword Military, Barnsley, South Yorkshire, 2006, p. 174.

6   Bean, *Anzac to Amiens*, p. 346–7.

7   C Harington, *Plumer of Messines*, John Murray, London, 1935, p. 86.

8   His motto was 'Trust, Training and Thoroughness': C Harington, *Plumer of Messines*, John Murray, London, 1935, p. 79.

9   ibid., pp. 80–2.

10   ibid., p. 82.

11   Quoted in G Powell, '*Plumer The Soldiers' General: A Biography of Field-Marshal Viscount Plumer of Messines*, Pen & Sword Military, Barnsley South Yorkshire, 2004, p. 155.

12   C Harington, *Plumer of Messines*, John Murray, London, 1935, p. 86; At the height of the war, there were 25 British tunnelling companies, including three Australian companies. Each company had up to 1000 men: G Corrigan, *Mud Blood and Poppycock*, Cassell Military Paperbacks, London 2003. p. 178.

13   A M Henniker, *Transportation on the Western front 1914–1918*, The Imperial War Museum, London, originally released 1937, p. 190: see also Haig's view of the importance of the railways quoted on p. 396.

14   I M Brown, *British Logistics on the Western Front 1914–1919*. Praeger, Westpoint Connecticut, 1998, p. 163.

15   ibid., p. 164.

16   ibid., p. 163.

17   N Wanliss, *The History of the Fourteenth Battalion, AIF Being the Story of the Vicissitudes of an Australian Unit during the Great War*, The Arrow Printery, Melbourne, 1929, pp. 218–19.

18   C Harington, *Plumer of Messines*, John Murray, London, 1935, p. 87.

19   ibid., p. 99.

20   ibid., 1935, p. 100

21   ibid., p. 101.

22   This could be done by a process of averaging. One shot was fired long and the next short. After the observer reported the results, the gunners took an approximate average of the difference. The process was repeated until the right range was struck.

23   R Crack, *Until a Dead Horse Kicks You*, Kangaroo Press, Sydney, 2000, pp. 85–8.

24   Bean, *Anzac to Amiens*, p. 348.

25   Monash, *Letters*, pp. 138–9.

26   N Wanliss, *The History of the Fourteenth Battalion, AIF Being the Story of the Vicissitudes of an Australian Unit during the Great War*, The Arrow Printery, Melbourne, 1929, p. 219.

27   M E David, *Professor David: The Life of Sir Edgeworth David*, Edward Arnold & Co, London, 1937, p. 294.

28 C Harington, *Plumer of Messines*, John Murray, London, 1935, pp. 90–1.

29 N Wanliss, *The History of the Fourteenth Battalion, AIF Being the Story of the Vicissitudes of an Australian Unit during the Great War*, The Arrow Printery, Melbourne, 1929, p. 219.

30 C Harington, *Plumer of Messines*, John Murray, London, 1935, p. 103.

31 ibid.

32 Although the smoke and dust of the battlefield tended to obscure the vision of the balloonists: Monash, *Australian Victories*, p. 15.

33 C Harington, *Plumer of Messines*, John Murray, London, 1935, p. 92.

34 ibid., p. 104.

35 ibid, p. 103–4.

36 Bean, *Anzac to Amiens*, pp. 355–6.

37 C Harington, *Plumer of Messines*, John Murray, London, 1935, p. 102.

38 Lord Birdwood, *Khaki and Gown: An Autobiography*, Ward, Lock & Co. Limited, London, 1941, reprinted, 1942, p. 313. General Holmes is my great-grandfather — the father of my father's mother.

39 Quoted in G Powell, *Plumer The Soldiers': General A Biography of Field-Marshal Viscount Plumer of Messines*, Pen & Sword Military, Barnsley South Yorkshire, 2004, p. 145.

40 Haig, *War Diaries*, p. 298.

Chapter 11 — Passchendaele

1 Bean, *Anzac to Amiens*, p. 376–377.

2 A A Wiest, *Haig: The Evolution of a Commander*, Potomac Books, Inc., Washington DC, 2005, p. 40.

3 Duff Cooper, Haig's 'authorised' biographer, claims that Lloyd George lost confidence in Haig from the beginning of 1917, and, from then on had 'no confidence in his own commander-in-chief, and he disbelieved the main strategic principle upon which the governments of France and England had decided and to which, in spite of him, they were to adhere': D Cooper, *Haig*, Doubleday, Doran & Company, Inc, New York, 1935, p. 122.

4 Bean, *Anzac to Amiens*, p. 360.

5 Hankey, *Supreme Command*, p. 670–671.

6 ibid., p. 675–676.

7 ibid., p. 682.

8 Hankey, *Supreme Command*, p. 676.

9 ibid., pp. 677–8.

10   ibid., p. 678.

11   ibid.

12   ibid., p. 678–9.

13   ibid., p. 679–80.

14   ibid., p. 682.

15   ibid., p. 680.

16   Haig, *War Diaries*, p. 300.

17   ibid., p. 300.

18   ibid, p. 301.

19   Hankey, *Supreme Command*, p. 682.

20   ibid., p. 683.

21   Haig, *War Diaries*, p. 302.

22   K Jeffery, *Field Marshal Sir Henry Wilson*, Oxford University Press, Oxford, 2006,
      p. 195.

23   Hankey, *Supreme Command*, p. 683.

24   ibid., p. 684.

25   General Haig's *Third Despatch*, p. 111–112.

26   *Official History*, vol. IV, p. 699–701.

27   ibid., p. 697.

28   ibid., p. 696.

29   J E Edmonds, *Military Operations France and Belgium 1917*, Imperial War Museum,
      London, 1948, vol. II, p. 127.

30   *Official History*, vol. IV, p. 697.

31   R Prior and T Wilson, *Command on the Western Front: The Military Career of Sir
      Henry Rawlinson 1914–1918*, Pen & Sword Military Classics, Barnsley, South
      Yorkshire, 1992, p. 150.

32   Haig, *War Diaries*, p. 307.

33   Bean, *Anzac to Amiens*, p. 357–8; *Official History*, vol. IV, p. 711.

34   General Haig's *Fourth Despatch*, p. 116.

35   B H Liddell Hart, *The Real War 1914–1918*, Little Brown & Company, Boston,
      1930, p. 339.

36   *Official History*, vol. IV, p. 723.

37   ibid., p. 722.

38   Bean, *Anzac to Amiens*, p. 362.

39   Hankey, *Supreme Command*, p. 694.

40   J H Johnson, *Stalemate! Great Trench Warfare Battles*, Rigel, London, 1995, p. 148.

41   Hankey, *Supreme Command*, p. 697.

42   ibid., p. 701.

43   A A Wiest, *Haig: The Evolution of a Commander*, Potomac Books, Inc., Washington DC, 2005, p. 86, R Prior and T Wilson, *Passchendaele: The Untold Story*, Yale University Press, New Haven, 2nd ed, 2002, p. 155.

44   Hankey, *Supreme Command*, p. 693.

45   Bean, *Anzac to Amiens*, p. 367.

46   C Edmonds, *A Subaltern's War*, Peter Davies Limited, London, 1929, p. 145.

47   W H Downing, *To the last Ridge*, Duffy & Snellgrove, Sydney, 1998, p. 71–72.

48   L Mann, *Flesh in Armour A novel*, Robertson & Mullen Ltd, Melbourne, 1944, p. 45.

49   W D Joynt, *Breaking the Road for the Rest*, Hyland House, Melbourne, 1979, p. 134.

50   L Mann, *Flesh in Armour: A novel*, Robertson & Mullen Ltd, Melbourne, 1944, p. 35.

51   A M Henniker, *Transportation on the Western front 1914–1918*, The Imperial War Museum, London, originally released 1937, pp. 122, 279.

52   Bean, *Anzac to Amiens*, p. 368.

53   C Harington, *Plumer of Messines*, John Murray, London, 1935, p. 117.

54   P Yule (ed.), *Sergeant Lawrence goes to France*, Melbourne University Press, Melbourne, 1987, p. 131.

55   Bean, *Anzac to Amiens*, p. 369. Five Australian divisions attacked together in 1918.

56   F C Trotter, *Tales of Billyac, being Extracts from a Digger's Diary*, Robert McGregor & Co, Brisbane, 1923, p. 23–24; W D Joynt, *Breaking the Road for the Rest*, Hyland House, Melbourne, 1979, p. 136–45.

57   Bean, *Anzac to Amiens*, p. 370.

58   ibid., p. 371.

59   W D Joynt, *Breaking the Road for the Rest*, Hyland House, Melbourne, 1979, p. 146.

60   Haig, encouraged by Colonel Charteris, his intelligence officer, often assumed that German morale was worse than it in fact was.

61   Bean, *Anzac to Amiens*, p. 374.

62   *Official History*, vol. IV, p. 928.

63   C Harington, *Plumer of Messines*, John Murray, London, 1935, p. 127.

64   Except for the old problem that it was the British who were exposing themselves by hopping the bags, while the Germans remained in the protection of their defences.

65   Bean, *Anzac to Amiens*, p. 374.

66   Monash, *Letters*, p. 153.

67   ibid., p. 154.

68   ibid., pp. 154–5.

69   *Official History*, vol. IV, p. 910.

70   Haig, *War Diaries*, p. 336.

71   Bean, *Anzac to Amiens*, p. 376. In the *Official History*, vol. IV, p. 875, he wrote that, 'An overwhelming blow had been struck and both sides knew it.'

72   General Haig's *Fourth Despatch*, p. 133.

73   C Harington, *Plumer of Messines*, John Murray, London, 1935, p. 130.

74   J Terraine, *Douglas Haig The Educated Soldier*, Cassell, London, 1963, reprinted 2005, p. 387.

75   T Travers, *The Killing Ground The British Army, The Western Front & the Emergence of Modern War 1900–1918*, Pen & Sword Military Classics, Barnsley, South Yorkshire, 1987, pp. xxi, xxiii. Tim Travers also claims that Haig may have forbidden his officers to visit the front line: ibid, pp. 108–09.

76   D Cooper, *Haig*, Doubleday, Doran & Company, Inc, New York, 1935, pp. 169–70.

77   A Behrend, *As From Kemmel Hill An Adjutant in France and Flanders, 1917 & 1918*, Eyre & Spottiswoode, London, 1963, p. 40.

78   General Haig's *Fourth Despatch*, p. 133.

79   General Haig's *Fourth Despatch*, p. 134.

80   General Haig's *Fourth Despatch*, p. 134.

81   Lord Birdwood, *Khaki and Gown: An Autobiography*, Ward, Lock & Co. Limited, London, 1941, reprinted, 1942, p. 309.

Chapter 12 — Prisoners of War

1   *Official History*, vol. VI, p. 1099.

2   ibid., vol. III, p. 514.

3   ibid., vol. V, p. 396–397.

4   ibid., p. 397.

5   ibid., p. 397.

6   ibid., p. 397. Bean does not name the Australian officer.

7   *Official History*, vol. IV, p. 629. Again, Bean does not name the Australian officer.

8   Meaning a German concrete fortification, dug into the ground, with only the firing ports protruding above the ground. Many of these can still be seen on the battlefield today, including one at Tyne Cot cemetery, and another at Pozières.

9   *Official History*, vol. IV, p. 771–2.

10   W D Joynt, *Breaking the Road for the Rest*, Hyland House, Melbourne, 1979, pp. 128–9.

11   Monash, *Australian Victories*, p. 229.

12   For examples of this logic, see *Official History*, vol. III, p. 541; and N Wanliss, *The History of the Fourteenth Battalion, AIF Being the Story of the Vicissitudes of an Australian Unit during the Great War*, The Arrow Printery, Melbourne, 1929, pp. 323–4.

13   J Maxwell, *Hell's Bells and Mademoiselles*, Angus & Robertson Limited, Sydney, 3rd ed, 1933, p. 214.

14   N Wanliss, *The History of the Fourteenth Battalion, AIF Being the Story of the Vicissitudes of an Australian Unit during the Great War*, The Arrow Printery, Melbourne, 1929, p. 121.

15   W H Downing, *To the last Ridge*, Duffy & Snellgrove, Sydney, 1998, p. 119.

16   N Wanliss, *The History of the Fourteenth Battalion, AIF Being the Story of the Vicissitudes of an Australian Unit during the Great War*, The Arrow Printery, Melbourne, 1929, p. 294.

17   *Official History*, vol. V, p. 246n.

18   Cf *Official History*, vol. IV, p. 504n.

19   *Official History*, vol. V, p. 91.

20   C Harington, *Plumer of Messines*, John Murray, London, 1935, p. 95. Fifty one guns, 242 machine guns and 60 trench mortars were also captured: ibid, pp. 95–6.

21   *Official History*, vol. IV, p. 595.

22   ibid., p. 342.

23   ibid.

24   ibid., p. 342. On this subject, see: D Blair, 'No Quarter Unlawful Killing and Surrender in the Australian War Experience', Ginninderra Press, Canberra, 2005, pp. 5–6.

25   E J Rule, *Jacka's Mob*, Angus & Robertson Limited, Sydney, 1933, p. 70.

26   A W Keown, *Forward with the Fifth*, The Specialty Press Pty Ltd, Melbourne, 1921, p. 232.

27   Monash, *Australian Victories*, pp. 229–30.

28   A W Keown, *Forward with the Fifth*, The Specialty Press Pty Ltd, Melbourne, 1921, p. 233.

29   A pistol for firing flares.

30   W E Harney, *Bill Harney's War*, Currey O'Neil, Melbourne, 1983, pp. 46–8.

31   M Henry, *Notes of a Veterinary Officer with the AIF 1914–18*, 1932, Volume VIII *The Australian Veterinary Journal*, p. 17.

32 S E Dent, *Fourteen Months a Prisoner of War*, The North Western Courier Print, Narrabri, 1919, ch. 1.

33 ibid.

34 ibid., ch. 2.

35 R H Knyvett, *'Over There' with the Australians*, Charles Scribner's Sons, New York, 1918, p. 274.

36 The United States did not come into the war until 6 April 1917.

37 S E Dent, *Fourteen Months a Prisoner of War*, The North Western Courier Print, Narrabri, 1919, ch. 2.

38 ibid., ch. 2.

39 ibid., ch. 3.

40 ibid.

41 ibid.

42 ibid.

43 ibid., ch.4.

44 ibid. My father, Captain W H Travers, received similarly generous treatment from the Swiss when he was repatriated from a German prisoner of war camp in January 1945. Indeed, Captain Dent's account of his time as a German prisoner of war bears many similarities to my father's.

Chapter 13 — Leave

1 S Sassoon, *Memoirs of a Fox-hunting Man*, in *The Complete Memoirs of George Sherston*, Faber and Faber 1937, 1972 reprint, pp. 269–70.

2 J S Linton, *A Soldier's Tale: One Man's War 16 February 1916–12 June 1919*, J S Linton, Kalamunda WA, 1997, p. 68.

3 M Campbell and G Hosken, *Four Australian at War Letters to Argyle*, Kangaroo Press, Sydney, 1996, p. 149.

4 One estimate is that, at the rate of one leave per man per year, there would be 40 000 men on the move at any one time: A Rawson, *British Army Handbook 1914–1918*, Sutton Publishing, London, 2006, p. 342.

5 Bean, *Anzac to Amiens*, p. 203.

6 R & L Denning, *Anzac Digger: An Engineer in Gallipoli and France*, Australian Military History Publications, Sydney, 2004, p. 84ff.

7 ibid., p. 85.

8 ibid.

9 ibid., p. 86.

10 ibid., pp. 86–87.

11 ibid., p. 87.

12 ibid., p. 95.

13 ibid., p. 97.

14 P Yule (ed.), *Sergeant Lawrence goes to France*, Melbourne University Press, Melbourne, 1987, p. 111–12. Soap-dodging!

15 B Bishop, *The Hell, the Humour and the Heartbreak. A Private's View of World War 1*, Kangaroo Press, Sydney, 1991, p. 191.

16 ibid.

17 J Maxwell, *Hell's Bells and Mademoiselles*, Angus & Robertson Limited, Sydney, 3rd ed, 1933, p. 87.

18 ibid., p. 88.

19 ibid., p. 88.

20 ibid., p. 90.

21 ibid., p. 91.

22 ibid., pp. 93–4.

23 Lord Birdwood, *Khaki and Gown: An Autobiography*, Ward, Lock & Co. Limited, London, 1941, reprinted, 1942, p. 311.

24 ibid.

25 A M Nixon, *Somewhere in France Letters to Home The War Years of Sgt Roy Whitelaw*, The Five Mile Press, Melbourne, 1989, p. 104.

26 ibid., p. 105.

27 ibid., p. 105.

28 ibid., p. 108.

29 W S Oliver, *The Great White Father The biography of a great Australian*, Fast Proof Press Brisbane, 1999, p. 115.

30 P Yule (ed.), *Sergeant Lawrence goes to France*, Melbourne University Press, Melbourne, 1987, p. 112.

31 H R Clay, *Letters and Memoirs of the late Sergeant Harold Richard Clay*, T J Higham, Blackburn, 1928, p. 88.

32 ibid., pp. 88–92.

33 R Howell (ed.), *Signaller at the Front The War Diary of Gunner Arthur G. Howell M.M. First Australian Field Artillery Brigade and his Impressions of he Great War 1915–1918*, Hesperian Press, Perth, 2001, p. 55.

34 ibid.

35 P Yule (ed.), *Sergeant Lawrence goes to France*, Melbourne University Press, Melbourne, 1987, p. 109–10.

36   J S Linton, *A Soldier's Tale One Man's War 16 February 1916–12 June 1919*, J S
     Linton, Kalamunda WA, 1997, p. 59.

37   ibid.

38   As opposed to the halfpenny, which was the most the YMCA charged soldiers
     for a meal, albeit a small one: ibid., p. 60, 63.

39   ibid. pp. 59–60.

40   ibid, p. 61–62.

41   ibid, p. 65.

42   ibid.

43   ibid., p. 63.

44   ibid., p. 66

45   A. Donnell, *Letters of an Australian Army Sister*, Angus & Robertson Limited,
     Sydney, 1920, p. 211.

46   The main northern railway station in Paris.

47   R Howell (ed.), *Signaller at the Front The War Diary of Gunner Arthur G. Howell
     M.M. First Australian Field Artillery Brigade and his Impressions of he Great War
     1915–1918*, Hesperian Press, Perth, 2001, p. 63.

48   ibid., p. 62.

49   Absent without leave.

50   E J Rule, *Jacka's Mob*, Angus & Robertson Limited, Sydney, 1933, pp. 192–5.

51   P Yule (ed.), *Sergeant Lawrence goes to France*, Melbourne University Press,
     Melbourne, 1987, p. 103.

52   ibid., p. 103.

53   ibid., p. 104.

54   ibid.

55   ibid., p. 105.

56   ibid., p. 106.

57   ibid., p. 107.

58   ibid.

Chapter 14 — The Birth of the Australian Corps

1   Hankey, *Supreme Command*, p. 711.

2   Lloyd George, quoted in Hankey, *Supreme Command*, p. 562.

3   General Haig's *Fifth Despatch*, p. 157.

4   Churchill, *World Crisis*, p. 1190.

5   Monash, *Australian Victories*, p. 54–55.

6   Bean, *Anzac to Amiens*, p. 449–450.

7   Haig, *War Diaries*, p. 364.

8   Churchill, *World Crisis*, p. 1219.

9   Bean, *Anzac to Amiens*, p. 393.

10   According to Bean, this led to the Russians being forced to sign a 'robber's treaty' at Brest Litovsk: Bean, *Anzac to Amiens*, pp. 399–400.

11   ibid., pp. 398–9.

12   ibid., 399.

13   ibid.

14   ibid., p. 393.

15   ibid.

16   Churchill, *World Crisis*, p. 1220.

17   Haig, *War Diaries*, p. 369.

18   ibid., pp. 370–71.

19   *Official History*, vol.V, p. 50.

20   K Jeffery, 'Field Marshal Sir Henry Wilson', Oxford University Press, Oxford, 2006, p. 202.

21   *Official History*, vol.V, p. 50.

22   Churchill, *World Crisis*, p. 1220.

23   ibid., p. 1221.

24   Quoted in J Terraine, *Douglas Haig The Educated Soldier*, Cassell, London, 1963, reprinted 2005, p. 389. Haig himself had taken to threatening to resign. He made the threat to Lord Milner on Boxing Day 1917: Haig, *War Diaries*, p. 363; and to Lord Hankey on 22nd January 1918: Hankey, *Supreme Command*, p. 556.

25   Bean, *Anzac to Amiens*, p. 395.

26   *Official History*, vol.V, pp. 21–2.

27   Bean, *Anzac to Amiens*, p. 401.

28   ibid., p. 294.

29   ibid., p. 437.

30   72 399 to 58 894 in 1916: Bean, *Anzac to Amiens*, p. 294; and 103 789 to 93 910: *Official History*, vol.V, p. 22.

31   Bean, *Anzac to Amiens*, p. 437.

32   ibid., p. 287.

33   *Official History*, vol.V, p. 28.

34   ibid., p. 30; I D Chapman, *Iven G. Mackay Citizen and Soldier*, Melway Publishing Pty Ltd, Melbourne,1975, p. 105.

35   ibid., p. 27.

36   Bean, *Anzac to Amiens*, pp. 287–8.

37   ibid., p. 288.

38   To encourage (or, rather, to discourage) the others.

39   *Official History*, vol.V, p. 31.

40   B Bishop, *The Hell, the Humour and the Heartbreak. A Private's View of World War 1*, Kangaroo Press, Sydney, 1991, pp. 103–4.

41   Bean, *Anzac to Amiens*, p. 289.

42   Monash, *Letters*, p. 157.

43   Monash, *Australian Victories*, p. 5.

44   'This...was something we had long wanted and that our leaders had striven for': W D Joynt, *Saving the Channel Ports 1918*, Wren Publishing, Melbourne, 1975, p. 118.

45   Monash, *Australian Victories*, p. 9.

46   *Official History*, vol.V, p. 11.

47   Monash, *Australian Victories*, p. 10.

48   Haig, *War Diaries*, p. 385.

49   ibid.

50   ibid., p. 388.

51   Churchill, *World Crisis*, p. 1245.

52   ibid., p. 1249.

53   C E Callwell, *Field Marshal Sir Henry Wilson His Life and Diaries*, Cassell and Company Ltd, 1927, vol 2 p. 73.

54   Haig, *War Diaries*, p. 385.

55   ibid., p. 386.

56   ibid.

57   Monash, *Australian Victories*, p. 22.

Chapter 15 — The German Offensive — Spring 1918

1   Many of the eyewitnesses give the time of the attack, but very few give the time accurately. The times differ by as much as 15 minutes either way.

2   Churchill, *World Crisis*, p. 1251–1252.

3   ibid., p. 1247–1248.

4   ibid.

5   ibid., p. 1247. Churchill used this assertion as the premise for an argument that the German offensive was a failure — a supreme example of heroic advocacy: see Churchill, ibid., p. 1259.

6   ibid., p. 1246.

7   *Official History*, vol.V, p. 106.

8   Haig, *War Diaries*, p. 394.

9   *Official History*, vol. V, p. 106.

10   Edmonds, British *Official History*, 1918, vol. I, p. 61.

11   G Chapman (ed.), 'Vain Glory', Cassell and Company Limited, London, 1937, p. 540.

12   ibid., p. 541.

13   ibid., p. 551–4.

14   A Behrend, *As From Kemmel Hill An Adjutant in France and Flanders, 1917 & 1918*, Eyre & Spottiswoode, London, 1963, p. 103.

15   ibid., p. 103.

16   H Essame, *The Battle for Europe 1918*, B T Batsford, London, 1972, p. 112.

17   A Behrend, *As From Kemmel Hill An Adjutant in France and Flanders, 1917 & 1918*, Eyre & Spottiswoode, London, 1963, p. 84. There were, for example, 1000 'Chinese labour' employed on the docks of Dunkirk: A M Henniker, *Transportation on the Western front 1914–1918*, The Imperial War Museum, London, originally released 1937, p. 321.

18   Haig, *War Diaries*, pp. 389–90.

19   ibid., p. 391.

20   ibid.

21   C E Callwell, *Field Marshal Sir Henry Wilson His Life and Diaries*, Cassell and Company Ltd, 1927, vol. 2 p. 74.

22   Haig, *War Diaries*, p. 391.

23   Bean, *Anzac to Amiens*, p. 407.

24   Haig, *War Diaries*, p. 391.

25   A M Henniker, *Transportation on the Western front 1914–1918*, The Imperial War Museum, London, originally released 1937, p. 364.

26   *Official History*, vol. V, p. 257.

27   Bean, *Anzac to Amiens*', p. 408.

28   ibid., p. 409.

29   W D Joynt, *Saving the Channel Ports 1918*, Wren Publishing, Melbourne, 1975, pp. 1–2.

30   Churchill, *World Crisis*, p. 1232.

31   *Official History*, vol. V, p. 119.

32   Not necessary now — you will hold them.

33   *Official History*, vol. V, p. 120.

34   T A White, *The History of the Thirteenth Battalion, AIF*, Tyrells Limited, Sydney, 1924, p. 122.

35   *Official History*, vol.V, p. 128.

36   Monash, Letters, p. 166–169.

37   *Official History*, vol.V, p. 246.

38   Monash, *Australian Victories*, p. 24–25.

39   Town hall.

40   Monash, *Letters*, p. 170.

41   G B Edmunds, *Somme Memories: Memoir of an Australian Artillery Driver,
     1916–1918*, Arthur H Stockwell Ltd, Devon, undated, pp. 23–4.

42   As Lord Gowrie, General Hore-Ruthven was later Governor-General of
     Australia.

43   Monash, *Letters*, pp. 173–174. Sinclair-MacLagan, commanding the 4th division,
     arrived as Monash was leaving, and received similarly brief orders: Monash,
     Australian Victories, p. 29.

44   Monash, *Letters*, p. 174–175.

45   ibid., p. 175.

46   ibid.

47   ibid.

48   *Official History*, vol.V, p. 184.

49   Monash, Letters, p. 170.

50   *Official History*, vol.V, p. 174.

51   M Campbell and G Hosken, *Four Australians at War*, Kangaroo Press Pty Ltd,
     Sydney, 1996, p. 172.

52   Town hall.

53   A M Henniker, *Transportation on the Western front 1914–1918*, The Imperial War
     Museum, London, originally released 1937, p. 363.

54   *Official History*, vol.V, p. 175.

55   G B Edmunds, *Somme Memories: Memoir of an Australian Artillery Driver,
     1916–1918*, Arthur H Stockwell Ltd, Devon, undated, pp. 25–6.

56   Monash, *Letters*, p. 176.

57   P Gibbs, *The War Dispatches*, Times Press Limited, 1964, p. 336.

58   Monash, *Letters*, pp. 176–177.

59   Bean, *Anzac to Amiens'*, p. 416.

60   *Official History*, vol.V, p. 235.

61   Monash, Letters, p. 177.

62   Bean, *Anzac to Amiens*, pp. 423–4.

63   ibid., p. 424.

64   ibid., p. 426.

65   Churchill, *World Crisis*, p. 1259.

66   ibid., p. 1247.

67   Edmonds, British *Official History*, 1918, vol. I, p. 61

68   J Terraine, *Douglas Haig The Educated Soldier*, Cassell, London, 1963, reprinted 2005, p. 435.

69   I M Brown, *British Logistics on the Western Front 1914–1919*, Praeger, Westpoint, Connecticut, 1998, p. 189.

Chapter 16 — Villers-Bretonneux

1   B Bishop, *The Hell, the Humour and the Heartbreak. A Private's View of World War 1*, Kangaroo Press, Sydney, 1991, pp. 146–7.

2   Quoted in J Terraine, *Douglas Haig The Educated Soldier*, Cassell, London, 1963, reprinted 2005, pp. 432–3; for a facsimile of the handwritten version, see Churchill, *World Crisis*, p. 1273.

3   G Powell, *Plumer The Soldier's General*, Pen & Sword Military Classics, Barnsley, South Yorkshire, 1990, p. 263.

4   Bean, *Anzac to Amiens*, p. 427.

5   ibid., pp. 428–9.

6   A M Henniker, *Transportation on the Western front 1914–1918*, The Imperial War Museum, London, originally released 1937, pp. 382, 393.

7   Bean, *Anzac to Amiens*, p. 428–429.

8   Harington thought the enemy 'had shot his bolt in Flanders'. He thought the attack there was aimed at local success. But for the Portuguese breaking, the attack would readily have been contained: C Harington, *Plumer of Messines*, John Murray, London, 1935, p. 159.

9   Bean, *Anzac to Amiens*, p. 430.

10   *Official History*, vol. V, pp. 694–5.

11   ibid., p. 693–701.

12   Monash, *Letters*, pp. 181–2. After von Richthofen's death, the command of his flight passed to none other than Hermann Goering, who was a decorated fighter pilot in the first war and the commander of the Luftwaffe in the next. Von Richthofen was buried with fill military honours and great respect.

13   J Maxwell, *Hell's Bells and Mademoiselles*, Angus & Robertson Limited, Sydney, 1933, p. 209.

14   Bean, *Anzac to Amiens*, p. 431.

15   ibid., p. 432.

16 Lord Birdwood, *Khaki and Gown: An Autobiography*, Ward, Lock & Co. Limited, London, 1941, reprinted, 1942, p. 322.

17 G Blaxland, *Amiens: 1918*, Star, London, 1968, pp. 128–9.

18 R McMullin, *Pompey Elliott*, Scribe Publications, Melbourne, 2002, pp. 400–01.

19 Adapted slightly from the *Official History*, vol. V, p. 574–575.

20 *Official History*, vol. V, pp. 577–8.

21 ibid., p. 579.

22 Bean, *Anzac to Amiens*, p. 433. Sixty four Australians were awarded the Victoria Cross in the Great War: one in East Africa; one in Palestine; nine at Gallipoli; and 53 on the western front. Of the 53 Victoria Crosses awarded on the western front, six were awarded in 1916; 18 in 1917; and 29 in 1918: N Brasch, 'Australia's Victoria Cross Recipients, Book 1, World War I', Echidna Books, Melbourne, 2003.

23 Sergeant R A Fynch, quoted in *Official History*, vol. V, p. 603.

24 W H Downing, *To the last Ridge*, Duffy & Snellgrove, Sydney, 1998, p. 118.

25 ibid., p. 120.

26 *Official History*, vol. V, p. 637.

27 Lord Birdwood, *Khaki and Gown: An Autobiography*, Ward, Lock & Co. Limited, London, 1941, reprinted, 1942, p. 322.

28 E J Rule, *Jacka's Mob*, Angus & Robertson Limited, Sydney, 1933, p. 269.

29 ibid., p. 271.

30 Haig, *War Diaries*, p. 370–371.

Chapter 17 — Hamel

1 Bean, *Anzac to Amiens*, p. 435.

2 No good; very good; very, very, very, good: J S Linton, *A Soldier's Tale*, Published privately, Perth, 1997, p. 91

3 The description that follows is taken from *Official History*, vol. VI, p. 8–18. Brewery Farm was the headquarters of the Australian press correspondents, including Bean: *Official History*, vol. VI, p. 196.

4 ibid., p. 9.

5 ibid., p. 11.

6 Teasing.

7 *Official History*, vol. VI, p. 11.

8 A W Keown, *Forward with the Fifth: The Story of Five Years' War Service with the Fifth Infantry Battalion, AIF*, The Specialty Press Pty Limited, Melbourne, 1921, p. 310.

9 Monash, *Australian Victories*, p. 39.

10   G Powell, *Plumer The Soldiers' General: A Biography of Field-Marshal Viscount Plumer of Messines*, Pen & Sword Military, Barnsley South Yorkshire, 2004, p. 159.

11   ibid. If Monash ever attempted to justify his magnificent quarters at Bertangles, it was another example of heroic advocacy. The sense of 'inevitable alienation' on comparing Bertangles with the accommodation of the troops is as strong in 2006 as it must have been in 1918.

12   *Official History*, vol. VI, p. 14.

13   A W Keown, *Forward with the Fifth: The Story of Five Years' War Service with the Fifth Infantry Battalion, AIF*, The Specialty Press Pty Limited, Melbourne, 1921, p. 305.

14   *Official History*, vol. VI, p. 16–17.

15   Bean, *Anzac to Amiens*, p. 455.

16   Bean, *Anzac to Amiens*, p. 455.

17   *Official History*, vol. VI, p. 42.

18   ibid.

19   Monash, *Australian Victories*, p. 40.

20   I D Chapman, *Iven G. Mackay Citizen and Soldier*, Melway Publishing Pty Ltd, Melbourne, 1975, pp. 106–7; The 1st division also used the crops as camouflage in Flanders: W D Joynt, *Saving the Channel Ports 1918*, Wren Publishing, Melbourne, 1975, p. 123.

21   *Official History*, vol. VI, p. 188.

22   ibid., pp. 196–7.

23   Lord Birdwood, *Khaki and Gown: An Autobiography*, Ward, Lock & Co. Limited, London, 1941, reprinted, 1942, p. 325–326; *Official History*, vol. VI, p. 184–191.

24   Bean, *Anzac to Amiens*, p. 458.

25   W D Joynt, *Saving the Channel Ports 1918*, Wren Publishing, Melbourne, 1975, pp. 113–4. Joynt added, 'We had no complaints about other British Army Generals, only Gough. We respected Plumer of the Second Army under whom we fought throughout the terrible battles of 1917 and the terrific Passchendaele operations': ibid, p. 117.

26   *Official History*, vol. VI, p. 207.

27   Monash, Letters, p. 139.

28   *Official History*, vol. IV, p. 562.

29   Great work.

30   *Official History*, vol. IV, p. 578.

31   ibid., p. 580.

32   Monash, *Australian Victories*, p. 56.

33   G Powell, *Plumer The Soldier's General*, Pen & Sword Military Classics, Barnsley, South Yorkshire, 1990, pp. 186–7.

34   Letter to Walter Rosenhain, 14 June 1917, quoted in P A Pedersen, *Monash as Military Commander*, Melbourne University Press, Melbourne, 1985, p. 176.

35   Monash, *Australian Victories*, p. 104.

36   General Haig's Final Despatch, p. 326.

37   *Official History*, vol. III, p. 643.

38   General Haig's *Second Despatch*, p. 32.

39   But only if, as Bean pointed out, Sinclair-MacLagan was accounted a member of the AIF': Bean, *Anzac to Amiens*, p. 458n.

40   Monash, *Australian Victories*, p. 323.

41   ibid., p. 48.

42   Bean, *Anzac to Amiens*, p. 459–460.

43   The letter is quoted in full in Monash, *Australian Victories*, p. 48–52.

44   Monash, *Australian Victories*, p. 50.

45   ibid., p. 52.

46   'The word 'tank' was anathema to us': W D Joynt, 'Saving the Channel Ports 1918, Wren Publishing, Melbourne, 1975, p. 120.

47   Monash, *Australian Victories*, pp. 53–4.

48   ibid., p. 54.

49   ibid., pp. 54–5.

50   ibid., p. 56.

51   ibid., p. 56–7.

52   C Harington, *Plumer of Messines*, John Murray, London, 1935, p. 100

53   N Wanliss, *The History of the Fourteenth Battalion, AIF Being the Story of the Vicissitudes of an Australian Unit during the Great War*, The Arrow Printery, Melbourne, 1929, p. 304.

54   Monash, *Australian Victories*, p. 64.

55   ibid., p. 59.

56   N Wanliss, *The History of the Fourteenth Battalion, AIF Being the Story of the Vicissitudes of an Australian Unit during the Great War*, The Arrow Printery, Melbourne, 1929, p. 306.

57   Monash, *Australian Victories*, p. 62.

58   N Wanliss, *The History of the Fourteenth Battalion, AIF Being the Story of the Vicissitudes of an Australian Unit during the Great War*, The Arrow Printery, Melbourne, 1929, p. 310.

59   'Stunts' was the slang word for attacks.

60   J S Linton, *A Soldier's Tale*, Published privately, Perth, 1997, p.96.

61   E J Rule, *Jacka's Mob*, Angus & Robertson Limited, Sydney, 1933, p. 308.

62   Monash, *Australian Victories*, p. 63.

63   E J Rule, *Jacka's Mob*, Angus & Robertson Limited, Sydney, 1933, p. 306.

64   Monash, *Australian Victories*, p. 63.

65   ibid., p. 65.

66   ibid., p. 66.

67   ibid., p. 74.

68   ibid., p. 70.

69   Privates, not officers, it will be noted, acted as bookies. N Wanliss, *The History of the Fourteenth Battalion, AIF Being the Story of the Vicissitudes of an Australian Unit during the Great War*, The Arrow Printery, Melbourne, 1929, p. 311.

70   E J Rule, *Jacka's Mob*, Angus & Robertson Limited, Sydney, 1933, pp. 309–10.

Chapter 18 — 8 August 1918

1   Monash, *Australian Victories*, p. 79.

2   ibid., p. 91.

3   ibid.

4   ibid., p. 92.

5   ibid., p. 94.

6   ibid., pp. 95-6.

7   ibid., p. 96

8   ibid., p. 82.

9   ibid., p. 99.

10   ibid., p. 99.

11   ibid., p, 101-2.

12   ibid., p.104.

13   ibid., p. 106-8.

14   As indicated by the dawn start times for many battles: 3.10 am for Messines and 3.30 am for operation Michael, for example.

15   Monash, *Australian Victories*, p. 111.

16   ibid., p. 113.

17   ibid., pp. 113-4.

18   ibid., p. 127.

19   W D Joynt, *Saving the Channel Ports 1918*, Wren Publishing, Melbourne, 1975, p. 126.

20 J S Linton, *A Soldier's Tale: One Man's War 16 February 1916–12 June 1919*, J S Linton, Kalamunda WA, 1997, p. 101.

21 Monash, *Australian Victories*, p. 79-82.

22 J S Linton, *A Soldier's Tale: One Man's War 16 February 1916–12 June 1919*, J S Linton, Kalamunda WA, 1997, pp. 101-02.

23 W D Joynt, *Saving the Channel Ports 1918*, Wren Publishing, Melbourne, 1975, pp. 127-8.

24 J Maxwell, *Hell's Bells and Mademoiselles*, Angus & Robertson Limited, Sydney, 3rd ed, 1933, p. 211.

25 ibid., p. 212.

26 Monash, *Australian Victories*, p. 133.

27 ibid., p. 137.

28 G B Edmunds, *Somme Memories Memoir of an Australian Artillery Driver, 1916-1918*, Arthur H Stockwell Ltd, Devon, undated, pp. 36-38.

29 Monash, *Australian Victories*, p. 137.

30 T A White, *The History of the Thirteenth Battalion AIF*, Tyrrells Ltd, Sydney, 1924, pp. 150-1.

31 N Wanliss, *The History of the Fourteenth Battalion, AIF Being the Story of the Vicissitudes of an Australian Unit during the Great War*, The Arrow Printery, Melbourne, 1929, p. 324.

32 ibid., p. 323.

33 Monash, *Australian Victories*, p. 136.

34 ibid., p. 118.

35 T A White, *The History of the Thirteenth Battalion AIF*, Tyrrells Ltd, Sydney, 1924, p. 149.

36 H Essame, *The Battle for Europe 1918*, B T Batsford, London, 1972, p. 136.

37 N Wanliss, *The History of the Fourteenth Battalion, AIF Being the Story of the Vicissitudes of an Australian Unit during the Great War*, The Arrow Printery, Melbourne, 1929, p320.

38 T A White, *The History of the Thirteenth Battalion AIF*, Tyrrells Ltd, Sydney, 1924, p. 150.

39 R and L Denning, *Anzac Digger An Engineer in Gallipoli and France*, Australian Military History Publications, Sydney, 2004, p. 118.

40 W H Downing, *To the last Ridge*, Duffy & Snellgrove, Sydney, 1998, p. 146.

41 Quoted in Monash, *Australian Victories*, pp. 141-2.

42 H Essame, *The Battle for Europe 1918*, B T Batsford, London, 1972, p. 136.

43 ibid.

44   Monash, *Australian Victories*, p. 143.

45   C E Callwell, *Field Marshal Sir Henry Wilson His Life and Diaries*, Cassell and
      Company Ltd, 1927, vol 2, p. 121.

46   Haig, *War Diaries*, p. 440.

47   ibid, pp. 440-1.

48   Bean, *Anzac to Amiens*, p. 532.

49   Monash, *Australian Victories*, p. 144. A surprising number of Englishmen and
      women find this attainment beyond them.

50   Monash, *Australian Victories*, p144.

51   R Prior and T Wilson, *Command on the Western Front, The Military Career of Sir
      Henry Rawlinson 1914-1918*, Pen & Sword Military Classics, Barnsley, South
      Yorkshire, 1992, p. 318.

52   N Wanliss, *The History of the Fourteenth Battalion, AIF Being the Story of the
      Vicissitudes of an Australian Unit during the Great War*, The Arrow Printery,
      Melbourne, 1929, p. 329.

53   T A White, *The History of the Thirteenth Battalion AIF*, Tyrrells Ltd, Sydney, 1924,
      p. 150.

54   Haig, *War Diaries*, p. 448.

55   ibid.

56   Although the cavalry was used on 8 August 1918 to good effect, their new
      whippet tans were superseding their role.

57   Quoted in T Travers, *How the Was Won Factors that Led to Victory in World War I*,
      Pen & Sword Military Classics, Barnsley, South Yorkshire, 1992, p. 141.

58   Quoted in: J Tolland, *No Man's Land The Story of 1918*, Eyre Methune London,
      1980, pp. 370-1.

59   Haig, *War Diaries*, p. 448.

60   ibid., p. 453.

61   ibid.

62   ibid.

63   ibid. What did Haig expect? Lloyd George was a politician, after all.

64   ibid.

65   ibid.

66   Hankey, *Supreme Command*, p. 838.

67   The unemotional Hankey, who was a civil servant, not a politician, and should
      not have had an axe to grind, went so far as to name the chapter in his memoirs
      covering the last three months of the war 'Knocking away the Props', and to
      headline the surrender of Bulgaria: THE FIRST OF THE PROPS HAD

FALLEN; Turkey: THE SECOND PROP HAD CRASHED!; and Austria: THE
LAST OF THE PROPS HAD FALLEN! as though the military successes on the
western front counted for nothing: Hankey, *Supreme Command*, ch. LXXXI.

68   J Buchan, *Memory Hold the Door*, Hodder and Stoughton Ltd, London, 1940, p. 178.

69   *Official History*, vol. VI, p. 11.

Chapter 19 — Mont St Quentin and Péronne

1   N Wanliss, *The History of the Fourteenth Battalion, AIF Being the Story of the
     Vicissitudes of an Australian Unit during the Great War*, The Arrow Printery,
     Melbourne, 1929, p. 330.

2   Monash, *Australian Victories*, p. 159.

3   ibid.

4   ibid. p. 161; Haig, *War Diaries*, p. 448.

5   ibid.

6   Monash, *Australian Victories*, p. 161; Haig, *War Diaries*, p. 446.

7   Monash was particularly of this school. He knew how tired his men were, and he
     agonised over asking them to persist on the offensive, but, in the end, decided
     that the rewards on offer were too valuable to forgo: Monash, *Australian Victories*,
     p. 181, 201ff.

8   R and L Denning, *Anzac Digger: An Engineer in Gallipoli and France*, Australian
     Military History Publications, Sydney, 2004, p. 120.

9   J Maxwell, *Hell's Bells and Mademoiselles*, Angus & Robertson Limited, Sydney,
     3rd ed, 1933, p. 223.

10   Canal of the north.

11   Monash, *Australian Victories*, p184.

12   ibid., p. 162.

13   ibid.

14   ibid., p. 162-3.

15   J Terraine, *Douglas Haig The Educated Soldier*, Cassell Mititary Paperbacks, London
     1963, reprinted 2005, p. 179.

16   ibid., p. 54-5.

17   Leonard Mann describes this willingness as 'civilian adaptability': L Mann, *Flesh in
     Armour: A novel*, Robertson & Mullen Ltd, Melbourne, 1944, p. 212. It is an
     interesting speculation that civilians, as a group, might be more responsive to
     criticism than soldiers.

18   K Jeffery, *Field Marshal Sir Henry Wilson*, Oxford University Press, Oxford, 2006,
     p. 214.

19   Monash, *Australian Victories*, p. 163.

20   ibid., p. 170.

21   ibid., p. 171.

22   ibid., p. 174-175.

23   ibid., p. 176.

24   ibid., p. 179-180.

25   ibid., p. 180.

26   ibid., p. 181.

27   ibid., p. 182–184.

28   ibid., p. 184-185.

29   H Essame, *The Battle for Europe 1918*, B T Batsford, London, 1972, p. 158.

30   Monash, *Australian Victories*, p. 187–8.

31   ibid., p. 189.

32   ibid., p. 191, 197.

33   ibid., p. 195.

34   Haig, *War Diaries*, p. 448.

35   Monash, *Australian Victories*, p. 200.

36   ibid., p. 203.

37   B Bishop *The Hell, the Humour and the Heartbreak. A Private's View of World War 1*, Kangaroo Press, Sydney, 1991, p. 215.

38   ibid., p. 231.

39   Monash, *Australian Victories*, p. 203-4.

40   ibid., p. 206-7.

41   ibid., p. 208.

42   ibid.

43   J Maxwell, *Hell's Bells and Mademoiselles*, Angus & Robertson Limited, Sydney, 1933, p. 220.

44   Monash, *Australian Victories*, p210-213.

45   ibid., p. 223.

46   ibid.

47   ibid., pp. 223-4.

48   ibid., p. 251.

49   ibid., p. 248.

50   ibid., p. 251; N Wanliss, *The History of the Fourteenth Battalion, AIF Being the Story of the Vicissitudes of an Australian Unit during the Great War*, The Arrow Printery, Melbourne, 1929, pp. 343-4.

51   ibid., p. 252.

52   ibid., p. 253.

53   ibid., ch. XIV.

54   ibid., p. 275-9.

55   ibid., p. 279-80.

56   ibid., p. 282.

57   ibid., p. 283.

58   ibid., p. 283-8.

59   ibid., p. 291-2.

60   ibid., p. 292.

61   ibid.

62   ibid., p. 298-300.

63   J Maxwell, *Hell's Bells and Mademoiselles*, Angus & Robertson Limited, Sydney, 1933, p. 225.

64   ibid., p. 225, 231.

65   Monash, *Australian Victories*, p. 301.

Chapter 20 — Victory

1   Bill Harney, *A Bushman's Life An Autobigraphy*, Viking O'Neil, Melbourne, 1990, p. 54–5.

2   Haig, *War Diary*, p. 487.

3   Lt.-Col. F Lushingham quoted in G Chapman (ed.), *Vain Glory*, Cassell and Company Limited, London, 1937, pp. 683–4.

INDEX